# Designs for Disciplines

I dwell in Possibility—
A fairer House than Prose—
More numerous of Windows—
Superior—for Doors—

—Emily Dickinson, "I Dwell in Possibility"

# Designs for Disciplines

A Guide to Academic Writing

SECOND EDITION

Steven C. Roe and Pamela H. den Ouden

Canadian Scholars' Press

Toronto

Designs for Disciplines: A Guide to Academic Writing, Second Edition
by Steven C. Roe and Pamela H. den Ouden

First published in 2015 by
**Canadian Scholars' Press Inc.**
425 Adelaide Street West, Suite 200
Toronto, Ontario
M5V 3C1

**www.cspi.org**

**Library and Archives Canada Cataloguing in Publication**

Roe, Steven C. (Steven Charles), 1960-. Author
    Designs for disciplines : a guide to academic writing / Steven C. Roe and Pamela H. den Ouden.
— Second edition.

Issued in print and electronic formats.

ISBN 978-1-55130-888-3 (paperback).—ISBN 978-1-55130-889-0 (pdf).—ISBN 978-1-55130-890-6 (epub)

    1. English language—Rhetoric. 2. Academic writing. I. Den Ouden, Pamela H., author  II. Title.

PE1408.D48 2015         808'.042         C2015-905836-8         C2015-905837-6

Text design by Susan MacGregor
Cover design by Em Dash Design

15   16   17   18   19          5   4   3   2   1

Printed and bound in Canada by Webcom

Canada

MIX
Paper from
responsible sources
FSC
www.fsc.org    FSC® C004071

We dedicate this book to our families:
Thank you for your constant support and encouragement.

—S. R.
—P. D.

# Table of Contents

Acknowledgements ... xi

Preface ... xiii

Chapter 1:   What's the Occasion? Genre and Voice ... 1

Chapter 2:   Hitting the Books: Research and Topic ... 11

Chapter 3:   Moving Forward: Compiling a Research Notebook ... 41

Chapter 4:   A Trial Run: Proposals as Research Bids ... 71

Chapter 5:   Hello, Reader! Rhetorical Moves in Scholarly Introductions ... 111

Chapter 6:   Hills and Valleys: The Big Country of Core Paragraphs ... 181

Chapter 7:   Crossing the Finish Line: Rhetorical Moves in Scholarly
             Conclusions ... 243

Chapter 8:   Freight-Train Nouns: The Density of Scientific Writing ... 268

Chapter 9:   A Last Review: Revising and Proofreading ... 294

Copyright Acknowledgements ... 308

Index ... 311

# Acknowledgements

Our work has been made possible by the many students we have learned with over the years and by colleagues who have shared their time and disciplinary experience. We would also like to express our appreciation for the help provided by the dedicated people at Canadian Scholars' Press.

# Preface

This preface is written for students and instructors. We want to explain what the second edition of this book will do and how it fits into approaches to teaching academic writing at colleges and universities. The book will be useful not only to first-year students but also to upper-level undergraduates and perhaps even to graduate students. We focus on "academic writing" in the strict sense of that phrase, meaning that we discuss the kind of writing that actually occurs in scholarly disciplines such as criminology, English, history, and women's studies.

Historically, students starting out in university have taken "composition" courses that provide instruction in writing essays that are grouped into various categories (or "rhetorical modes") such as narration, description, division, comparison and contrast, process analysis, persuasion, and so on. In such courses, essays enable students to express their own ideas and to show that they understand the basic rules of formal writing. These courses may also include some instruction on how to use and acknowledge sources.

Here, we are doing something different. *Designs for Disciplines* examines academic writing as a more specialized form of communication aimed at a more limited audience. In particular, we discuss patterns that occur in scholarly writing from academic journals. Our emphasis is on research prose in the humanities and social sciences, and we also acknowledge some of the distinctive characteristics of scientific writing. In this book, then, discipline-based research papers replace rhetorical-mode essays as the medium for teaching writing. The goal is to have students join a genuinely academic community of writers by developing an original, sustained research paper that resembles writing published in discipline-based books and journals.

The second edition of *Designs for Disciplines* is arranged as follows. Chapter 1 provides a foundation by exploring ideas about genre. Chapters 2, 3, and 4 discuss preliminary steps such as research, compiling a research notebook, note-taking, summarizing, and drafting a proposal. The centre of the book—chapters 5, 6, and 7—trace the development of scholarly papers through introductions, core paragraphs, and conclusions. Chapter 8 addresses writing in the sciences. Chapter 9 covers revision and proofreading. Throughout, instructional commentary is accompanied by annotated passages that illustrate aspects of academic style. In using the book, instructors may wish to supplement *Designs for Disciplines* with full-length sample papers that they choose.

Looking back on our work of over a decade ago, we think the first edition of *Designs for Disciplines* was part textbook, part research project. At that time, a discipline-based approach to first-year writing courses had not been widely adopted, and we found ourselves addressing students while simultaneously wanting to persuade instructors through a critique of writing pedagogy. Today, however, an emphasis on research prose has gained a firmer foothold in the undergraduate writing curriculum, and we no longer feel the need to advocate for a pedagogical shift. That shift has occurred, and it's enabled us to keep our student audience more firmly in mind throughout the second edition. Indeed, while we continue to regard student readers of this book as apprentice scholars, the level of discourse is now more student-friendly. We think this is important because even as the bar has been raised by a move from traditional composition to research prose, the challenges of teaching and learning university-level writing may be greater than ever before. Factors such as the prevalence of writing practices in social media and the growing internationalization of the student populace have certainly not made things any easier. In any event, our enthusiasm remains keen. This text presents students with an opportunity to move beyond schoolroom essays and to join scholarly conversations that enrich our knowledge economy. This is valuable and exciting work for everyone involved.

In this second edition, readers will meet Jenna Sin, a Korean student who studied at Northern Lights College. Jenna started in the English as a Second Language (ESL) program and progressed to university-level courses, including an academic writing course taught by Dr. Greg Lainsbury. With Jenna's permission and help, we have presented a construction of her thoughts and personal experience as she moved through the course. The original work that Jenna developed along the way, with the guidance of her instructors, was very impressive. Again with Jenna's permission, we have added to and revised her work to further reflect the patterns and instructional purposes of this textbook. We have also gathered and augmented the feedback on Jenna's work, resulting in comments that originate from Dr. Lainsbury, from Jenna's ESL instructors, and from our own observations. We refer to Jenna's material as "The Jenna Files." We've also enriched the selection of sample academic passages from a variety of disciplines and embellished instructional commentary on key rhetorical features in scholarly prose. The illustrations are new as well. They have been created by Laney Tenisci.

Steve Roe

Pamela den Ouden

## The Jenna Files

Notes to self:

– I am so excited to take this course. I heard it is very hard to pass, but I cannot wait to see myself with a big improvement in English at the end of the semester. Always remember to keep challenging yourself, do your best, and never give up!

# CHAPTER 1

# What's the Occasion?

## Genre and Voice

> The strength of the genie comes of being confined in a bottle.
>
> —Anonymous

Following the approach of Janet Giltrow (2002), we begin our book by discussing the concept of genre (from French: *type*, *kind*, or *style*) because this concept is a foundation for understanding and practising the kind of writing that actually occurs in scholarly communities. Let us explain.

Contemporary genre theory tells us that all effective acts of human communication are sensitive to social values and situations. In other words, genre theory tells us, "know your audience." This advice can be found in almost every composition textbook. However, genre theory calls for a more thoughtful awareness of audience—of who the readers are—and how language reflects social values. For example, Karen wants to invite a friend to meet her at a nearby coffee shop. Karen sends a text: "Hey, can u meet me @ Starbucks. Noon." Later that day, Karen asks her Economics 101 professor for a meeting during the professor's office hours. This time, Karen sends an email: "Hi Dr. Brown, Could I meet you today at 3 p.m. to discuss my paper topic? Please let me know. Thank you, Karen Samuels." The tone and content of Karen's two messages are different because of the different social circumstances. The text message is brief and informal, and assumes consent because Karen is speaking to a close friend. The tone and content of the email are still fairly informal, but this message is more deferential because of the professor's position. The different social circumstances can even be used to explain the finer details of the two messages. Note, for example, the implication of "u" versus "you." "U" is more informal than "you," and Karen's social awareness tells her that "u" fits her friend, not her professor.

Similarly, when applied to academic writing, genre theory provides a way of understanding the distinctive features of scholarly discourse. Features such as a methods section, long noun phrases, explicit announcements of argument, extensive source documentation, acknowledgements of previous studies, and technical language may appear strange to newcomers, yet all of these telltale signs of scholarly work serve an overarching social need to generate knowledge. The appearance of these features, as knowledge-making gestures, is the subject of this book and will occupy all of the chapters that follow. In this respect, the concept of genre explains why academic writing looks the way it looks. But let's not get ahead of ourselves.

Because genre theory functions as a "theoretical framework" for what's to come, it would be worthwhile to pause and consider genre theory in more detail.

There was a time when the discussion of genre in English classes may have been confined to an analysis of poetic types, for example, epic, ode, dramatic monologue, sonnet, lyric, and so on. Today, however, the concept of genre has been broadened and revitalized by intellectuals who insist that *all* language, literary or not, must be evaluated within its social context. This proposition implies that one form of communication is not inherently better than another, only different. It follows that each communicative act should be judged by the way it meets the demands of specific situations. As Carolyn Miller (1984) explains, when we use language, most of the time, we engage in a "social action" that takes place in a "discourse community":

> What we learn when we learn a genre is not just a pattern of forms or even a method of achieving our own ends. We learn, more importantly, what ends we may have: we learn that we may eulogize, apologize, recommend one person to another, instruct customers on behalf of a manufacturer, take on an official role, account for progress in achieving goals. We learn to better understand the situations in which we find ourselves and the potentials for failure and success in acting together. As a recurrent, significant action, a genre embodies [a cultural exchange].

For the critic, genres serve as both an index to cultural patterns and as tools for exploring the achievements of particular speakers and writers; for the student, genres serve as keys to understanding how to participate in the actions of a community. (p. 165)

The contemporary concept of genre, therefore, measures "good writing" by considering particular settings or social circumstances, turning style into both a relative and a practical consideration.

"I like reading Alice Munro because her style is so clear.
Why doesn't this rental agreement sound like that?"

Such an approach exchanges universal rules for situation-based conventions that achieve desired effects. Because of this exchange, genre theory also allows for stylistic flexibility: the forms of discursive effectiveness may change just as social conditions and expectations change. "The result," according to Carolyn Miller, "is that the set of genres is an open class, with new members evolving, old ones decaying" (p. 153). For example, new genres include blogs, tweets, and Facebook status updates. Similarly, genres may also undergo internal changes. Many wedding invitations, for example, are more informal today than before. Viewed through the lens of genre theory, style becomes a matter of choice rooted in social needs and values.

Effectively applied, then, genre theory requires a thoughtfulness on the part of instructors and students, a joint commitment to investigate content and form in relation to context. Such an investigation is challenging, to be sure, and does not always yield definitive answers. Yet the perspective that a genre-based approach offers—communication as a social activity rooted in a social context—can make writing more practical and more meaningful. Students who engage in such an inquiry should not be simply better writers, but writers who have gained a better awareness of the demands of particular discursive situations.

## The Jenna Files

Notes to self:

- This was the first week of class, and I'm a little worried. The instructor and the textbook use words I've never heard. It took me a long time to read through this chapter because I had to keep checking my dictionary. I feel like I'm in a foreign language class. (I don't think I can make it. This class will be a lot harder and more work than ESL writing class.)
- I understand that "genre" is related to the idea of "know your audience," but now I'm hearing about "discourse communities," "social needs," "situation-based conventions," and "cultural patterns."
- I'm asking myself what all this is really about. I feel the concept of genre theory is connected to something bigger. Do we create language or does language create us?

The contemporary concept of genre calls for a rigorous, sustained inquiry into the social rationale for virtually every aspect of style, reminding us that language is always situated in a social context. The following exercise has been adapted from Janet Giltrow's book *Academic Writing: Writing and Reading in the Disciplines* (2002, pp. 21–26). Read the following passages with genre theory in mind.

Your analysis should comprise three steps: (1) choose a term or phrase to describe the genre; (2) note the social purposes that motivate the writing; (3) comment on how the form and content of each passage are related to the various social purposes.

## Example 1

With a love and respect
for the completeness
we shall gain as a couple
and with the blessings of our parents
we will be joined in marriage
on Saturday, the second of August
nineteen hundred and ninety-seven
at two o'clock in the afternoon
Calvary Baptist Church
You are invited to share
This day of happy beginnings
Diana Grace den Ouden
and
Michael Mohninger

## Example 2[1]

Illusion Rose Tee: Roses bloom beautifully on soft illusion knit; sheer 3/4 sleeves. Lined body. High-hip length. Polyester/cotton, machine wash. Imported. [K23922] Feminine silhouette, 3/4 sleeves. High-hip length. Machine wash for easy care. $39.95-$44.95.

## Example 3[2]

Misuse of Library or Information Technology Resources

(a) No student shall knowingly remove books or other library material from a University library without proper authorization, mutilate or deface library books or material, purposely misplace them or in any other way purposely deprive other members of the University of the opportunity to have access to library resources, or knowingly behave in a way that interferes with the proper function and use of the library, as described in the McGill Libraries' "Users' Code of Behaviour."

# Example 4[3]

"Introduction to Poetry" by Billy Collins

> I ask them to take a poem
> and hold it up to the light
> like a color slide
>
> or press an ear against its hive.
>
> I say drop a mouse into a poem
> and watch him probe his way out,
>
> or walk inside the poem's room
> and feel the walls for a light switch.
>
> I want them to waterski
> across the surface of a poem
> waving at the author's name on the shore.
>
> But all they want to do
> is tie the poem to a chair with rope
> and torture a confession out of it.
>
> They begin beating it with a hose
> to find out what it really means.

# Example 5

Romantic and creative SWF, young-looking, 42, 5' 9", 130 lbs., long blonde hair and green eyes. I enjoy movies and music. Seeking a smart, funny, sensitive, and passionate SM, 21-45, N/S. Ad#: 1791

# Example 6[4]

| | |
|---|---|
| *Gale:* | What if they did it? Just one year. What if everyone just stopped watching. |
| *Katniss:* | They won't, Gale. |
| *Gale:* | What if they did? What if we did? |
| *Katniss:* | It won't happen. |
| *Gale:* | You root for your favourites, you cry when they get killed. It's sick! |
| *Katniss:* | Gale. |
| *Gale:* | If no one watches, then they don't have a game. It's as simple as that. What? |
| *Katniss:* | Nothing. |
| *Gale:* | Fine, laugh at me. |
| *Katniss:* | I'm not laughing at you. |
| *Gale:* | We could do it you know. Take off, live in the woods, it's what we do anyway. |
| *Katniss:* | They'd catch us. |
| *Gale:* | Well, maybe not. |
| *Katniss:* | Cut out our tongues or worse. We wouldn't make it five miles. |
| *Gale:* | No, I'd get five miles. I'd go that way. [Gale points to the woods] |
| *Katniss:* | I have Prim and you have your brothers. |
| *Gale:* | They can come too. |
| *Katniss:* | Prim in the woods? |
| *Gale:* | Ha, maybe not... |
| *Katniss:* | I'm never having kids. |
| *Gale:* | I might. If I didn't live here... |
| *Katniss:* | But you do live here. |
| *Gale:* | I know, but if I didn't. Oh I forgot. Here, [Gale pulls out a bread roll and hands it to Katniss] |
| *Katniss:* | Oh my god! Is this real? |
| *Gale:* | Yeah, it better be! Cost me a squirrel. Happy hunger games! |
| *Katniss:* | And may the odds be ever in your favour. How many times is your name in today? |
| *Gale:* | Forty-two. I guess the odds aren't exactly in my favour. |

## Example 7

Spacious Condo, New West. 2BR, 2 ba, 1,217 sf, with private entry, 9½ ft ceilings & grt layout. Finished professionally for an exclusive atmosphere. Immaculate. Amens: swimming pool, Sauna, Jacuzzi, fitness room, U/G parking, near skytrain & schls. Safe neighbourhood.

## Example 8[5]

I'm in need of some greens. The gnarly kind. The kind that bite back.

Clearly kale is the answer. It's clean and crunchy and that's where we're starting for today.

The very back of the pantry is like a treasure trove of forgotten bottles and spices. I dug out my neglected bottle of sesame oil and rice wine vinegar for this clean and crunchy salad. They're just the right ingredients to tame the taste and texture of raw kale.

Fresh ginger is grated and whisked together with minced garlic, sesame oil, and rice wine vinegar. A little honey to balance the spicy-ness of ginger, too! Salt and pepper, of course. Making fresh salad dressing is just that easy.

Before tossing the dressing onto the kale, I massaged the kale with a bit of olive oil. This helps soften the fibrous leaves further.

Chopped roasted almonds and sesame seeds for crunch and this salad is a go! It's simple, satisfying, and totally green! What a way to make a pound of kale go down easy.

## Example 9[6]

In the past decade, graphic novels—book-length narratives written in the medium of comics—have emerged as a popular form of reading material and have been credited with serving a variety of educational functions. Like the comic book, their older sibling, graphic novels interweave word and image to convey a story. Yet whereas educators have historically held the comic book in low esteem (Hajdu 2008; Nyberg 1998), a recent spate of books and journal articles suggests that a growing number of them are willing to entertain the idea of using graphic novels in classroom settings.

There is certainly no shortage of arguments for using graphic novels with students. Indeed, one may well sense that they constitute a sort of panacea for literacy education. Teachers are encouraged to use them to motivate so-called reluctant readers (e.g., Crawford 2004; Snowball 2005), foster the development of skills associated with visual literacy (e.g., Gillenwater 2009; Versaci 2008), and support students who struggle with literacy as it is traditionally conceived (e.g., Frey and Fisher 2004). Others regard graphic novels as a complex form of reading material capable of challenging readers of varying ability levels (e.g., Carter 2007; Connors 2010; Versaci 2001, 2007). Despite the enthusiasm some educators—particularly those of us in higher education—have shown for graphic novels, however, there remain those who continue to regard the medium of comics as "a way station on the road to 'higher' forms of literacy and to more challenging and, by implication, worth-while texts" (Jacobs 2007, 20). My own experience using graphic novels with pre-service teachers in the context of a young adult literature class confirms this point.

## Ideas for Further Study

1. In your own words, write a one-sentence definition of genre theory in 25 words or less.
2. Select a genre of discourse and analyze how its features fit a particular social situation.

## Notes

1. Coldwater Creek (2014), Spring 2014 Catalogue.
2. McGill University (2013), *Code of Student Conduct and Disciplinary Procedures*.
3. Collins (1988), "Introduction to Poetry."
4. Ross, Collins, & Ray (2012), *The Hunger Games* movie script.
5. Wilson (2014), Web blog post.
6. Connors (2012), "Altering Perspectives: How the Implied Reader Invites Us to Rethink the Difficulty of Graphic Novels."

## References

Coldwater Creek. (2014). Coldwater Creek online catalogue: Spring 2014. Retrieved from www.coldwatercreek.com/product-detail/ 68207/75297/illusion-rose-tee. aspx?colorid=L87&refLink=search.aspx

Collins, B. (1988). Introduction to poetry. In *The apple that astonished Paris* (p. 58). Fayetteville, AR: University of Arkansas Press.

Connors, S. P. (2012). Altering perspectives: How the implied reader invites us to rethink the difficulty of graphic novels. *The Clearing House: A Journal of Educational Strategies, Issues, and Ideas, 85*(1), 33–37. doi:10.1080/00098655.2 011.607476

Giltrow, J. (2002). *Academic writing: Writing and reading in the disciplines* (3rd ed.). Scarborough: Broadview.

McGill University. (2013). *Code of student conduct and disciplinary procedures.* Retrieved from www.mcgill.ca/ secretariat/sites/mcgill.ca.secretariat/files/ code_-student_-conduct-discipline-procedures_april_2013_final_revised_3.pdf

Miller, C. (1984). Genre as social action. *Quarterly Journal of Speech, 70*(2), 151–167.

Ross, G., Collins, S., & Ray, B. (2012). *The hunger games.* Script. Retrieved from awesomeness.forumotion.com/t2-the-hunger-games-script

Wilson, Joy. (2014, March 17). Sesame kale salad with roasted almonds [Web blog post]. Retrieved from http://joythebaker.com/2014/03/sesame-kale-sal-ad-with-roasted-almonds/#more-14049

# CHAPTER 2

# Hitting the Books:
## Research and Topic

> Before you can do any research, you must set yourself a direction—
> a general area to investigate. That direction can, and probably will,
> change with time and knowledge—at least it will become
> more specific and focused. But with the first step,
> as the cliché goes, begins the journey.
>
> —Charles Bazerman, *The Informed Writer:*
> *Using Sources in the Disciplines*

Courses that focus on academic writing in the disciplines often involve a research paper. Instructors who assign research papers in such courses do so on the assumption that something important is at stake. Evidently, this assumption is shared by instructors across the academic curriculum because students are also asked to write research papers in courses on anthropology, criminology, gender studies, history, literature courses, men's studies, sociology, and women's studies. The importance of research papers is reflected in the percentage of marks allotted to them: sometimes, research papers may comprise 30 percent or more of an overall grade for a course. In terms of marks, then, a research paper deserves to be taken seriously. Ideally, however, marks should not be regarded as ends in themselves.

What is at stake (aside from marks) in college and university courses that involve writing research papers? The answer to this question lies in the discipline-based training and practices of instructors themselves, many of whom have been writing research papers for most of their professional lives. Instructors have been taught to regard research papers (or articles published in academic journals) as a kind of highly valued disciplinary currency, second in value only to full-length books.

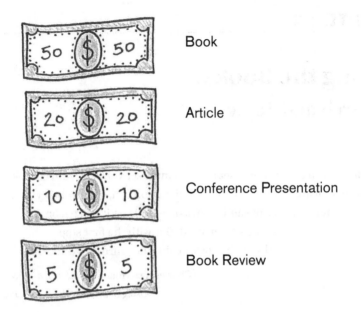

Like all analogies, our currency analogy breaks down if taken literally. In reality, there usually isn't any monetary value associated with a journal article, and conferences frequently leave academics with out-of-pocket expenses. Scholarly writing isn't the way to get rich! However, research papers have a high value in scholarly communities because they are the primary medium for presenting new knowledge and participating in ongoing scholarly conversations. So, as suggested earlier, we could regard research papers as the signature product of scholarly work. The résumés of senior academics often list page after page of research articles that represent a lifetime of academic achievement.

Accordingly, when students are faced with research papers in post-secondary academic courses, such assignments are steeped in cultural expectations. Whether they say so or not, most instructors probably have high hopes for student work and would like to see students produce papers that have much in common with articles in academic journals. Indeed, while papers written by undergraduate students are not usually accepted by scholarly journals, such papers may still share some of the characteristics of published research. In effect, students who are asked to write a research paper at the undergraduate level are being invited to join in scholarly conversations about the state of knowledge in a given area. Rather than a make-work project, such an exercise can be a meaningful initiation, one that gives students the privilege of working on their own or in groups, closing the gap between student and professional responsibilities.

This chapter explores the process of getting started on a research project. It addresses the search for direction, how to construct a firm sense of topic, and how to find relevant sources. This business of searching, constructing, and finding is not always a neat, linear process. It often involves backtracking and uncertainty about how to proceed. Nevertheless, we encourage students to embrace the challenges of research with both determination and an open mind, for the difficulties of the process mark a passage beyond the world of personal writing—essays, journals, blogs—into the domain of knowledge-making.

## Searching for Direction

The ground rules for selecting a topic may vary from course to course. Some instructors may limit student choices to a list of given topics. Other instructors might invite students to think of their own topics. Still others might provide a list of suggestions and allow for innovation. Whatever approach is taken, decisions about topic are vital to the success of a paper. Such decisions can be among the hardest to make. Embarking on the research enterprise, writers may feel paralyzed—set adrift in an ocean of possibility, without a compass and with no shoreline in sight.

Here are some general guidelines for getting to shore safely. First, writers should be engaged by their topic. Even at the undergraduate level, a research paper often involves a sustained commitment of time and energy over several months, and such prolonged effort tends to be easier to sustain when the writer has an interest in the topic. However, the criterion of personal interest should be accompanied by a cautionary note: more so than a personal essay or blog entry, which displays private convictions, the knowledge-making aims of a research paper call for a careful logic that could be compromised by excessive emotional involvement. "If you are going through a divorce," advises Linda Deutschmann, a sociology instructor, "now is not the time to write on divorce" (Garrett-Petts, 1996). Second, most instructors have something to say about the importance of focus. Echoing advice that appears in the epigraph to this chapter, English instructor William Garrett-Petts regards carefully focused writing as "emblematic" of the best writing in the disciplines (Garrett-Petts, 1996). Third, academic writers, unlike bloggers, need external evidence to support their points. Thus, the search for a topic goes hand in hand with a search for sources. The issue of sources deserves extended discussion a little later. In the meantime, a few other preliminary considerations are worth mentioning.

As student writers formulate topics, they should discuss their ideas with peers, instructors, and librarians early in the term. Ask for advice. Where the curriculum permits, opportunities to engage in original research can be enhanced when writers remain open to topics close to home, involving their local or regional surroundings. If you're in a history program, for example, you could consider doing research in a local museum that may house unique archival material.

Looking further afield, one can sample the diversity and flavour of scholarly research by using the Internet to examine "calls for papers" in a variety of disciplines or subject areas. Let's say you have an interest in writing on some aspect of popular culture. If you were to employ a search engine and use "calls for papers film television" as a search phrase, you might find the following:

---

### Outer Space

This 2-day conference seeks to explore the significance of 'outer space' in textual and visual culture, including literature (fiction/non-fiction/scientific or legal texts), film (cinema/documentary/youtube/television/NASA or ISS clips or broadcasts), digital media (games/twitter/social media), photography, material culture, ephemera and popular culture.

We especially welcome papers that move beyond the paradigms of science-fiction studies, and engage with geographical or historical approaches to visual or textual cultures of 'outer space'. We invite papers on the following themes (but not limited to):

- 20th century and post-millennial representations of outer space
- Poetics/poetries of outer space
- Non-fiction and outer space, from film documentary to the non-fiction novel ( for example, Al Reinert's For All Mankind, Patricio Guzmán's Nostalgia for the Light, Oriana Fallaci's If the Sun Dies, Norman Mailer's Of a Fire on the Moon)
- Digital games and outer space
- Visual/textual representations of rockets, satellites, telescopes, the International Space Station, and other material technologies of outer space
- Posthumanism – visual/textual representations of sentient/non-sentient life
- Weird fictions and outer space
- Papers that seek to establish frameworks for a cinematic or literary geography of outer space
- Papers that examine terms such as 'cosmography', 'celestial space', 'astroculture', in relation to literature, film, other visual/textual media
- Visual/textual gendering of 'outer space'
- Governance, laws, and capital of outer space in visual/textual culture
- Discourse analysis of space law, treaty, governance in technical literature
- Non-western/Non-Soviet space programs and their representation ( for example Cristina De Middel's Afronauts (2012) http://www.icp.org/support-icp/infinity-awards/cristina-de-middel)
- Space tourism/personal space flight
- Heritage and outer space (archaeologies of outer space, space debris, heritage sites, museum orbit)
- Ecology and outer space (space as wilderness or environment, terraforming, pollution, waste, life, texts such as Charles Cockell's Space on Earth (Palgrave 2006)

*Source:* http://call-for-papers.sas.upenn.edu/node/56297

And this:

---

# Border Crossings

In an age of media convergence, international co-productions, and social networking, the borders traditionally used to define the cinema are constantly being re-examined within evolving discourses on film and moving image studies.... Paper topics may include but are not limited to national borders and transnational cinema, digital cinema, VOD and other digital platforms for the distribution of films, television, transmedia storytelling, generic hybridity, interdisciplinarity, and new approaches to moving image history. By hosting discussions as diverse as these, we hope to engender reflection on the wide scope of the topic itself.

In the spirit of border crossing, we encourage students from outside of film studies to submit their work to the symposium. Papers from such disciplines as art history, music, religious studies, sociology, history and English with a focus on visual culture and the moving image are welcome.

*Source:* http://carleton.ca/filmstudies/bordercrossings/

---

And this:

---

# AX Anime and Manga Studies Symposium

Japanese animation (anime) and comics (manga) represent one of the major contributions that Japan has made to global visual and popular culture. Indeed, for many people, their first—and sometimes only—contact with Japanese culture is through Japanese visual culture.

The field of anime and manga studies is young, only about 30 years old, but extraordinarily vibrant. It welcomes a wide range of interpretations and approaches, draws on different disciplines and methodologies, and can involve both academics, industry professionals, independent scholars, and fans/enthusiasts.

A major goal of the Anime and Manga Studies Symposium is to bring together speakers from diverse backgrounds, fields and areas to exchange ideas, explore new directions, and contribute to building a community of anime and manga studies. Uniquely, the Anime and Manga Symposium is an integral part of the schedule of Anime Expo, the largest gathering of fans of Japanese popular culture in the U.S. This will give speakers an opportunity to present their research and scholarship directly to a public, non-academic audience, to interact with fans of anime and manga from around the world, and to become participants in a celebration and appreciation of Japanese popular culture. In turn, the Symposium also serves to introduce convention attendees to the ideas and practices of formal scholarship of Japanese visual culture.

Submissions on a wide range of topics dealing with anime and manga will be considered. Possible areas to explore can include—but are not limited to:

- Critical studies of individual creators, directors and animators, especially in larger contexts such as anime/manga as a whole, animation, comics, Japanese literature/film, science fiction, war literature, etc.
- Close readings of particular works, with a focus on genre conventions and subversions and relationships to previous works in anime/manga and other media
- Gender and Sexuality: Fan service and objectification, the male and female gaze, the interplay of male and female creators, producers, and audiences
- Age, class, race, ethnicity/nationality and other social differences
- Reflections on current social, political and ecological issues
- Responses to the world and to Japanese history: The 3.11 Tohoku Disaster, World War II, interactions between Japan and other countries
- The impact of new technologies (wireless communication, augmented reality, mobile computing) on storytelling in anime/manga
- The use of remix culture: Adaptation and interpretation of Eastern, Western and other literatures and visual media in Japanese popular culture
- Copyright, obscenity, and other legal issues
- Anime and manga as tools of globalization and agents of promoting Japanese culture
- The history and evolution of anime/manga fandom outside Japan: Fan practices and experiences—clubs, conventions, cosplay, fansites, fansubbing, anime music videos
- The future of anime/manga consumption—streaming, online comics, crowdsourcing, etc.
- Potentials for anime/manga as platforms for social change and anime/manga fans as actors of social change
- The ethics and challenges of presenting Japanese popular culture products around the world

The Symposium particularly welcomes presentations on newer/emerging works and creators.

Speakers are also welcome to submit proposals for roundtable discussions on these and related topics. Potential roundtables can include:

- Differences in theoretical approaches to anime and manga
- Anime/manga fan practices and activities in different countries, cultures and regions
- New directions, new opportunities, and new challenges in thinking, writing, and teaching about anime/manga

*Source:* https://call-for-papers.sas.upenn.edu/node/55513

Switching subjects, we Googled "call for papers weather" and found this invitation:

# Modernism, Weather, and Climate (SCMLA Panel; Abstracts due 2/22)

This panel seeks papers about the significance of weather and/or climate in modern literature. Open to a wide range of topics (including American, British, and world literatures) and approaches. Submissions might address (but certainly are not limited to):

- The depiction of weather/climate in traditional and avant-garde forms.
- The construction of weather/climate as a specific interest of modernity.
- The importance of predicting and/or forecasting weather.
- Major climatological/meteorological events (e.g., the American Dust Bowl).
- The relation of weather/climate to race, gender, and class formations.
- Ecocritical approaches to modernist literature.
- The connection between weather/climate and genre.
- The differing appearances of relative stability (climate) and unpredictability (weather).
- The links between weather/climate and other modernist themes.

*Source:* http://call-for-papers.sas.upenn.edu/node/55511

As you can see, calls for papers present a "movable feast" of possibilities drawn from the real world of academic research and can be used by students in search of their own topics.

Another way to scout out topics is by looking through titles of articles in academic journals. Choose journals related to your area of interest. You can go to your college or university library and look at the current or back issues of journals, or you can access these online, either through searching the title of a specific journal (if you know it), "subject area" journals (for example, social work journals, nursing journals, forestry journals), or you can access them through your school library catalogue. Even if the full-text article is not available, reading the titles will give you a good idea of the kinds of topics being written about in your field.

## Constructing a Topic

In the previous pages, the word *topic* has been used loosely, to indicate a general understanding of what a research paper is or could be about. From here on, however, we treat *topic* as a technical term that involves specific elements. Our approach can be used across the humanities and social sciences, in different courses. Indeed, even when instructors do not explicitly seek this more

technical understanding of topic, students can successfully use the strategy on their own. And there are good reasons for doing so, since researchers do not really *have* a topic until it can be clearly articulated.

In this text, we treat "topic" as a concept that involves *two* components: a *research site* and a *prestige abstraction*. Our use of these terms follows Janet Giltrow's lead (1995, pp. 241–243, 370–372; 2002, pp. 119–122, 125, 371–372, 380). We have built on Giltrow's insights by developing them into a practical and sophisticated pattern.

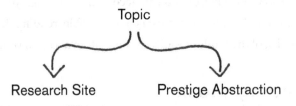

## Research Site

In everyday usage, *site* usually refers to a place where something occurs. In turn, a *research site* is a "place" chosen for scholarly activity. It is the thing under investigation, the phenomenon that is to be studied. Alternatively, a research site might be defined as the raw material on which a paper is based. The phrase is commonly used in the social and natural sciences, where research often takes place in a specific physical setting. In archaeology, for example, a research site could consist of a carefully marked-off area in which archaeologists dig for artifacts.

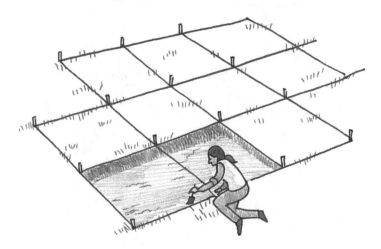

In these cases, research sites are very much "places," in the normal sense of the word. In other academic disciplines, however, the spatial reality of a research site might look a little different. In medical research, for example, biologists may investigate a single cell that can only be seen under a microscope. Alternatively, in English and history, research site-as-place might be a textual "space"—Milton's *Paradise Lost* or old issues of newspapers. In sociology, on the other hand, a researcher may study the behaviour of children on an elementary school playground during recess.

**Research sites** are the physical area, text, or event that is under consideration. Even though they can sometimes be hard to see, they have a concrete reality.

When you are at liberty to choose your own topic, you can consult your own life, your own field of interests for possible research sites. In any event, a focused topic involves a carefully narrowed research site:

- mind-mapping in elementary mathematics education
- writing instruction for kindergarten children with learning challenges
- images of Mary in medieval English prose
- micro- and macro-level intervention during the 2008 financial crisis
- lodgepole pine forests during the red stage of mountain pine beetle attack
- clothing imagery in William Golding's *Lord of the Flies*
- steam power and British influence in Baghdad, 1820–1860
- gender imagery in 20th-century U.S. presidential wartime speeches
- the eastern grey squirrel in the United States
- New York's Irish famine immigrants

Narrow research sites, such as these, help to create focused topics that permit in-depth analysis, one of the hallmarks of academic research. Unlike a sound bite or a newscast that covers a range of stories, research articles frequently focus on one item—on one event, thing, or place. It is this careful scrutiny of one thing, rather than a cursory survey of many, that permits academics to make a contribution to knowledge.

## Abstractions and Prestige Abstractions

If the research site is the carefully demarcated raw material on which a study is based, the prestige abstraction is an *idea* or *concept* that makes the research site meaningful in academic culture. Thus, while research sites have some physical reality, prestige abstractions cannot be touched or seen in and of themselves: their reality is mental rather than physical. For example, if children on a recess playground are a physical reality, concepts such as hope, freedom, power, authority, and change are ideas that we might use to interpret that physical reality.

In order to distinguish the two ingredients of topic, we could pay closer attention to the word *abstraction*, breaking down its parts this way:

$$(\textbf{AB})\ (S\textbf{\textit{TRACT}}\,ION)$$

The prefix *ab-* means to lift away, remove, or take from. *Tract* means a stretch of territory—a place. Hence, *abstraction* involves a lifting away from concrete realities—a movement upward, if you will, into the airier realm of ideas. Thus, the verb "to abstract" means to remove or to take away. Abstractions are ideas that emerge from the raw material of life. They are the categories or mental boxes that we create for ourselves, in order to understand and interpret the world around us.

## Short Exercises

1. Working in small groups, come up with abstractions that could arise out of the situations or circumstances listed below:
   (a) Every lunch hour, thousands of children across North America line up in their school cafeteria, awaiting free lunches.
   (b) Teenagers in both small towns and large cities tend to be very aware of brand-name clothing.
   (c) Last summer, a record number of bear attacks occurred throughout North America.
   (d) Many people watch television sports on Sunday.
2. At home, make a collection of related items from one room in your house— you could, say, collect study materials from a desk area. Then arrange the items on a plate or some other flat surface. Bring the collection to class and ask people to think of an abstraction that applies to the collection as a whole.
3. For some movies you have seen, or novels you have read, think of one or more abstractions that express the theme of the work.

Once the basic concept of abstractions is clear, it is a short step to "prestige abstractions." Prestige abstractions are a select group of ideas or mental categories that enjoy a privileged existence in academic circles. Prestige abstractions are Big Issues that most academics immediately recognize as relevant to academic concerns. However, the appeal of prestige abstractions relates to shifting interests, so that prestige abstractions themselves are a reflection of currents in economic, political, and cultural thought. Right now, some of the most fashionable abstractions in the humanities and social sciences include the following:

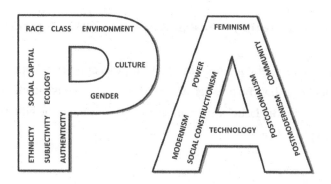

In any given discipline, at any given time, there is no fixed list or limited field of prestige abstractions. Nevertheless, some abstractions are noticeably "hot" insofar as they receive more attention than others. According to Janet Giltrow (1995), "It is hard now to foresee a time when *race* and *gender* will not be big issues, or when *community* will not give research rhetorical force, but there was a time when they did not have the prestige they have now" (p. 243).

You could try to identify the "hot" abstractions in your field by perusing article titles of relevant journals. You will find that certain abstractions recur more than others. You will even find special issues devoted entirely to the development or exploration of a single abstraction. Similarly, calls for papers, such as those previously noted, are fertile ground for abstractions. Sometimes a host of abstractions hover around a single research site, such as that of John F. Kennedy ( for example, heroic mythology, conspiracy, negation, cultural renaissance, tragedy). Prestige abstractions further refine or narrow topic, specifying ideas that can be brought to bear on research sites.

A **prestige abstraction** signals the scholarly importance of a research site by creating a partnership between the raw stuff of life and the concerns of the academic community. Prestige abstractions, therefore, are Big Issues that strategically position the research site in relation to academic culture.

To recap, a research site and a prestige abstraction fully articulate topic— the specific subject or "aboutness" of a paper. According to this pattern, topic consists of something concrete (some raw material from life) and something abstract (some idea or mental category). For the sake of brevity, the pattern can be expressed as a simple equation:

**Research Site (RS) + Prestige Abstraction (PA) = Topic (Top)**

When you apply the formula in an attempt to construct your own topic, you may discover that the prestige abstraction wants to push itself to the front of the lineup. As a Big Issue, it may press for first billing, so the equation might actually look like this:

**Prestige Abstraction (PA) + Research Site (RS) = Topic (Top)**

Moreover, we recommend that students use simple connecting words—coordinate conjunctions or prepositions—to join prestige abstractions and research sites. Accordingly, the plus sign in the topic formula might be replaced by words such as *and, for, in, among, between,* and so on. Consider the following example:

Community formation + the Williams Lake Museum

becomes

Community formation **and** the Williams Lake Museum

In cases like this, the topic formula clearly shows the basic rhetorical building blocks of a university-level research paper. The careful construction of topic will provide you with a clear idea of what your paper is about, while at the same time signalling its relevance to the academic community. If you have a carefully defined topic, you have a base for the paper as a whole, and you can be sure that your central focus will interest other scholars.

## The Jenna Files

Notes to self:

– Help! I thought my instructor was going to tell me what to write about! Now I'm supposed to find my own topic.
– I did read something on the Internet news about a girl who was bullied on the Internet. Kids in her school posted really mean things about her. This made me think of what happened to my friend last year. Maybe I could write something about that. (Wait ... if I want to write about bullying, I'll have to use APA style and will need to learn about that.)
– I need something called a research site and something called a prestige abstraction. My instructor says these two elements will help me find a very narrow and specific topic.
– I think it will save me time if I highlight important paragraphs and sentences as I'm reading through my sources.

We think Jenna's notes hold the promise of an effective topic. Now, she just needs to refine the language of prestige abstraction and research site. Below, we present a case study of an emerging topic for another paper.

# A Case Study:
# The Making of a University-Level Research Paper

## Research Site

The behaviour of nurses on acute-care wards

## Pondering Prestige Abstractions

[The research site should be framed in a way that makes it relevant to the scholarly community.]

One might begin to think of nurse behaviour in terms of social responsibility, time management, stress, gender, discrimination, bullying, collaboration, patient care, and so on.

## Potential Topic

A brief search on Academic Search Premier reveals that, in academic studies, the abstractions above and many others are associated with nursing behaviours. In particular, we noticed numerous references to a concept linked to bullying. In the scholarly literature, this concept is identified as "horizontal violence." We are intrigued by this and think it would be an effective prestige abstraction. Accordingly, our topic-in-the-making would sound like this:

Horizontal violence in the behaviour of nurses on acute-care wards

## The Emerging Paper

### Uncaring Caregivers: Horizontal Violence in the Behaviour of Nurses on Acute-Care Wards

Throughout North America, the nursing profession is experiencing budget cutbacks, longer shifts, an expanding scope of practice, and increasing rates of burnout. These stressors take a toll on nurses in many working environments, but the challenges appear to be particularly severe in certain areas of practice, such as acute care. On acute-care wards and elsewhere, nurses may respond to the stresses of their workplace by engaging in peer-to-peer bullying, a concept known as horizontal violence. Accordingly, my paper will analyze horizontal violence among nurses on acute-care wards. I will show that horizontal violence emerges from a pervasive sense of oppression caused by the strict hierarchies in the health care system.

## Reading for Topic

The topic formula that we have discussed here is evident in published research, particularly within the humanities and social sciences. In a paper on Feng Shui and village property development in Hong Kong, for example, C. M. Tam, Tony Tso, and K. C. Lam (1999) explicitly label their abstraction as an abstraction. "Feng Shui," the authors write, "is ancient Chinese geomancy. It is abstract, invisible, untouchable, and intangible—as the wind, hard to see, and as water, difficult to be grasped" (p. 152).

However, a topic, as we have defined it, is not always readily visible. In some papers, for instance, one might be able to identify a research site, but the prestige abstraction could be harder to pinpoint. On occasion, prestige abstractions may be implied rather than explicitly stated. This is the case in "Thrice-Told Tales: The Exploration Writing of John Franklin," Richard C. Davis's paper about Sir John Franklin's second overland expedition to the Arctic. Here's a passage from the introduction:

### Richard C. Davis, "Thrice-Told Tales: The Exploration Writing of John Franklin"

When John Franklin journeyed across the North American continent to explore the shores of the Polar Sea on his second land expedition of 1825-1827, he kept—in accordance with British Admiralty convention—an official journal of his experience. Later, perhaps during the lengthy Atlantic crossing on his return to England, Franklin prepared what appears to be a fair copy of this official journal. The fair copy encompasses roughly the same geographical and temporal scope as does the journal, but through selective editing, it condenses the account by half. In 1828, John Murray published Narrative of a Second Expedition on the Shores of the Polar Sea. This narrative, based on the original journal and the fair copy, was composed for a popular audience with an appetite for travel writing and an exotic interest in the far reaches of the Empire. We have, then, three accounts of the same experience, all told by the same author, or, as my title suggests, "thrice-told tales"—a journal, a fair copy, and a narrative.

A crucial assumption made in this paper is that the variations between these three accounts grow out of the author's sense of audience—of who reads the account and what they want to hear.... The truth is that all three accounts bear a tedious similarity; Franklin's laboring imagination rarely capitalizes on the rich rhetorical possibilities offered by the different audiences he addresses. Perhaps encouraged by his military training, Franklin instead strived for an unattainable objectivity in his writing, resulting in a literary personality that is thin and obscure.... Yet even though Franklin can hardly be said to take full advantage of the rhetorical situation, his accounts are not totally innocent of literary manipulation. His excessive self-effacement veils the process, but close scrutiny of the tales reveals an indisputable shaping of the narrative to meet the expectations of his audience. A full examination from this perspective must consider Franklin's perceptions of landscape, duty and leadership, native people, Canadians, and the experience in North America. This brief paper, however, focuses only on Franklin's portrayal of the Indians and Inuit.

Subtly but consistently, as one moves from journal through fair copy to narrative, one encounters an image of native people that grows gradually more disparaging and condemning. The narrative casts Indian and Inuit in the role of predatory antagonist to civilization and portrays them as the chaotic, irrational enemy of order, a disapprobation that is considerably intensified from what appears in the journal. I must emphasize that the differences are not extreme: Franklin's desire to avoid subjective evaluations prevents any dramatic alterations. Nevertheless, it seems fair to say that many of the indigenous North Americans who appear in the narrative are portrayed as savages opposed to such European virtues as industry, trust, and reason.

*Source:* Davis (1989, pp. 15–16)

Although this is very much a paper about racism, racist discourse, and ethnocentrism, none of these high-powered words (or synonyms for them) appears in the introduction or anywhere else in the paper.

On other occasions, general references to concrete phenomena seem to stand in for abstractions. This happens in Nancy Theberge's paper about media coverage of a hockey brawl. This paper is entitled "A Feminist Analysis of Responses to Sports Violence: Media Coverage of the 1987 World Junior Hockey Championship." In this article, Theberge situates her research site in relation to "sports violence," a Big Issue, to be sure, but not exactly an abstraction. In fact, to think of violence as an abstraction (as something intangible) is problematic. "Sports violence" certainly rises above specific reference, but its generality hovers somewhere *between* specific instances of violence and the concept of violence. In the case of Theberge's paper, then, we might again have to go searching for an abstraction, and that search might bring into view phrases like "masculinity" or the "social construction of masculinity." All of this suggests that the effort to identify topic in someone else's work might not yield immediate and transparent answers. Among a community of readers, there may be some disagreement over what constitutes the prestige abstraction or even the research site. Accordingly, all of us should be prepared to tolerate different versions of topic, although some versions may be more persuasive than others. We would like to suggest that what matters most is not having everyone agree on precisely the same phraseology, but that readers try to identify topic according to the structural pattern described here. In this respect, the topic pattern under consideration becomes a strategy to enhance reading comprehension of academic literature.

As you encounter other people's research papers (and think about writing your own) there are certain places where the topic is likely to appear. Frequently, for example, an announcement of topic will occur in the title of a paper, and the topic will then be reaffirmed in a sentence somewhere within the introduction. Sentence-level announcements of topic often begin with subject-predicate patterns such as "This paper examines," "I will examine," "I investigate," "My paper focuses on," and "This paper describes." These constructions, which refer to the activity of the paper or author, represent self-conscious moments in the presentation of research. In passages such as this, readers encounter language about language or *meta*discourse, which can be envisioned as a flag that alerts readers to key moments in the development of knowledge. The following excerpts display the topic formula at work. Note that metadiscursive flags are underlined, research sites are in bold, and abstractions are in italics:

---

## Ismail Aydogan, "Favoritism in the Classroom: A Study on Turkish Schools"

.... this study examines the **use of wireless laptop technology** to support the application of *problem-based learning (PBL)* in a special education methods course.

*Source:* Aydogan (2008, p. 169)

---

## John McCreery, "Getting to Persuasion"

This study describes **Japanese youth in their late teens and early twenties** as preferring a style of communication the researchers label *"silent appeal."*

*Source:* McCreery (2001, p. 167)

---

The topic formula is also discernable in the next example by D. P. Pierson (2005). In this case, however, topic is dispersed throughout long and complicated sentences. In advising students, we would recommend simpler constructions:

---

## D. P. Pierson, "'Hey, They're Just Like Us!': Representations of the Animal World in the Discovery Channel's Nature Programming"

Analyzing a week of prime-time nature programming yielded the thematic discourse of nature, or the natural world as familiar domain. The **Discovery Channel's nature programming** engages its viewers and creates an identifiable cable identity because the discourses are already a recognizable part of a viewer's social and imaginative worlds. These discourses do not exist just in Discovery's nature programming, but are in fact represented in many other social and media forms. *Evaluating animals through human moral values (good, evil, lazy)* is also represented in Hollywood films (e.g., *The Lion King*), circuses, children's books, songs, and other popular cultural forms.

*Source:* Pierson (2005, p. 699)

Or, more simply:

This essay explores *anthropomorphism* in **Discovery Channel's nature programming.**

# Finding Sources

Decisions about topic will be influenced by the availability of sources. In fact, the success of academic papers written by students and professors depends in large part on their ability to find appropriate sources. Without appropriate sources, a good grade for a student or publication for a professor is very unlikely. Careful research is one way that scholarly writers indicate a respect for the knowledge-making practices of their discipline.

## Primary, Secondary, and Tertiary Sources

We will begin with a distinction between kinds of sources. Primary sources "are written by people who have direct knowledge of the events or issues under discussion; they were participants in or observers of those events" (Rosen & Behrens, 1995, p. 570). Let's say that someone's research site involves the life of writer and diarist Anne Morrow Lindbergh. Although Lindbergh herself is now deceased, a number of primary sources from her era are available. In this case, Lindbergh's own diaries, for example, would count as a primary source (if the research site were redefined as the diaries themselves, Lindbergh's diaries would do double duty as both research site and primary sources). Journals or diaries by people who knew Lindbergh or who lived in her time and place would also count as primary sources, as would historical documents such as newspaper articles or photographs from her time. Similarly, interviews with Lindbergh's friends and family members would belong to the category of primary sources.

Secondary sources, on the other hand, have a "secondary" or more distant relationship to the research site—"authors of secondary sources have only indirect knowledge; they rely on primary or other secondary sources for their information" (Rosen & Behrens, 1995, p. 570). Following through on the prospect of a paper about Anne Morrow Lindbergh's life, scholarly discussions of Lindbergh or of matters that relate to her would count as secondary sources. Such sources, whether books or articles, may be valuable, but they do not provide first-hand access to the subject; they are products of reflection and research. Secondary sources, which consist of someone else's research, involve a "re-seeing" or "re-envisioning" of someone or something.

Finally, tertiary sources include dictionaries, encyclopedias, almanacs, bibliographies, indexes, guidebooks, textbooks, and manuals. These sources are often a useful place to start when researching a topic as they can help students locate primary and secondary sources.

> **Primary sources** provide first-hand observation or investigation. They are produced by people who have direct experience of the events or issues under discussion. **Secondary sources** are created by people who have indirect or second-hand experience of the subject. **Tertiary sources** are compilations, including encyclopedias, bibliographies, and the like.

It may be tempting to assume that primary sources are inherently truer or more accurate than secondary or tertiary sources, or vice versa, that secondary or tertiary sources are more accurate than primary sources, thanks to the benefit of hindsight. However, it would be unwise to generalize in this manner. Often in very obvious ways, diaries and journals are coloured by the personalities of the people who wrote them. Such colouring can reveal all sorts of biases and distortions. Nor is the more distant reflection afforded by secondary sources any guarantee of impartiality. Primary, secondary, and tertiary sources are simply constructed in different ways, and the best papers often contain a mix.

In the case of secondary sources, it is important to make a further distinction between popular and academic material. Usually, the distinction is evident. For one thing, academic sources tend to look different from popular sources: the covers and texts of academic journals often have a more formal appearance. In any event, an academic article will probably have more in-depth and focused information than an article in *Time* or *Newsweek* magazine. Instructors in college and university classes will be inclined to respond favourably to the former source but may wonder about the relevance of the latter one. Accordingly, in relation to secondary sources, students should move beyond popular, journal-istic fare and access academic material. Scholarly research will make a greater contribution to the form and content that students should be attempting to cultivate in their own writing.

## Computer-Based Research

The Internet plays a central role in the search for sources for a paper and other aspects of scholarly research. Informal searches can be made by entering a search term into an Internet search engine, such as Google or Firefox. Formal searches involve access to academic databases that are usually linked to college and university library websites.

### Informal Searches

Surfing the Internet as a way of doing research for a paper has its pitfalls. Anyone can put just about anything on the Internet. Anyone can create a blog about anything! No one monitors the individual pages and websites. This means that the information may or may not be accurate. Even Wikipedia, with its countless contributors supposedly holding every other contributor to a high level of accuracy, may contain errors of fact or be biased.

In 2006, *Google* officially entered the English language as a verb, being included in an update to the *Oxford English Dictionary*, usually considered the most authoritative English dictionary. Although Google is perhaps the most widely used Internet search engine, others, such as Firefox, may give slightly different results. In addition, putting terms or phrases in quotation marks, for example, normally results in a narrower "exact phrase" search that yields fewer hits than the same search term without the quotation marks. The results will only be as good as the search terms. Try to think of different ways to express the concept or thing that you are researching.

The Internet can also be used to conduct other kinds of informal research. Email, for example, is an excellent means of communicating with people who may know about a topic. Rather than being aloof, experts are usually willing to share their expertise. Email addresses can be tracked down in a variety of ways. University and college websites often list professors by department.

Blogs are another source encountered during the informal search stage. Browsing through the titles of blogs on a site like blogger.com or wordpress.com will give an idea of the variety and number of blogs. Because bloggers can respond quickly to incidents with facts and opinions, blogs often contain up-to-the-minute perspectives. Again, no one is monitoring for accuracy or bias, so blogs should be taken with a grain of salt.

Sites like LinkedIn, Facebook, and even Twitter can offer some help at this stage of research. LinkedIn can help you find experts in an area that you are researching. You can join a Facebook group that is interested in a certain topic. Finally, many people—politicians, writers, artists, entertainers, sports stars—tweet their opinions about a wide variety of things. If you want a fresh quote, Twitter is the place to look.

All these may be a good place to start, but more formal research is needed for an academic paper.

## Formal Searches

Formal searches are more selective and frequently involve two types of databases: library catalogues and article databases. On the whole, public libraries tend to contain books and magazines, most of which are less academic in nature, but it is wise, at an early stage in the research process, to check the book and magazine holdings at your local public library. However, the best place for scholarly researchers to start formal searches is at their own educational institution. Talk to the librarian! He or she is trained to help you find the information you need. Librarians know the ins-and-outs of searching for academic sources and avoiding less valuable sources. Tell your librarian the scope of your paper. He or she will not do your research for you but will be able to help you. If your course does not include a library orientation, ask the librarian for one. Next, you can use your computer or mobile device to check the book catalogue and article indexes at your school library. If the book or article you are looking for is not held at your school library, it may be available as an electronic book or through an interlibrary loan. Depending on your location, interlibrary loans may be delivered within a few days. Individual libraries have their own interlibrary loan policies and procedures, so make sure that you are aware of the practices at your institution.

Article databases, which contain full-text articles as well as references to millions of others, are maintained by private companies. Universities and colleges buy the right to display these indexes. For the academic researcher, article indexes are vital because they provide references and access to up-to-date articles published in academic journals. Since most journals are published several times a year, they identify the frontiers of knowledge. The "newness" of information tends to be more important in the sciences than in the humanities, but even in the humanities, there is considerable value placed on the most recent knowledge claims.

The databases themselves vary in scope. Some, like Academic Search Premier, are multidisciplinary, meaning that they cover many disciplines. Others, like the MLA Bibliography for English Studies, focus on particular disciplines. These discipline-specific article databases are probably the most valuable, and even small colleges have access to some. Talk to your librarian to find out about access. As noted above, some libraries provide access to full-text e-books. In addition, one database that is very useful is Google Scholar (scholar.google.ca for Canada or scholar.google.com). This contains partial or full texts of books. Sometimes you can read enough there to know whether you should request the book.

## Using Sources to Find a Topic

We know there is an important link between sources and topic. In fact, sources often lead academic writers to their topic. Let's say, for example, that a student has an interest in writing on some aspect of the North American oil industry (research site). Through interlibrary loan, the student has requested and received *Oil and Ideology: The Cultural Creation of the American Petroleum Industry* by Roger M. Olien and Diana Davids Olien (2000). The research site is still quite general, but the book could help to generate an abstraction. The title, for example, refers to "ideology"—an intriguing yet ambiguous word.

Further, the table of contents for *Oil and Ideology* has suggestive chapter headings like this: "Manhood against Money," "Hasting to Get Rich," "Numerous Offences against Common Morality," "Running Out of Oil," "Visions of Chaos," and so on. Accordingly, gender and/or masculinity, already familiar abstractions, again appear to be relevant. Concepts such as wealth, competition, ethics, resource sustainability, and industrial regulation may also be hovering in the background.

The preface to the book is complex, leaving no doubt that this is a genuinely academic text (not coincidentally, the publisher is the University of North Carolina Press). In the preface, we find out that this is a book about "discourse"—about the language and imagery used to describe the American petroleum industry. The authors say that they are going to investigate various "channels of discourse" (Olien & Olien, 2000, p. xiii) and that such channels involve the themes implicit in the table of contents.

Thus, *Oil and Ideology* suggests that a prestige abstraction for a 10-page paper could highlight a particular "channel of discourse" in the petroleum industry. Skimming other sources as they become available, it would be a good idea to watch for overlapping concepts or issues. Ideally, clusters of related material will emerge. If, for example, other sources also have something to say about wealth, particularly the language and imagery of wealth, a useful abstraction might be on the horizon. Granted, a student wanting to write on the oil industry may still have a lot of research to do. Such a student could generate primary sources by interviewing oil company executives. Students wishing to conduct personal interviews as part of their research should check their institution's research ethics guidelines before commencing their interviews.

As mentioned in the previous chapter, there is often no easy or linear route to finding a topic. The process may involve uncertainty and changes of direction. It will probably involve a mix of intuition and expedient decision-making.

## Creating a Portfolio of Sources

You've probably already been thinking about a topic (abstraction + research site) for a paper of your own. After considering potential sources and gaining a sense of what your own topic might be, create a "portfolio of sources." Gather your sources (articles, book chapters, and so on) either in an online folder or in printed form. If you're printing the articles, a binder is a handy way to keep them organized. The goal is to have your sources easily accessible when you start the next step of the research process. On a cover sheet at the front of your portfolio, present your abstraction, research site, and topic, with an alphabetical list of the sources that you've gathered. There are style manuals and websites that help academic writers to format lists of sources, and we'll talk about this in greater detail in the chapters to come.

Here's the cover sheet for Jenna's portfolio of sources.

## The Jenna Files

Research Site: Teenage Girls and Suicide
Abstraction: Cyberbullying
Topic: Cyberbullying among Teenage Girls and Suicide

### References

Alvarez, L. (2013, September 13). Girl's suicide points to rise in apps used by cyberbullying. *The New York Times*. Retrieved from http://www.nytimes.com

Bauman, S., Toomey, B. R., & Walker, L. J. (2013). Associations among bullying, cyberbullying, and suicide in high school students. *Journal of Adolescence, 36*, 341-350.

Bhat, C. S., Chang, S., Linscott, J. A. (2010). Addressing cyberbullying as a media literacy issue. *New Horizons in Education, 58*, 34-43.

Dooley, J. J., Pyzalski, J., & Cross, D. (2009). Cyberbullying versus face-to-face bullying. *Journal of Psychology, 217*(4), 182-188. doi: 10.1027/0044-3409.271.4.182

Hinduja, S., & Patchin, J. W. (2010). Bullying, cyberbullying, and suicide. *Archives of Suicide Research, 14*(3), 206-221. doi:10.1080/13811118.2010.494133

Hinduja, S., & Patchin, J. W. (2011). Overview of cyberbullying. White Paper. *White House Conference on Bullying Prevention*. Washington, DC. Retrieved from Cyberbullying Research Centre.

Lindfors, P. L., Kaltiala-Heino, R., & Rimpelä, A. H. (2012). Cyberbullying among Finnish adolescents—a population-based study. *BMC Public Health, 12*(1), 1-5. doi:10.1186/1471-2458-12-1027

Schneider, S. K., O'Donnell, L., Stueve, A., & Coulter, R. W. (2012). Cyberbullying, school bullying, and psychological distress: A regional census of high school students. *American Journal of Public Health, 102*(1), 171-177. doi:10.2105/AJPH.2011.300308

Thom, K., Edwards, G., Nakarada-Kordic, I., McKenna, B., O'Brien, A., & Nairn, R. (2011). Suicide online: Portrayal of website-related suicide by the New Zealand media. *New Media & Society, 13*(8), 1355-1372. doi:10.1177/1461444811406521

# Ideas for Further Study

1. Conduct formal searches for books and journal articles on one of two historical figures in 20th-century North American culture: John F. Kennedy and Madonna. Compile a bibliography that lists five books and five journal articles on the person you are researching. In looking for journal articles, distinguish between popular and academic sources, and choose the latter. Be prepared to explain elements of the topic formula (abstraction + research site) in some of the titles that you find.

2. The following passage is taken from the introduction to "Lords of the World," a research article by Heather Smyth. Smyth's article appeared in a special issue of *Studies in Canadian Literature*. Read through Smyth's introduction and identify her articulation of topic. Is the topic clearly stated? Can you differentiate topic (aboutness) from thesis (knowledge claim)?

---

## Heather Smyth, "Lords of the World"

A feeling persisted that I never should discover what I sought for unless I could travel in the wild, unpeopled parts of the world ... (Vyvyan, *Roots and Stars* 131)

Women, too, have spirits which crave the adventure of the unknown and the silence of the northern wilderness. (Hoyle 117)

The adventurer is in flight from women. (Zweig 61)

The epigraphs that introduce this paper juxtapose a number of ideas about travel and travel writing: the traveler seeks to "discover" something in far-away or foreign places; these destinations are often scripted as "wild," "unpeopled," and "unknown"; women as well as men have the urge for travel and adventure; and, paradoxically, the persona of the traveler or adventurer has historically been masculine. This last point is the starting place for my reading of C.C. Vyvyan's *Arctic Adventure* (1961), a travel narrative of a journey through what is now northern Canada and Alaska, ... taken in 1926 by C.C. Vyvyan, born Clara Coltman Rogers (1885-1976), and her friend Gwendolyn Dorrien-Smith.[1] The "adventure" portion of the trip involved the two English women and two Loucheux (now Gwich'in) guides named Lazarus Sittichinli and Jim Koe canoeing up the Rat River bridging the Yukon Territory and Alaska, and then the two women alone canoeing the 115 miles downriver from

LaPierre House to Old Crow. Although *Arctic Adventure* has received little critical attention,[2] it is significant for being arguably the first travel narrative written about the Canadian Arctic by a white professional writer (MacLaren, "Land" 2); and Vyvyan and Dorrien-Smith are notable for being among the first recreational arctic travelers, so that Vyvyan's travel book marks a transition from centuries of arctic discovery and exploration narratives. *Arctic Adventure*, however, is also important for the ways in which Vyvyan manipulates her travelling and writing personae in a genre that has historically been masculine, and for the ways in which she both resists and reproduces the imperial baggage that accompanies travel writing. Vyvyan's representations of the northern space that she often calls "unpeopled" or "uncharted" are implicated in these negotiations.

I will therefore look at *Arctic Adventure* in terms of the intersections of gender and imperialism.[3] I will be starting from the premise that, although women have always travelled and often written about their travels, the activity of travelling and the genre of travel literature have historically been coded as masculine. This has meant that the conventions of travel writing have supported a reading of the adventurer or traveler as male. Travel writing has also often been accompanied by imperial interests. Earlier exploration ventures in what is now the Canadian Arctic were inspired by mercantile and imperial institutions,[4] and the interests of those institutions often inflect the resulting exploration narratives. In the same way, although Vyvyan travelled independent of any particular institution, her journey was largely facilitated by the institutions, transportation, and communications put in place by the gradual settlement and administration of the Canadian landscape. Her narrative also includes reflections on the legal and religious administration of the north and relations between Native, Inuit, and non-Native northerners.

[Thus,] although Vyvyan has inherited a genre that has historically interpellated the narrator and traveler as male and (to a greater or lesser degree) imperialist, she appears to be adjusting her personae to both fit and work against these confines.

*Source:* Smyth (1998, pp. 32–33)

3. Check a multidisciplinary index, such as Academic Search Premier, and compile a list of prestige abstractions. Do some abstractions seem discipline-specific? Do you notice densely recurring abstractions in certain disciplines?
4. Following the guidelines in this chapter and Jenna's example, create your own portfolio of sources.

# References

Aydogan, Ismail. (2008). Favoritism in the classroom: A study on Turkish schools. *Journal of Instructional Psychology, 35*(2), 155–168.

Bazerman, C. (1995). *The informed writer: Using sources in the disciplines* (5th ed.). Toronto: Houghton Mifflin.

Davis, R. (1989). Thrice-told tales: The exploration writing of John Franklin. In J. Carlsen & B. Streijffert (Eds.), *The Canadian North: Essays in culture and literature* (pp. 15–26). Lund: Lund University Press.

Garrett-Petts, W. (Producer). (1996). *Writing your "self" into the disciplines* [video]. Canada: UCC Media Production Services. Available from Thompson Rivers University Library.

Giltrow, J. (1995). *Academic writing: Writing and reading across the disciplines* (2nd ed.). Peterborough: Broadview.

Giltrow, J. (2002). *Academic writing: Writing and reading in the disciplines* (3rd ed.). Peterborough: Broadview.

McCreery, J. (2001). Getting to persuasion. *Anthropological Quarterly, 74*(4), 163–169.

Olien, R. M., & Olien, D. D. (2000). *Oil and ideology: The cultural creation of the American petroleum industry.* Chapel Hill: University of North Carolina Press.

Pierson, D. P. (2005). "Hey, they're just like us!": Representations of the animal world in the Discovery Channel's nature programming. *Journal of Popular Culture, 38*(4), 698–712.

Rosen, L. J., & Behrens, L. (1995). *The Allyn and Bacon handbook* (2nd ed.). Toronto: Allyn and Bacon.

Smyth, H. (1998). "Lords of the world": Writing gender and imperialism on northern space in C. C. Vyvyan's *Arctic Adventure. Studies in Canadian Literature, 23*(1), 32–52.

Tam, C. M., Tso, T. Y., & Lam, K. C. (1999, December). Feng Shui and its impacts on land and property developments. *Journal of Urban Planning and Development, 125*(4), 152–163.

Theberge, N. (1989). A feminist analysis of responses to sports violence: Media coverage of the 1987 World Junior Hockey Championship. *Sociology of Sport Journal, 6*(3), 247–256.

# CHAPTER 3

# Moving Forward:
## Compiling a Research Notebook

> Knowledge never stands alone. It builds upon and plays against the
> knowledge of previous knowers and reporters, whom scholars call
> "sources." These are not, in scholarly papers, the source of your
> particular argument (you are), but rather persons or documents
> that help you arrive at and support your argument. They are sources
> of information that you interpret; of ideas that you support, criticize,
> or develop; of vivid language that you quote and analyze.
>
> —Gordon Harvey,
> *Writing with Sources: A Guide for Students*

Since academic writers depend heavily on sources, they must wade through a lot of information. Professors and graduate students sometimes spend months, even years, doing research that precedes writing. Undergraduate students work under more severe time constraints, but the ability to find texts, to extract and repackage information, and to record where the information came from remains crucial. Good academic writers must develop special skills as readers. In this chapter, we'll discuss compiling a research notebook, and note-taking and summary-writing as part of this process.

## Building a Research Notebook

We advise using your portfolio of sources (see Chapter 2) as the foundation for a "research notebook." In a research notebook, academic writers quote, paraphrase, summarize, critique, and sort information that appears in their sources. This important process marks the early development of a paper. Indeed, the research notebook will provide a foundation for your upcoming work on a proposal and introduction. Eventually, it will also be vital to your work on core paragraphs because many of the low-level details that fill core paragraphs will have made their first appearance in your research notebook. Thus, as you build your research notebook, try to cluster details that belong together, details that could form the basis of core paragraphs. Perhaps you'll even begin to detect potential paragraph groupings that will become major sections in the core of your paper. Further, a research notebook can yield signs of an argument (or thesis) in the making. Remember, too, that research and writing are not neatly linear. As you continue through the semester, you will come back to your research notebook, building or revising it as you gain fresh insights about how to sort and arrange the material for your paper.

Below, we present two research notebooks at various stages of development. The first sample is by Jenna, a student we are now familiar with. Jenna's research notebook, presented here with instructor feedback, is in an early stage of development and consists of unsorted and primarily paraphrased passages. Jenna's efforts at paraphrasing are impressive, but we think quotation marks are likely needed around certain phrases. Although the use of quotation marks is something Jenna could review as she begins drafting, we encourage students to clearly distinguish between paraphrased and quoted material even as they are making their research notebooks. We'll have *much* more to say about paraphrase and quotation later on, in Chapter 6. The instructor comments on Jenna's research notebook are gathered at the end and correspond to numbers that appear throughout the assignment.

## The Jenna Files

### Research Notebook (in progress)

**Topic:**

Cyberbullying among Teenage Girls and Suicide

**Thesis:**

I argue that cyberbullying can lead to suicide among teenage girls. ✓

**Notes:**

- Because cyberbullying has arisen as a social issue recently, there is no exact definition for it. However, in general, cyberbullying is a harmful and

- aggressive action through the Internet or any electronic devices (Dooley, Pyzalski & Cross, 2009, p. 182). ✓
- The studies examining the connection between cyberbullying and suicide are relatively small, because <u>it only has been 20 years researchers studied deep into this connection</u>[1] (Bauman, Toomey & Walker, 2013, p. 342).
- Cyberbullying and traditional bullying both involve victims and offenders. However, the similarities end at this. Cyberbullying only occurs through telecommunication devices. Offenders do not have to expose their information, and this gives them more freedom to express themselves without weighing the costs. This can be very humiliating for the victims, as it is not only a dispute between victims and the bullies, but between victims and the whole community (Schneider K. S., O'Donnell L., Stueve A., & Coulter W. S, 2010, p. 171). ✓
- In America, youth suicide is the third leading cause of death among teenagers, 13.8% of ~~which~~ high school students reported seriously considering suicide; 6.3% reported[2] 12 months before the survey attempted[3] to commit suicide (Bauman, Toomey & Walker, 2013, p. 341).
- Victims of cyberbullying continuously feel low <u>self-esteem, worthless, and it may lead to a higher suicidal risk</u> ([4]Bauman, Toomey & Walker, 2013, p. 341).
- Over 1.8 billion people used the Internet in 2009. 42.4% of <u>which being</u>[5] Asian users, 23.6% European users, and 14.4% North American users (Bhat, Chang & Linscott, 2010, p. 35).
- In a study conducted by Bhat, Chang, and Linscott, 30-40% of youth who were bullied did not consider they would need help. If they did, they would rather seek help from their friends than teachers and parents; where 19% of witnesses told adults about cyberbullying, only 9% of victims actually reported their situation to guardians (Bhat, Chang & Linscott, 2010, p. 35-36). ✓
- Out of 54% of youth that witnessed cyberbullying first hand, 25% were victims, 15% were cyberbullies themselves (Bhat, Chang & Linscott, 2010, p. 36). ✓
- Because the incidents happen through the Internet, victims still have to deal with it out of school. It is very hard for victims to evade (Bhat, Chang & Linscott, 2010, p. 37).
- Those who have committed suicide may influence others who are being bullied to commit suicide (Hinduja and Patchin, 2010, p. 206). ✓

- According to Hinduja and Patchin, ~~in their studies~~, 4% of boys who were bullied at least once a week attempted to commit suicide, whereas the girls' rate was twice as high as the boys' rate. Also, bullied boys had suicidal thoughts 3.8 times more than non-bullied boys <u>when</u>[6] bullied girls had suicidal thoughts 8 times more than those who were not bullied. This study shows that boys and girls have different reactions to cyberbullying, and girls take such situations more seriously (Hinduja and Patchin, 2010, p. 209).
- <u>Due to the fact that</u>[7] adolescents are continuously connected to the Internet, they have a high chance of being victimized; 20% of 11 to 18 year old students have been victims of cyberbullying (Hinduja and Patchin, 2011, p. 2).
- Many victims of cyberbullying have mentioned ~~the~~ feelings of being bullied;[8] depression, sadness, anger, frustration, embarrassment, and suicidal thoughts ~~being among them~~ (Hinduja and Patchin, 2011, p. 2).
- Depressive thoughts may lead to suicidal behavior among teenage girls (Schneider, K. S., O'Donnell, L., Stueve, A., & Coulter, W. S, 2010, p. 284).

## List of References[9]

Alvarez, L. (2013, September 13). Girl's suicide points to rise in apps used by cyberbullying. *The New York Times*. Retrieved from www.nytimes.com

Bauman, S., Chang, H., & Linscott, A. (2013). Associations among bullying, cyberbullying, and suicide in high school students. *Journal of Adolescence, 36*, 341-350.

Bhat, C. S., Chang, S., & Linscott, J. A. (2010). Addressing cyberbullying as a media literacy issue. *New Horizons in Education, 58*, 34-43.

Dooley, J. J., Pyzalski, J., & Cross, D. (2009). Cyberbullying versus face-to-face bullying. *Journal of Psychology, 217*(4), 182-188. doi: 10.1027/0044-3409.271.4.182

Hinduja, S., & Patchin, J. W. (2010). Bullying, cyberbullying, and suicide. *Archives of Suicide Research, 14*(3), 206-221. doi:10.1080/13811118.2010.494133

Hinduja, S., & Patchin, J. W. (2011). Overview of cyberbullying. White Paper. *White House Conference on Bullying Prevention*. Retrieved from Cyberbullying Research Centre.

Lindfors, P. L., Kaltiala-Heino, R., & Rimpelä, A. H. (2012). Cyberbullying among Finnish adolescents—a population-based study. *BMC Public Health, 12*(1), 1-5. doi:10.1186/1471-2458-12-1027

Schneider, S., O'Donnell, L., Stueve, A., & Coulter, R. W. S. (2012). Cyberbullying, school bullying, and psychological distress: A regional census of high school students. *American Journal of Public Health, 102*(1), 171-177. doi:10.2105/AJPH.2011.300308

Thom, K., Edwards, G., Nakarada-Kordic, I., McKenna, B., O'Brien, A., & Nairn, R. (2011). Suicide online: Portrayal of website-related suicide by the New Zealand media. *New Media & Society, 13*(8), 1355-1372. doi:10.1177/1461444811406521

**Instructor comments:**

1. Syntax. You must be paraphrasing here?
2. Syntax again. You need a relative phrase describing a span of time.
3. This verb needs a subject.
4. Use parallel structure here.
5. People? Use whom + simple past.
6. Wrong connector. Use "while" instead of "when."
7. Wordy.
8. Improper use of semi-colon. Use a comma and "including" to introduce your list.
9. Nice work on your list of references. It's carefully compiled. You're already paying attention to APA style.

Notes to self:

– Maybe this isn't going to be so hard after all. I got my second assignment back with lots of check marks. My instructor noted some grammatical things, such as non-parallel structures and poor syntax in a couple of places, but he liked all of my low-level details. He also said my Reference List was "carefully compiled."

The second sample research notebook, by Talia Miller, is at a later stage of development, with passages already sorted under subheadings. Talia, however, has relied strictly on quotation for the time being. Further, Talia realizes that her research notebook needs more work. When she submitted her assignment electronically, she sent the following note to her instructor: "I've divided the notes into some categories, but at the moment they are still quite large, so I still need to analyze them further. In other words, it's still in progress ☺." It's also important to notice that the quoted passages in Talia's research notebook do not have page numbers, which should have been included at this stage in the process. Talia may have these passages highlighted in her portfolio of sources, but omitting page numbers here creates additional work later on at the writing stage. By coincidence, Talia's research notebook also deals with a form of bullying.

---

# Research Notebook

## Topic:

Victimization of Obese Adolescents

## Thesis:

I will show that obese adolescents are more likely to be bully victims than their normal-weight peers, and that this victimization leads to future emotional and mental issues.

## Notes:

### Bullying of Overweight Teens

- "Relational victimization ... was significantly associated with ... weight concerns" (Compian, Laura J., 2009)
- "[There is] a link between being overweight or obese and bullying/peer victimization" (Fox, C. L., & Farrow, C. V., 2009)
- "Certain behavioral characteristics do seem to increase children's vulnerability, for example, those behaviors which mark them out as 'easy targets', as well as those behaviors which 'reward' and 'reinforce' the bully's behavior" (Fox, C. L., & Farrow, C. V., 2009)
- "Thus, it is not simply being overweight or obese that appears to put children at risk of being victimized by their peers, but these other factors seem to account for this relationship" (Fox, C. L., & Farrow, C. V., 2009)
- "... being overweight or obese would predict increases in all types of bullying (verbal, physical and social forms) and that these relationships would be mediated by the child's physical and global self-esteem and body dissatisfaction" (Fox, C. L., & Farrow, C. V., 2009)
- "Weight focused victimization is associated with increased weight concerns and poor body image satisfaction among early adolescent girls" (Compian, Laura J., 2009)

- "More physically mature girls reported greater overt victimization and lack of prosocial treatment" (Compian, Laura J., 2009)
- "... making negative self-evaluations about their own appearance and weight if they are not experiencing acceptance within the peer group" (Compian, Laura J., 2009)
- "Global self-worth self-esteem for physical appearance and body dissatisfaction mediate the relationships between being overweight and experiencing verbal bullying, and between overweight and experiencing physical bullying" (Fox, C. L., & Farrow, C. V., 2009)
- "... and also between obesity and adjustment problems such as low self-esteem and body dissatisfaction" (Fox, C. L., & Farrow, C. V., 2009)
- "Obese children have consistently been shown to have lower self-esteem specifically related to their *physical appearance* and report higher levels of body dissatisfaction" (Fox, C. L., & Farrow, C. V., 2009)
- "Overweight and obese children who suffer from body dissatisfaction and low self-esteem either globally or related to their appearance may therefore be at a greater risk of being bullied" (Fox, C. L., & Farrow, C. V., 2009)
- "Adolescence is a time when children's peer relationships are valued highly and with the onset of puberty body image is likely to become more salient. Given this it may be a particularly difficult time to be overweight, obese and/or a victim of bullying" (Fox, C. L., & Farrow, C. V., 2009)
- "Common weight-related problems among adolescent girls include obesity, body dissatisfaction, and the use of disordered eating behaviors, such as unhealthy weight control behaviors and binge eating" (Neumark-Sztainer, D., & Bauer, K. W., 2010)
- "These weight-related problems are a concern, given their high prevalence and harmful consequences for physical health and emotional well-being" (Neumark-Sztainer, D., & Bauer, K. W., 2010)
- "Girls who were either overweight or obese had significantly lower levels of perceived competence than did normal or underweight girls" (Craft, L. L., & Pfeiffer, K., 2003)
- "Adolescence is generally associated with an increase in body weight for girls. Early maturing girls often have more body fat than other girls their age and it may be this change in body shape that leads to negative feelings regarding their physical appearance" (Alasker, 1992; Brooks-Gunn, 1988 as cited in Craft, L. L., & Pfeiffer, K., 2003)

- "Encouraging heavier girls to participate in sport and exercise should increase their feelings of competence in the physical domain and positively impact their feeling of self-worth" (Craft, L. L., & Pfeiffer, K., 2003)
- "Women and men do not perceive their body size in the same manner, and this disparity may be influenced by social and cultural messages that portray women's and men's bodies differently" (Gucciardi, E., 2007)
- "Overweight or obese children reported experiencing significantly more verbal and physical (but not social) bullying than their non-overweight peers" (Fox, C. L., & Farrow, C. V., 2009)
- "This proposes that children are bullied because of some external negative deviation" (Fox, C. L., & Farrow, C. V., 2009)
- "Ethnographic research, including individual interviews, focus groups, and participant observation, was conducted to examine how adolescents define and negotiated the boundaries between normal/acceptable weight and overweight through direct and indirect teasing" (Taylor, N. L., 2011)
- "... girls' body fat was more closely monitored and criticized than boys' by both male and female peers" (Taylor, N. L., 2011)
- "Overweight bodies came to represent laziness, weakness, and a lack of impulse control whereas thin, toned bodies indexed discipline and willpower" (Bordo, 1993, 1999; Connel, 1996; etc. as cited in Taylor, N. L., 2011)
- "... body image ideology continues to dictate that bodies be thin, toned, and fat free" (Taylor, N. L., 2011)
- "Obesity represents an incorrect 'attitude,' a willful failure to adhere to the norm, and is therefore a source of social stigma" (Taylor, N. L., 2011)
- "... there is no social space within which it is considered normal or attractive for girls to be large" (Taylor, N. L., 2011)
- "Gossip ... functions as a means for keeping track of social norms and keeping track of individual's behavior in relation to those norms" (Eckert, 1993 as cited in Taylor, N. L., 2011)
- "... if boys responded emotionally to being teased by another boy, the exchange would immediately escalate to more serious insulting" (Taylor, N. L., 2011)
- "Thus, the phrase 'I was just joking' allows speakers to say virtually anything without taking responsibility for potentially negative or hurtful effects of their utterances" (Taylor, N. L., 2011)
- "... girls used humour to insult each other indirectly" (Taylor, N. L., 2011)
- "... hide their hurt feelings for fear of being thought of as hypersensitive" (Taylor, N. L., 2011)

- ".. allowed adolescents of all sizes to construct boundaries that mark fat teens (or teens who simply display body fat) as 'different' and reaffirm their subordinate status within the high school's social hierarchy" (Taylor, N. L., 2011)
- "... continually renegotiate body fat norms, which they largely did through direct and indirect teasing" (Taylor, N. L., 2011)

**Bullying Leads to Psychological Difficulties (Dissatisfaction)**

- "The child develops psychological problems related to the comments and jokes to which they become subject on the part of their colleagues" (State University of Campinas, 1997) (de Sousa, Pedro Miguel Lopes, 2008)
- "Women and men do not perceive their body size in the same manner, and this disparity may be influenced by social and cultural messages that portray women's and men's bodies differently" (Gucciardi, E., 2007)
- "... body dissatisfaction ... may then lead to emotional eating and further weight gain" (Fox, C. L., & Farrow, C. V., 2009)
- "... higher body weight challenges social norms about acceptable body size; individuals with higher body weight that do not conform to the norm are discredited, treated as physically deformed and subjected to discrimination" (Sobal, 1999; as cited in Curtis, P., 2008)
- "... excess body weight is necessarily undesirable, the programme prioritizes key areas of activity which emphasize individual responsibility for the prevention of body deviance" (Monaghan, 2007; as cited in Curtis, P., 2008)
- "The young people with obesity, particularly girls, perceived themselves to be under constant scrutiny from their peers, a scrutiny that was experienced as highly judgmental" (Curtis, P., 2008)
- ".... felt themselves to be on the 'outside' of local peer culture" (Curtis, P., 2008)
- "The overweight body has come to be considered as undesirable and, indeed, abhorrent, by many non-overweight young people and adults (Wardle et al. 1995) and this morally laden, value judgment sets apart young people within the school and helps to create the circumstances of their isolation" (Curtis, P., 2008)
- "Adolescents with excessive weight or obesity perceive their difference, and hear rude, even offensive comments from classmates, causing them to limit their athletic activities and social life" (de Sousa, Pedro Miguel Lopes, 2008)

- "One potential factor that may exacerbate the difficulties faced by obese children is social interaction at school and difficulties with peer relationships, particularly bullying" (Fox, C. L., & Farrow, C. V., 2009)
- "When adolescents experience negative peer relationships, with their weight status becoming the target of the harassment, the short and long term effects could be particularly devastating" (Fox, C. L., & Farrow, C. V., 2009)
- "Perceptions of lack of acceptance by the peer group may be salient in the formation of weight concerns and depression symptoms in early adolescence" (Compian, Laura J., 2009)
- "... victimization would predict later depression and increases in body mass over the course of the study and that these links would be mediated by adolescents' perceptions of their physical appearance" (Adams, R. E., 2008)
- "Obese adolescents are more likely to be depressed ..." (Adams, R. E., 2008)
- "Obese adolescents are a target of preconception and discrimination, attend school for fewer years, have a lower probability of being accepted into more competitive schools or jobs, have lower salaries, and less stable romantic relationships" (Segal et al., 2002; as cited in de Sousa, Pedro Miguel Lopes, 2008)
- "Some social consequences are discrimination, difficulty with cultural integration, and deterioration of the self-image" (Cruz, 1983; as cited in de Sousa, Pedro Miguel Lopes, 2008)
- "The adolescents who considered themselves "fat" tend to have less functional families, and those with families with elevated levels of dysfunction tend to have more adolescents considered "fat" than the remainder" (Rodriguez et al., 2004; as cited in de Sousa, Pedro Miguel Lopes, 2008)
- "Emotional consequences associated with weight-based teasing among youth are serious and can reach into adulthood. Studies show that overweight youth who are teased by peers are at great risk for developing negative body images and low self-esteem (Crocker & Garcia, 2005; Eisenberg et al., 2003) and tend to have greater levels of body dissatisfaction as adults" (Grilo, Welfly, Brownell, & Rodin, 1994; as cited in Taylor, N. L., 2011)

**Other Facts: Types of Bullying, Family Influence, etc.**

- "Bullying is commonly defined as a subset of aggressive behavior characterized by repetition and by an imbalance of power where the victim cannot defend himself ..." (Fox, C. L., & Farrow, C. V., 2009)

- "Whereas bullying encompasses both relational and indirect forms and both overt and covert forms, it is viewed in terms of its goal—to do social harm" (Fox, C. L., & Farrow, C. V., 2009)
- "Obese boys more likely to experience overt victimization and obese girls being more likely to experience relational victimization compared to their average weight peers" (Fox, C. L., & Farrow, C. V., 2009)
- "... girls reporting being on the receiving end of more verbal and social bullying than boys" (Fox, C. L., & Farrow, C. V., 2009)
- "boys are more likely to be overt victims, compared to their average weight peers" (Fox, C. L., & Farrow, C. V., 2009)
- "Teachers, parents and practitioners need to be aware of the links between children's weight, their psychological health and their risk of being bullied" (Fox, C. L., & Farrow, C. V., 2009)
- "... weight-teasing by family members or parental encouragement to diet may be more harmful than indirect factors, such as observing a parent dieting" (Neumark-Sztainer, D., Bauer, K. W., 2010)
- "... negative comments directed to a child might be more harmful than general weight talk in the home, such as parents talking about their own weight" (Neumark-Sztainer, D., Bauer, K. W., 2010)
- "Girls who were teased 'very often' about their weight were at much greater risk for binge eating than girls who were not teased by family members" (Neumark-Sztainer, D., Bauer, K. W., 2010)
- "... more likely to be targets of verbal bullying" (Wang, J., Iannotti, R. J., 2010)
- "... the main type of bullying toward overweight youth is through being called mean names and teased in a hurtful way" (Wang, J., Iannotti, R. J., 2010)
- "... described indirect teasing as making derogatory comments about someone's appearance, behavior, or character behind that person's back. Many informants likened indirect teasing with gossip and used the two terms interchangeably" (Taylor, N. L., 2011)
- "Like you'll be in a circle and let's say Suzi, the really fat girl, walks by. Everyone will get silent and they won't go, "Ha Suzi's fat!" [spoken loudly]. They'll go in the circle and whisper, "Guys, she's humongous!" [spoken in a whisper] ..." (Taylor, N. L., 2011)
- "... commenting to each other on people's appearance as they walk by as "thinking out loud" (Taylor, N. L., 2011)

- "Male and female informants from a variety of social groups and ethnic backgrounds reported engaging in indirect teasing" (Taylor, N. L., 2011)
- "Although indirect teasing may appear to be less publicly and immediately humiliating than being teased directly in front of one's peers, the emotional effects can be just as damaging for adolescents" (Taylor, N. L., 2011)
- "These comments were made quickly and quietly so that teachers did not notice" (Taylor, N. L., 2011)
- "Engaging themselves in direct and indirect teasing also enabled adolescents to distance themselves from everyday fatness by focusing attention on other people's bodies and away from their own" (Taylor, N. L., 2011)
- "... fuels female gossip, which functions to further heighten girls' insecurities about the way they look" (Taylor, N. L., 2011)
- ".... girls were most frequently teased by their male peers and that this teasing was primarily direct in nature" (Taylor, N. L., 2011)

## List of References

Adams, R. E., & Bukowski, W. M. (2008). Peer victimization as a predictor of depression and body mass index in obese and non-obese adolescents. *Journal of Child Psychology & Psychiatry, 49*(8), 858-866. Retrieved February 28, 2011, doi:10.1111/j.1469-7610.2008.01886.x

Compian, L. J., Gowen, L., & Hayward, C. (2009). The interactive effects of puberty and peer victimization on weight concerns and depression symptoms among early adolescent girls. *Journal of Early Adolescence, 29*(3), 257-375. Retrieved February 28, 2011, from Academic Search Premier database.

Craft, L. L., Pfeiffer, K. A., & Pivarnik, J. M. (2003). Predictors of physical competence in adolescent girls. *Journal of Youth and Adolescence, 32*(6), 431-438. Retrieved February 28, 2011, doi:10.1023/A:1025986318306

Curtis, P. (2008). The experiences of young people with obesity in secondary school: some implications for the healthy school agenda. *Health & Social Care in the Community, 16*(4), 410-418. Retrieved February 28, 2011, from Academic Search Premier database

Fox, C. L., & Farrow, C. V. (2009). Global and physical self-esteem and body dissatisfaction as mediators of the relationship between weight status and being a victim of bullying. *Journal of Adolescence, 32*(5), 1287-1301.

Retrieved February 28, 2011, doi:10.1016/j.adolescence.2008.12.006

Gucciardi, E., Wang, S. C., Badiani, T., & Stewart, D. E. (2007). Beyond adolescence: Exploring Canadian women and men's perception of overweight. *Women's Health Issues, 17*(6), 374-382. Retrieved February 28, 2011, doi:10.1016/j.whi.2007.05.007

Kim, Y., Boyce, W., Koh, Y., & Leventhal, B. (2009). Time trends, trajectories, and demographic predictors of bullying: A prospective study in Korean adolescents. *Journal of Adolescent Health, 45*(4), 360-367. Retrieved February 28, 2011, from Academic Search Premier database.

Neumark-Sztainer, D., Bauer, K., Friend, S., Hannan, P., Story, M., & Berge, J. (2010). Family weight talk and dieting: How much do they matter for body dissatisfaction and disordered eating behaviors in adolescent girls? *Journal of Adolescent Health, 47*(3), 270-276. Retrieved February 28, 2011, from Academic Search Premier database.

de Sousa, P. (2008). Body-image and obesity in adolescence: A comparative study of social-demographic, psychological, and behavioral aspects. *The Spanish Journal of Psychology, 11*(2), 551-563. Retrieved February 28, 2011, from Academic Search Premier database.

Taylor, N. L. (2011). "Guys, She's Humongous!": Gender and Weight-Based Teasing in Adolescence. *Journal of Adolescent Research, 26*(2), 178-199. Retrieved February 28, 2011, doi:10.1177/0743558410371128

Wang, J., Iannotti, R., & Luk, J. (2010). Bullying victimization among underweight and overweight U.S. youth: Differential associations for boys and girls. *Journal of Adolescent Health, 47*(1), 99-101. Retrieved February 28, 2011, doi:10.1016/j.jadohealth.2009.12.007

# Note-Taking

Note-taking is central to compiling a research notebook. The best note-takers are voracious, efficient readers who are able to digest large amounts of information. Go through as much material as you can, extracting information for your research notebook. Your goal is to gather quotes and to write paraphrases and summaries that might appear in the first draft. In other words, you should be able to write the draft mostly from your research notebook rather than having to go back to the sources themselves. Charles Bazerman (1995) offers this advice on note-taking: "The most precise form of note is an exact quotation. Whenever you suspect that you may later wish to quote the writer's exact words, make sure you copy the quotation correctly. And whenever you decide to copy exact words down in your notes—even if only a passing phrase—make sure you enclose

All due back in one week?

them in *quotation marks*. In this way you can avoid inadvertent plagiarism when you are working from your notes" (p. 305).

Although people's notes will have different characteristics, *everyone should carefully record where the extracted information came from.* In the days when scholars primarily relied on printed material, this information involved some basic bibliographical (or textual) data, such as author and/or editor, full title, publisher, date of publication, and page numbers. Today, when the full texts of some sources have been accessed through the Internet, the bibliographical fingerprint is more likely to involve author, title, access date, and URL. Different scholarly disciplines have different and elaborate rule-governed procedures for presenting bibliographical information in finished papers. Be sure that you accurately copy down all the information you will need. Choose a discipline-specific documentation style and format your entries the best you can.

Returning to the hypothetical paper on the discourse of wealth in the oil industry (see Chapter 2), notes taken from the preface of *Oil and Ideology* might look like this:

### Roger M. Olien and Diana Davids Olien, *Oil and Ideology: The Cultural Creation of the American Petroleum Industry*

**Notes on the Preface:**

- "College-level textbooks usually portray John D. Rockefeller, the archetypal oil man and CEO of Standard Oil, as a ruthless, 'robber baron'" (x).
- "In short, Standard's predations and the anticompetitive and anticonsumer identity of the domestic oil industry are largely taken as 'given'" (x).
- "As we studied what has been said about the domestic petroleum industry, we came to recognize broad rhetorical categories, or, as we prefer to call them, channels of discourse. These are identified in terms of the subject area speakers addressed, the focus they took within that area, and the themes and rhetoric they used. Each channel has specific contextual information and characteristic perspectives along with broader elements of ideology" (xiii).
- One of the main channels of discourse is economic (xiii).
- "As we shall demonstrate, though there were differing ways of talking about oil, a great many of them were negative and tied the industry to problems such as the abuse of economic power or waste of natural resources. And, as we shall describe, such negative ideas, a staple in [the] discourse, had a powerful influence on the impulse to regulate the industry" (xv).

Given that chapters 1 and 2 in *Oil and Ideology* seem to pay special attention to the discourse of wealth, these chapters might also deserve carefully recorded notes.

## Writing Summaries

Your research notebook will consist primarily of "notes" in the form of brief quotations and paraphrases. Eventually, however, the ability to compose summaries will assume greater importance as you begin drafting your paper. Indeed, the ability to write effective summaries will be crucial in your work on a proposal and introduction, and perhaps even more so as you begin drafting core paragraphs. At this point, then, in preparation for the work ahead, we'll spend some time discussing the summary process.

When you go through your sources, there's no telling what or how much you may want to use. In some cases, very short notes, like those above, will seem adequate: you may simply want to take a sentence here or there. In other cases, you may want to expand the note-taking process so that it encompasses larger amounts of material—paragraphs, say, or pages, perhaps even entire articles or books. This is where summary comes in.

When you summarize, you demonstrate your ability to condense and repackage extended blocks of information while preserving their "gist" or general meaning. The summary enables you to take charge of or manage your sources. It is a way for you to shape your paper (*to make your paper your own*) while at the same time relying on other voices. Thus, summary writing points to a crucial principle of academic writing. Summaries demonstrate that academic writing involves a kind of balancing act: on the one hand, academic writers tend to rely heavily on sources; on the other hand, they contribute something of their own. If a student paper consists of too many long passages pulled directly from sources, the balance is lost, resulting in what instructors refer to as a "cut-and-paste job."

Ten pages of stuff. What do I really need?

There is much more to say about the kind of contributions that academic writers make to their papers, but, for now, it is enough to acknowledge summarizing as an initial means of moving beyond passive copying. People who can write good summaries demonstrate that they can condense information by neatly packing it into usable bundles that can be sorted and arranged to enhance the development of a paper.

Summaries may turn up almost anywhere in a finished paper. For example, readers may encounter a summary in an introduction, when the author of the paper (the primary writer) is describing previous research on his or her subject. In such cases, as the primary writer describes *a tradition of inquiry*, articles and books may be summarized in a sentence or two. At other times, however, in the middle of a core paragraph, say, the primary writer may be inclined to delve more deeply into the work of others, devoting more space to smaller amounts of material. In any event, summary writing is a practical skill that you will need as you put together your own research paper.

## Summarizing a Portion of an Article

We'll begin modestly, by summarizing a section of an article. Harman, a student researcher, has a general subject or research site in mind: the Canadian North in Aboriginal cultures. While searching a database, using "North AND Aboriginal people" as search terms, Harman came across the article by Shelagh Grant (1989), entitled "Myths of the North in the Canadian Ethos." A section of this article deals with Aboriginal attitudes toward the Canadian North, and this is the section that Harman wants to preserve in his research notebook. The section, in its entirety, reads as follows:

> Perhaps the oldest and most enduring perception of the north is one shared by the indigenous peoples long before Europeans set foot on the shores of the western hemisphere. There are many cultures and subcultures among the Indian and Inuit of northern Canada, but they share similar attitudes towards the land, derived in part from the long experience of survival in what many southerners consider a hostile environment. The image of the north as a "homeland" is essentially

a southern expression for the intensely spiritual concept of land held by northern natives. To the Inuit, it is called *Nunassiaq*, meaning the beautiful land. Fred Bruemmer, who has lived and travelled extensively in the Arctic, describes the deeper meaning of *Nunassiaq*:

> He (an Inuk) was a part of it; it brought him sorrow and it brought him joy, and he lived in harmony with it and its demands, accepting fatalistically, its hardships, exulting in its bounty and beauty.[11]

Prior to European contact, everything within the Inuit's natural world had a spiritual connotation, a sanctity which must be respected. The infinite space and majestic grandeur of the Arctic "gave northern man a special awe for the might and mystery of the world, impressed upon him his own insignificance, and made him both mystically inclined and humble." This feeling of impotence was also the basis for the Inuit's belief in shamans to act as "intermediaries between the world of man and the world of the spirits." Any life form or inanimate object which had a sense of permanency was thought to have had a spirit or soul, a belief which explains his profound respect for nature.[12] He was not a separate entity arriving on earth; he was always there, at one with, and a part of the natural world.

The Dene Indians of the Northwest Territories have similar beliefs, perhaps more estranged due to a more prolonged and intensive contact with western man. Significantly, there is no word for wilderness in the Athapaskan dialects. Wherever they travelled, it was simply "home." In the words of one Dene, the land represented "the very spirit of the Dene way of life. From the land came our religion ... from the land came our life ... from the land came our powerful medicine ... from the land came our way of life."[13] There was also a strong mother image attached to the land and waters, which fed and protected them from adversity. To the Aborigines of the north, their land was never "owned" in the sense of western man. It was always there. Only with the intrusion of strangers who did not understand the bond between man and nature was there a disorientation in the symbiotic balance between humans, animals, plant life, and the earth. There was never an idea of frontier or imperial design. The land belonged to the Creator, and in the Dene expression, [was] only borrowed for their children's children.[14]

Because Harman is at the information-gathering stage, he could "note" or file this passage through a variety of shortcuts. One option would be to photocopy the passage, tape it onto a sheet of loose-leaf, and record the appropriate bibliographic data. Moreover, when it comes to drafting, Harman could again save time and effort by simply presenting Grant's information as one long *block quote*. However, Harman has been to a plagiarism seminar and knows that too many block quotes create a cut-and-paste impression. Moreover, his instructors have said that summary-writing is worth the effort: it will enable him to take charge of Grant's material.

In this case, Harman has decided to aim for an 80 percent reduction of the original word count. Since Grant's passage is approximately 500 words long, he will try to get it down to 100 words. He will use the following guidelines that can be applied, with minor variations, to almost every summary task:

- **Preparation:** Carefully read through the material that you are going to summarize.
- **Step 1:** Reread the material, highlighting or underlining the major point in each paragraph, typically found at the beginning of the paragraph, in a "guiding sentence." In other textbooks, guiding sentences are called topic sentences. However, we've steered clear of that phrase because "topic" has an important, specific meaning in this book, and we don't want to muddy the waters. As you read, you'll see that paragraph structure varies. The main point may also be recapped at the end of the paragraph, and this recap can be useful for summary writers as well. Accordingly, each paragraph should be individually analyzed. Do not highlight examples or details or include them in your summary.
- **Step 2:** Copy the main points (guiding sentences) onto a separate sheet of paper (or new word-processing document).
- **Step 3:** Study and revise the list of main points: reorder the list where appropriate, and condense the list if you can. Is there needless repetition? Can

some points be combined and condensed? Does the order of the points make sense—should you rearrange the points?

- **Step 4:** As much as possible, put the revised main points into your own words by paraphrasing them. Quote only where the exact words of the source are vital. Use transitions or logical connectives to ensure coherence.
- **Step 5:** Arrange the main points in a well-written paragraph. Begin your summary by introducing the title and author. Use this pattern:

---

In ["Title of Article,"] + [author's first name and last name] + [verb] + [thesis].

For example:

In "Myths of the North in the Canadian Ethos," Shelagh Grant contends that although there are different Aboriginal cultures in northern Canada, many communities have similar values concerning the land.

---

Then present the revised and paraphrased main points. As you write your summary, remember to intermittently attribute these points to the author of the original article through ongoing attributive verbs. See Harman's example below.

Harman applies these five steps to Grant's passage. See if you agree or disagree with the decisions he made.

## Step 1: Underlining Main Points

Perhaps the oldest and most enduring perception of the north is one shared by the indigenous peoples long before Europeans set foot on the shores of the western hemisphere. There are many cultures and subcultures among the Indian and Inuit of northern Canada, but they share similar attitudes towards the land, derived in part from the long experience of survival in what many southerners consider a hostile environment. The image of the north as a "homeland" is essentially a southern expression for the intensely spiritual concept of land held by northern natives. To the Inuit, it is called *Nunassiaq*, meaning the beautiful land. Fred Bruemmer, who has lived and travelled extensively in the Arctic, describes the deeper meaning of *Nunassiaq*:

> He (an Inuk) was a part of it; it brought him sorrow and it brought him joy, and he lived in harmony with it and its demands, accepting fatalistically, its hardships, exulting in its bounty and beauty.[11]

Prior to European contact, everything within the Inuit's natural world had a spiritual connotation, a sanctity which must be respected. The infinite space and majestic grandeur of the Arctic "gave northern man a special awe for the might and mystery of the world, impressed upon him his own insignificance, and made him both mystically inclined and humble." This feeling of impotence was also the basis for the Inuit's belief in shamans to act as "intermediaries between the world of man and the world of the spirits." Any life form or inanimate object which had a sense of permanency was thought to have had a spirit or soul, a belief which explains his profound respect for nature.[12] He was not a separate entity arriving on earth: he was always there, at one with, and a part of the natural world.

The Dene Indians of the Northwest Territories have similar beliefs, perhaps more estranged due to a more prolonged and intensive contact with western man. Significantly, there is no word for wilderness in the Athapaskan dialects. Wherever they travelled, it was simply "home." In the words of one Dene, the land represented "the very spirit of the Dene way of life. From the land came our religion ... from the land came our life ... from the land came our powerful medicine ... from the land came our way of life."[13] There was also a strong mother image attached to the land and waters, which fed and protected them from adversity. To the Aborigines of the north, their land was never "owned" in the sense of western man. It was always there. Only with the intrusion of strangers who did not understand the bond between man and nature was there a disorientation in the symbiotic balance between humans, animals, plant life, and the earth. There was never an idea of frontier or imperial design. The land belonged to the Creator, and in the Dene expression, [was] only borrowed for their children's children.[14]

## *Step 2: Copying out Main Points*

[Note that superscript numerals are now omitted.]

1. There are many cultures and subcultures among the Indian and Inuit of northern Canada, but they share similar attitudes towards the land ...
2. Prior to European contact, everything within the Inuit's natural world had a spiritual connotation, a sanctity which must be respected.
3. Any life form or inanimate object which had a sense of permanency was thought to have had a spirit or soul, a belief which explains his profound respect for nature. He was not a separate entity arriving on earth: he was always there, at one with, and a part of the natural world.
4. The Dene Indians of the Northwest Territories have similar beliefs, perhaps more estranged due to a more prolonged and intensive contact with western man. Significantly, there is no word for wilderness in the Athapaskan dialects. Wherever they travelled, it was simply "home."
5. There was never an idea of frontier or imperial design. The land belonged to the Creator, and in the Dene expression, [was] only borrowed for their children's children.

## *Step 3: Reordering and/or Condensing Main Points*

1. There are many cultures and subcultures among the Indian and Inuit of northern Canada, but they share similar attitudes towards the land ...
2. Prior to European contact, everything within the Inuit's natural world had a spiritual connotation, a sanctity which must be respected.
3. ~~Any life form or inanimate object which had a sense of permanency was thought to have had a spirit or soul, a belief which explains his profound respect for nature.~~ (Omitted) He was not a separate entity arriving on earth: he was always there, at one with, and a part of the natural world.
4. The Dene Indians of the Northwest Territories have similar beliefs, perhaps more estranged due to a more prolonged and intensive contact with western man. Significantly, there is no word for wilderness in the Athapaskan dialects. ~~Wherever they travelled, it was simply "home."~~ There was never an idea of frontier or imperial design. (Moved up from 5)

5. ~~There was never an idea of frontier or imperial design.~~ <u>Wherever they travelled, it was simply "home."</u> (Moved down, for emphasis, from 4) The land
belonged to the Creator, and in the Dene expression, [was] only borrowed
for their children's children.

## Step 4: Rewording the Original

[Now that paraphrasing enters the process, quotation marks distinguish Grant's
words from Harman's own.]

1. Aboriginal peoples in northern Canada have different "cultures and subcultures," "but they share similar attitudes toward the land."
2. For the Inuit, virtually everything in their world has a soul that "must be
   respected."
3. Accordingly, the Inuit did not feel superior to or apart from nature: they were
   a part of it.
4. Given their "prolonged and intensive contact with western man," the Dene
   peoples of the Northwest Territories do not feel as close to nature, but they
   share Inuit values. Indeed, the Dene have "no word for 'wilderness,'" no sense
   of "frontier or imperial design."
5. For them, nature is "simply 'home'"—something that belongs to "the Creator"
   and is "borrowed" for future generations.

## Step 5: The Complete Summary

[Attributive expressions have been placed in bold print, for emphasis.]

> In "Myths of the North in the Canadian Ethos," Shelagh Grant
> **contends** that although there are different Aboriginal cultures in
> northern Canada, many communities have similar values concerning
> the land. **Grant notes** that, for the Inuit, virtually everything in the
> natural world has a soul that "must be respected." Accordingly, the
> Inuit do not feel superior to or apart from nature: they are a part of it.
> Given their "prolonged and intensive contact with western man," **Grant
> observes** that the Dene peoples of the Northwest Territories do not feel
> as close to nature, but they share Inuit values. Indeed, the Dene, **Grant**

**says**, have "no word for 'wilderness,'" no sense of "frontier or imperial design." For them, nature is "simply 'home'"— something that belongs to "the Creator" and is "borrowed" for future generations.

Harman's summary sounds impressive, but it is a little long—around 130 words rather than 100. With a little more work, Harman could probably reduce the summary to the intended word count. Remember, too, that another student might have been inclined to make different decisions about what to highlight and what to leave, what to paraphrase and what to quote. Nevertheless, it is likely that other summaries would sound very similar to this one.

## Summarizing a Complete Article

The length of article summaries varies. As noted, the summaries that are presented as part of a tradition of inquiry within research papers tend to be very short—a sentence or two. Here, in order to allow for more elaborate summaries, the scope will be set at 250–300 words. We will be producing what could otherwise be called "abstracts"—paragraph-length summaries of an entire paper. Now that a complete article is now being considered, the summary process could be reconfigured as follows:

- **Preparation:** Read the entire article, and then divide it into major structural divisions. Draw solid lines to separate the introduction, core, and conclusion. Draw dotted lines to separate major subdivisions within the core of the essay. In some essays, these subdivisions will be clearly denoted by subheadings.
- **Step 1:** Reread the introduction. At a minimum, get the summary under way by formulating topic and thesis in a single sentence, using the pattern described earlier. In your summary of the introduction, you could also acknowledge additional rhetorical features, such as a theoretical framework (see chapters 4 and 5 for more information).
- **Step 2:** Block or highlight guiding sentences (main points) in core paragraphs (see Chapter 6 for more information). Ultimately, each section or subsection within the core will have to be reduced to a few sentences.

- **Step 3:** Copy guiding sentences in the core onto a sheet of paper or into a new word-processing document.
- **Step 4:** Study and revise the list of main points: reorder the list where appropriate, and condense the list if you can. Is there needless repetition? Can some points be combined and condensed? Does the order of the points make sense—should you rearrange the points?
- **Step 5:** As much as possible, put the revised main points into your own words by paraphrasing them. Quote only where the exact words of the source are vital. Use transitions or logical connectives to ensure coherence.
- **Step 6:** Reformat the main points in a well-written paragraph that consistently employs attribution.
- **Step 7:** Reread the conclusion, blocking and labelling its major rhetorical features (see Chapter 7). If a conclusion merely recaps a thesis or main points, it may not have to be included in the summary. However, if a conclusion contains other important features, such as a statement of relevance, this material should be incorporated into the summary.

Remember, a summary does not contain your opinion about the original article.

## Writing Critical Summaries

Writing an accurate, comprehensive summary of an entire article is a significant achievement. Having successfully undertaken such a task, the summary writer makes something new. The academic community respects such efforts because it understands the importance of gathering and compacting knowledge. Prestigious academic journals frequently publish papers that are devoted to a "literature review"—a survey and summary of research on a given topic.

Often, however, academic writers are expected to move beyond summary to critical commentary and evaluation. For students who are newcomers to a given knowledge domain, evaluation can be a daunting task. Nevertheless, while it is wise to approach evaluation with some humility, novice scholars are entitled to critique the work of more senior people. Such analysis fosters an exchange of ideas that is vital to the health of the academic community. Offering critical commentary does not put you in the position of a movie reviewer who gives a thumbs-up or thumbs-down, providing only praise or condemnation. The key in academic commentary is to provide reasoned, thoughtful analysis. Here are some perspectives to consider as you try to develop a critical point of view:

- Inspect the evidence: Is the evidence substantial or solid enough? Is it sufficient to support the writer's thesis? What kind of evidence is being presented? Is the evidence mainly anecdotal? Is it limited to one person's view? Is it circumstantial?
- What is the writer's relation to his or her own topic? Is the writer too emotionally involved in the material? Is there an unacknowledged personal bias in the paper? If so, how does this bias manifest itself?
- What is the other side of the argument? Are opposing views acknowledged and/or given fair treatment? What else can be said for the other view?
- Is there an underlying Big Issue in the article, one that is not fully acknowledged? Do you see any prestige abstractions that may be buried in the paper? If so, bring these to the light of day. Introducing related ideas is another form of critical commentary.
- Does the author seem to be working from unstated assumptions that you can call into question? Are stated assumptions worth questioning as well?
- Inspect the connections in the argument: Are there weak connections? Are there gaps in reasoning or logical fallacies?

When writing a critical summary, the critical comments may be added in a second paragraph at the end of the summary. Remember that your comments are your own: using the critical perspectives listed above, say what you think is pertinent. What catches your attention? Note that critical summaries closely resemble the well-established genre of the academic book review. In this respect, critical summaries are real-world work. Looking through almost any academic journal, you'll be able to find examples of book reviews, which are essentially critical summaries.

Below, Harman provides a critical summary of another article in his portfolio of sources. Note how he uses ongoing attribution in the summary section, and the clear delineation between the summary and the critical commentary.

---

In "Popular Images of the North in Literature and Film," **Frank Norris examines** authenticity in literature and movies about the north, from 1900 to the present. **Norris claims that** Hollywood's early images of the north were based on a mixture of "factual" and imaginative literature. Early travelogues and newspaper journalism celebrated the beauty of the north while the dime-store novels of London and Beach portrayed the north as a rugged frontier where heroes battled the environment and corporate corruption. **According to Norris,** the first Hollywood movies drew upon these written treatments of the north, and, in doing so, further simplified and stereotyped the north: heroes were "too white" and villains were "too black." Granted, Charlie Chaplin's *The Gold Rush* manages to present a moving account of the human condition, but tame bears and confetti blizzards show Hollywood's inability to grapple with the realities of northern life. After the formation of the Alaska Motion Picture Corporation in the 1920's, the quality of some films improved, but even the best movies tended to convey "a notoriously poor sense of northern life." Throughout the 1950's, **Norris observes,** Hollywood's representations of the north were largely take-offs on Westerns. From the 1960's to the present, **Norris suggests that** there have been "sporadic attempts to present the north in realistic ways, yet most of the films remain grossly inaccurate." In summary, **Norris argues that** Hollywood's treatment of the north has been guided by a desire to produce profitable entertainment rather than to achieve authenticity.

**In my view,** several assumptions underlying Norris's argument are questionable. **Norris appears to assume that** realism should be an ethical or artistic obligation for Hollywood filmmakers, yet, in presenting this assumption, he ignores the overarching genre function of Hollywood movies, which is to provide entertainment. **I also believe that,** ironically, the realism Norris advocates cannot escape the fictionalizing he condemns. All attempts to tell about the north in some way shape the north, creating a version of place rather than revealing its essence.

---

# Ideas for Further Study

1. Based on guidelines discussed in this chapter, begin compiling your research notebook. Your research notebook will likely consist primarily of short

quotations and paraphrases, but be sure to use quotation marks if you've quoted key words, phrases, or full sentences. Also try your hand at summarizing a paragraph or two from your sources.

2. In 100–120 words, summarize the following passage from Samuel J. Levine's "Portraits of Criminals on Bruce Springsteen's *Nebraska*: The Enigmatic Criminal, the Sympathetic Criminal, and the Criminal as Brother," published in the *Widener Law Journal*, 2005:

In some of the songs on Bruce Springsteen's *Nebraska* album, criminals recognize and regret their wrongful ways, while at the same time they provide an often sympathetic, if not convincing, explanation for their conduct. Indeed, in the context of the dark universe that envelops the characters who populate the album, we can begin to understand the forces that have driven these individuals to their criminal ways.

In "Atlantic City," another story told from the perspective of the criminal, the song's opening stanzas paint a world of crime and disorder, a world in which "they blew up the chicken man ... [and] his house"; fights are brewing on the boardwalk and the promenade; "there's trouble busin' in from outta state"; and even the district attorney and gambling commissioner seem unable or unwilling to perform their duties. This setting of chaotic lawlessness gives added meaning to the speaker's powerful declaration of utter desperation: "I got debts that no honest man can pay." The nearly paradoxical nature of this phrase suggests its own strangely compelling syllogism: the speaker wants to pay his debts, but his debts are so substantial that he cannot pay them if he remains an honest man; therefore, he will choose the only viable alternative, to pay his debts through dishonesty, manifesting itself in criminal activity.

In addition to the internal logic of the argument, Springsteen provides emotional depth to the narrator's position, describing the experiences that have contributed to a condition he can no longer endure. The speaker has tried earnestly to cling to and offer some semblance of hope, valiantly promising that "our luck may have died and our love may be cold/ But with you forever I'll stay." The promise, however, is not easily fulfilled because, as he explains tersely, in the tough and gritty world he inhabits, the stakes are high and the possibilities are starkly simple: "[I]t's just winners and losers and don't get caught on the wrong side of that line." Having failed too often in the past and "tired of comin' out on the losin' end," he searches for a way to keep his promise. Despite the lawlessness that surrounds him, his first choice is to "look for a job," but he concludes that "it's too hard to find." Thus, having exhausted his legal options, he finally succumbs to the temptation of the only remaining choice, vaguely but unmistakably depicted in the song's final line: "[L]ast night I met this guy and I'm gonna do a little favour for him."

The story that begins in "Atlantic City" seems to unfold again in the tale of generically named "Ralph," whose nickname provides the title for "Johnny 99." If "Atlantic City" depicts the forces that lead to a life of crime, "Johnny 99" continues with a complex exploration of the justice system the criminal will now face as a consequence of his actions. Employing third-person omniscient rather than first-person narrative, Springsteen moves effectively between description and dialogue. With the addition of plaintive singing accompanied by frantic guitar playing and wailing harmonica, he constructs a poignant mosaic of a legal system that serves only to increase our sense of sympathy for the criminal.

Echoing "Atlantic City," the beginning of "Johnny 99" paints a picture of the struggle for survival in an antagonistic and dangerous world. However, unlike the gradual process that culminates in the crime committed at the end of "Atlantic City," Ralph's evolution from a worker in an auto plant into a criminal is depicted in events that transpire in rapid succession. As the song opens, having lost his job and unable to find other work, Ralph quickly descends into drinking and shoots a night clerk, thereby earning the moniker "Johnny 99." He then seems to embrace lawlessness, emerging in a part of town typified in the telling image of a place "where when you hit a red light you don't stop." In a final act of violent desperation, he stands "wavin' his gun around and threatenin' to blow his top."

*Source:* Levine (2005, pp. 767–785)

---

3. Write a critical summary of one of the source articles used for your research notebook or an article assigned by your instructor. Is the evidence for the argument substantial? Is there an underlying Big Issue that's not mentioned? Is there another side to the story? Does the author have a hidden bias? Let your comments reflect your own engagement with the article.

# References

Bazerman, C. (1995). *The informed writer: Using sources in the disciplines* (5th ed.). Boston: Houghton Mifflin.

Grant, S. (1989). Myths of the North in the Canadian ethos. *The Northern Review, 3/4*, 15–41.

Harvey, G. (2011). *Writing with sources: A guide for students.* Cambridge, MA: Hackett.

Levine, S. J. (2005). Portraits of criminals on Bruce Springsteen's *Nebraska*: The enigmatic criminal, the sympathetic criminal, and the criminal as brother. *Widener Law Journal, 14*(3), 767–785.

Olien, R. M., & Olien, D. D. (2000). *Oil and ideology: The cultural creation of the American petroleum industry.* Chapel Hill: University of North Carolina Press.

# CHAPTER 4

# A Trial Run:
## Proposals as Research Bids

> Before you start your research, do not neglect another important resource: your professor. Schedule a conference or visit your professor during office hours. You may have little or no idea about what kind of paper you would like to write, but during the course of the discussion, something may occur to your professor or to you that piques your curiosity, that becomes the equivalent of [a] "burning question." Your conference may turn into a kind of verbal free-writing session—with several unresolved questions remaining at the end of the session—one of which may become the focus of your paper.
>
> —Leonard J. Rosen and Laurence Behrens,
> *The Allyn & Bacon Handbook* (2nd ed.)

As researchers move through the process of collecting information and securing a topic, the completion of a written proposal, accompanied by an annotated list of references, provides an opportunity to formalize plans, assess sources, and get more advice. Accordingly, this chapter comments on proposals and on the annotated list of references often associated with them. It also discusses some stylistic matters that might be overlooked by writers who are not yet familiar with discipline-based habits of expression.

## Proposals

Proposals are a common genre in the world of professional academic writing. As Giltrow (2002) notes, "seeking a place on a conference program, or a spot in a collection of essays that will be published on a particular topic, scholars answer 'Calls for Papers' with a proposal" (p. 381). Giltrow invites us to think of such proposals as "bids" (p. 382), as research offers that may be accepted or rejected by those who monitor the production of knowledge. In college and university classrooms, the context for "research bids" is somewhat different. Rather than seeking a place on a conference program, undergraduate students typically use a proposal to inform their instructor about a forthcoming paper. In both cases, a proposal offers a preliminary overview of a paper.

It's time to get some thoughts down on paper.

Instructors, like conference chairs or editors, evaluate proposals by using some criteria with which we are already familiar. For example, when reading proposals, instructors will watch for clearly articulated, viable *topics* that involve focused research sites and prestige abstractions or Big Issues. They will also want to see that the person submitting the proposal is aware of previous research relating to the topic. Such research forms what might be described as a *tradition of inquiry*. Especially in the humanities and social sciences, proposals also include rhetorical features that we have not yet discussed at any length, features such as a *two-part title*, a brief presentation of *context*, *theoretical framework*, *definition of key terms*, *knowledge deficit*, *forecasting*, a brief description of *methods*, a *research question*, *thesis*, and a *statement of relevance*. Some of these terms are self-explanatory, but brief descriptions are useful at this point:

**Two-Part Title:** Consists of an allusive phrase that indirectly relates to topic and an explanatory phrase that directly conveys the topic.

**Epigraph:** A brief quotation related to the topic.

**Context:** Background information.

**Definition of Key Terms:** Define important concepts (e.g., the prestige abstraction).

**Tradition of Inquiry:** Previous studies related to the topic.

**Knowledge Deficit:** A statement about what has not yet been covered by previous research. The articulation of a knowledge deficit may also identify points of disagreement or a lack of consensus.

**Topic:** Research Site + Abstraction = Topic; or, Abstraction + Research Site = Topic.

**General Forecasting:** A structural comment that provides a broad sense of direction. It may be difficult to distinguish general forecasting from topic. For this reason, we recommend relying on specific forecasting (see below) rather than general forecasting.

**Specific Forecasting:** Detailed structural comments that outline sections of the paper.

**Methods:** A description of specific procedures undertaken to generate knowledge.

**Theoretical Framework:** Consciously adopted perspectives or theories that can be imposed on the topic and influence a thesis claim.

**Research Question:** A central question that the paper will answer.

**Thesis:** A knowledge claim; that is, an answer to the research question.

**Statement of Relevance:** A comment about how the topic and/or the thesis relate to broad social concerns. Statements of relevance often have a moral overtone and can be regarded as the "So what?" factor.

**Solutions to a Problem:** This rhetorical feature will be discussed more in Chapter 7 on conclusions. For now, it's enough to say that research into any given topic may reveal problems that should be addressed. Proposals, therefore, may suggest possible solutions to such problems. These solutions can be evaluated or tested as the research proceeds.

While the rhetorical features described above are common building blocks used in proposals, these "blocks" can be combined in different ways. Thus, the precise architectural details of proposals will vary, but informed proposal writers understand that specific elements and time-tested patterns are necessary for a proposal to be well received. In a well-written proposal, there is an internal logic to the arrangement.

Nevertheless, a proposal by its very nature may have a tentative quality, showing signs that much of the work is ongoing. Firm decisions about structure and thesis, for example, may still be in process. Accordingly, after reading a student proposal, an instructor can offer valuable feedback that will help guide the development of the paper. For example, an instructor might suggest a refinement of the topic, new sources, alternate specific forecasting, or a different take on a thesis.

Looking ahead, it is helpful to think of a proposal as a draft introduction for the paper itself. Proposals and introductions, especially in the humanities and social sciences, share basically the same rhetorical function, and, in turn, share many of the same rhetorical features. From this perspective, the proposal is not simply a make-work exercise: it constitutes a tentative beginning, one that can be adjusted on the basis of comments or recommendations. Given the overlap between proposals and introductions, feel free at this point to consult the more comprehensive description of rhetorical features in introductions (Chapter 5). Presented with a range of options, proposal writers need to make careful choices, choices that are rooted in their discipline and topic.

An annotated list of references does not always accompany a proposal, but your instructor may ask you to submit one as further evidence of the progress you are making in your research notebook. We are using "list of references" as a generic term for an alphabetical list of sources, yet such lists assume different names, depending on the style of documentation you are using (APA, MLA, Chicago, CSE, and so on). It would be worthwhile to take a preliminary look at the various styles of documentation and to consider which style is appropriate for your paper (see chapters 5 and 6). You can refine your presentation of sources later in the term, but, even at this early stage in the writing process, you should have at least some idea of how to format your list, using available style manuals. Your instructor may also ask you "to annotate" the items that you plan to use. In an annotated list of references, academic writers provide a brief summary of each source, after the details of publication.

The following sample proposals with lists of references demonstrate different styles of documentation. Some of the lists are annotated; some are not. In these samples, students have included all of the sources from their research notebook even though all the sources have not been cited within the proposal itself. Practice in this respect may vary. As you proceed through the rest of this chapter, block and label features that appear in the proposals, and note the differences in styles of documentation. Also note how some of the rhetorical features can be presented within a sentence (for example, topic), while other features (tradition of inquiry, methods) occupy larger chunks of space. These patterns are common.

## Sample 1: MLA Style

Something that impressed us about Sample 1 is the narrowly focused research site. Also, while the interest value of research sites is subjective, we were intrigued by this one. It's something we never would have thought to write on, but we found ourselves being attentive, engaged readers. Remember to watch for the rhetorical features discussed in the preceding box and to block and label these features as they appear in Helen's proposal. It's best to delay blocking and labelling until you've read a proposal in its entirety.

---

### Helen Knott, "'Beauty Body Projects': Psychosocial Factors in Brazilian Plastic Surgery"

In Brazil, the demand for plastic surgery, also known as plástica, is growing at a steady rate. Brazil had the second highest number of plastic surgeries performed in 2003 (Finger 1560). In Brazil, there are both private and public clinics that offer cosmetic procedures and, in spite of a faulty health care system, some places even offer the service for free. Due to the expansion of service providers in the field of cosmetic surgery, there are also clinics that have payment plans and financing available to their patients. Many surgeons strongly believe that cosmetic surgery is something that everyone should be able to access (Edmonds, "The Poor" 363).

The emergence and popularity of plastic surgery in Brazil has attracted some scholarly attention. Edmonds has published two papers that combine ethnographic fieldwork and research on Brazilian culture and origins of beauty. Villares analyzes a popular Brazilian novel that portrays the protagonist's image in conflict with race, which reflects the stigmas attached to African phenotypes. In discussing racial inequality in Brazil, Santana Pinho states that media, songs, and novels in Brazil have perpetuated attributing interpretations of desirability to variations of skin tones and phenotypes. Graham states that race is not something that is easily assigned in Brazil but the phenotypic expressions of racial backgrounds are either praised or stigmatized. It is not just "black or white"—there exists a range of colours in between that creates categories for further classification (1718). However, "discrimination and prejudice" manifest themselves "with each small difference" (1717). Moreover, plástica in Brazil is driven by the very beauty ideals created by societal selection of aesthetically pleasing racial phenotypes. Race blending is seen as a viable option as it is supposed to deter "Africanoid exaggerations" and "Caucasoid deficiencies in the protuberances of the body" (Edmonds, "Triumphant Miscegenation" 88-89). The ideal Brazilian body could be said to have a small waist, round bottom, and small breasts. The surgeries, such as liposculpture or the Brazilian butt lift, reflect these preferences (92).

Additional studies offer a more comprehensive and theorized explanation of the Western desire for plastic surgery by aligning beauty with power. In *The Beauty Myth: How Images of Beauty are Used against Women*, Wolf states that beauty is a "currency system like a gold standard" (12). Adelman and Ruggi agree by stating that for women who are "socially denied power … over their lives," embarking on a body project allows them to take the reins over something they do control, and, by improving their appearance, gain new "social status, value, or appreciation" (559). Similarly, Certeau defines beauty body projects as a "tactic … performed by the weak on terrain defined by the strong" (qtd. in Edmonds, "Engineering" 166). Thus, beauty, and the need to pursue it, must be looked at in the context of the society to which it belongs. Cultural conditioning, current politics, and economic opportunities all play a role in the "market value of appearance" (Edmonds, "The Poor" 371).

Drawing on the foregoing studies, this paper focuses on psychosocial factors related to Brazilian plastic surgery. First, I will look at the stigma surrounding ethnic differences that influence the demand for plastic surgery in Brazil. Second, I will discuss beauty as a means to escape class oppression. Third, I will investigate perceived relationships between beauty and mental health. I will demonstrate that the motivation for plastic surgery in Brazil partly reflects assumptions common across Western cultures, but that somewhat unique attitudes toward race both distinguish and influence the drive for Brazilian plastic surgery.

## Works Cited

Adelman, Miriam, and Lennita Ruggi. "The Beautiful and the Abject: Gender, Identity, and Constructions of the Body in Contemporary Brazilian Culture." *Current Sociology* 56.4: 555-586. *Academic Search Premier.* Web. 17 Sept. 2009.

Edmonds, Alexander. "'Engineering the Erotic': Aesthetic Medicine and Modernization in Brazil." in Cressida J. Heyes and Meredith Jones (eds.) *Cosmetic Surgery: A Feminist Primer*, 153-169. Farnham, UK: Ashgate.

———. "The Poor Have the Right to Be Beautiful: Cosmetic Surgery in Neoliberal Brazil." *Journal of the Royal Anthropological Institute* 13.3: 363-81. *Academic Search Premier.* Web. 17 Sept. 2009.

———. "Triumphant Miscegenation: Reflections on Beauty and Race in Brazil." *Journal of Intercultural Studies* 28.1: 83-97. *Academic Search Premier.* Web. 17 Sept. 2009.

Finger, Carla. Reporting from Sao Paolo: Brazilian Beauty. *Lancet,* 362.9395. 1560. *Academic Search Premier.* Web. 22 Sept. 2009.

Freedman, Rita. *Beauty Bound: Why We Pursue the Myth in the Mirror.* New York: Harper and Row, 1986.

Graham, Richard. "Juggling Race and Class in Brazil's Past." *PMLA: Publication of the Modern Language Association of America* 123.5: 1717-1722. *Academic Search Premier.* Web. 22 Sept. 2009.

"The Globalization of Beauty." *Earth Island Journal* 11.4: 15. *Academic Search Premier.* Web. 29 Sept. 2009.

Santana Pinho, Patricia. "White but Not Quite: Tones and Overtones of Whiteness in Brazil." *Small Axe: A Caribbean Journal of Criticism* 29: 39-56. *Academic Search Premier.* Web. 22 Sept. 2009.

Villares, Lucia. (2009). "Racism and Performance of Whiteness in *A Hora de Estrela*." *Journal of Iberian and Latin America Studies* 24 (2-3): 77-85. *Academic Search Premier.* Web. 30 Sept. 2009.

Wolf, Naomi. *The Beauty Myth: How Images of Beauty are Used Against Women.* New York: Anchor, 1991.

## Sample 2: CSE Style

Bren Gage was likely drawn to his topic because of his intention of studying pharmacy. In Bren's proposal, watch for the strong presentation of a tradition of inquiry and knowledge deficit. Here, in particular, Bren's proposal sounds like published research. Near the end of the proposal, are you able to make a distinction between a preliminary thesis claim and a statement of relevance? In addition, the description of a questionnaire shows how first-year students can supplement their analysis of secondary sources by conducting their own original research. Again, block and label the rhetorical features you encounter.

---

## Bren Gage, "An Ounce of Prevention?: Social Resistance to Vaccination"

The invention of vaccines dates back to 1796 when a British physician, Edward Jenner, noted that milkmaids in his community had not been infected by a smallpox epidemic that was otherwise having widespread and devastating effects. Jenner then injected cowpox virus into several experimental subjects and the inoculated patients were also rendered immune to the smallpox disease. Since Jenner's discovery, vaccination programs have become part of a global disease-prevention strategy. Much medical literature associates the near-elimination of bubonic plague, polio, and smallpox with vaccination programs. Vaccination for influenza, pneumonia, meningitis, and human papillomavirus (HPV) is also common (Centers for Disease Control and Prevention [CDC], 1999, as cited in Diekema 2005). Bonanni has noted that, globally, "pediatric immunizations are responsible for preventing 3 million deaths in children each year" (as cited in Diekema, 2005, p. 1428). Today, there is overwhelming scientific consensus that vaccinations help to prevent a variety of diseases. Nevertheless, an increasing number of people in North America and Europe are refusing available inoculations, either for themselves or for their children (see, for example, the "Vaccine Resistance Movement"), a phenomenon that may be responsible for a resurgence of vaccine-preventable diseases (Dannetun, Tegnell, Hermansson, & Giesecke, 2005, p. 149; Miller, Kourbatova, Goodman, & Ray, 2005, p. 650; Roberts et al., 1996, p. 1155; Salmon et al., 2009, p. 22).

Popular attitudes toward vaccination have received increasing scholarly attention. A growing number of studies delve into parental concerns about vaccination (Alfredson, Svenson, Trollfors, & Borres, 2004; Blum & Talib, 2006; Dannetun et al., 2005; Diekema, 2005; Gust, Darling, Kennedy, & Schwartz, 2008; Salmon et al., 2009). Related studies investigate skepticism among vulnerable senior populations (Dannetun, Tegnell, Normann, Garpenholt, & Giesecke, 2003; Gosney, 2000; Mangtani et al., 2006). Further articles analyze opposition to specific vaccines, such as the HPV inoculation (Brabin, Roberts, & Kitchener, 2007; Toffolon-Weiss et al., 2008). Despite such research, there remains a lack of expert consensus as to the specific causes for and effective resolutions to decreasing vaccination rates. Indeed, Alfredson et al. (2004) have observed that "knowledge of factors influencing [attitudes toward] vaccination in western societies, where vaccines are easily accessible and free of charge, is limited" (p. 1233). What, then, are the key underlying factors that influence social resistence to inoculation programs?

This paper synthesizes the available research, providing an overview of social resistance to vaccination programs. First, I will discuss concerns about side effects for children, with emphasis on a perceived relationship between vaccination and autism. Next, I will discuss skepticism toward vaccination among seniors. Subject to approval by the appropriate research ethics committees, I further intend to augment existing research by designing a questionnaire that will elicit qualitative information from two sample groups. Group A will consist of soon-to-be parents participating in pre-natal classes at a nearby community college. Group B will consist of seniors who reside in a nearby seniors housing complex. All voluntary participants will have the option of providing written or verbal responses. Responses will be grouped according to themes. In the conclusion, I will consider solutions to vaccine refusal, exploring how carefully focused educational efforts by healthcare professionals could significantly improve immunization rates. Current research suggests that much of the resistance to vaccination can be regarded as an expression of Western individualism and a related belief that personal well-being is constructed in opposition to external authority. While educational efforts will almost certainly encounter ongoing resistance, they are critical to the health and well-being of people around the globe.

### References

Alfredsson R, Svensson E, Trollfors B, Borres M. (2004, September). Why do parents hesitate to vaccinate their children against measles, mumps and rubella?. Acta Paediatr (Oslo, Norway: 1992), 93(9), 1232–1237. Retrieved September 28, 2009, from MEDLINE with Full Text database.

Benin A, Dembry L, Shapiro E, Holmboe E (2004, January). Reasons physicians accepted or declined smallpox vaccine, February through

April, 2003. J Gen Intern Med, 19(1), 85–89. Retrieved September 28, 2009, from MEDLINE with Full Text database.

Blum J, Talib N. (2006, June). Balancing individual rights versus collective good in public health enforcement. Medicine and Law, 25(2), 273–281. Retrieved September 28, 2009, from MEDLINE with Full Text database.

Brabin L, Roberts S, Kitchener H. (2007, January). A semi-qualitative study of attitudes to vaccinating adolescents against human papillomavirus without parental consent. BMC Public Health, 7, 20–7. Retrieved September 28, 2009, from Academic Search Premier database. doi:10.1186/1471-2458-7-20

Dannetun E, Tegnell A, Hermansson G, Giesecke J. (2005, September). Parents' reported reasons for avoiding MMR vaccination. A telephone survey. Scand J Prim Health, 23(3), 149–153. Retrieved September 28, 2009, from MEDLINE with Full Text database.

Dannetun E, Tegnell A, Normann B, Garpenholt O, Giesecke J. (2003). Influenza vaccine coverage and reasons for non-vaccination in a sample of people above 65 years of age, in Sweden, 1998–2000. Scand J Infect Dis, 35(6–7), 389–393. Retrieved September 28, 2009, from MEDLINE with Full Text database.

Diekema D. (2005, May). Responding to parental refusals of immunization of children. Pediatrics, 115(5), 1428–1431. Retrieved September 28, 2009, from Academic Search Premier database. doi:10.1542/peds.2005-0316

Gosney M. (2000, October). Factors affecting influenza vaccination rates in older people admitted to hospital with acute medical problems. J Adv Nurs, 32(4), 892–897. Retrieved September 28, 2009, from Academic Search Premier database.

Gust D, Darling N, Kennedy A, Schwartz B. (2008). Parents with doubts about vaccines: which vaccines and reasons why. Pediatrics, 122(4), 718–725. Retrieved September 25, 2009, from Academic Search Premier database. doi:10.1542/peds.2007-0538

Mangtani P, Breeze E, Stirling S, Hanciles S, Kovats S, Fletcher A. (2006, October 11). Cross sectional survey of older peoples' views related to influenza vaccine uptake. BMC Public Health, 6, 249 [7 pages]. Retrieved September 28, 2009, from MEDLINE with Full Text database.

Miller L, Kourbatova E, Goodman S, Ray S. (2005, July). Brief report: risk factors for pneumococcal vaccine refusal in adults. J Gen Intern Med, 20(7), 650–652. Retrieved September 28, 2009, from Academic Search Premier database. doi:10.1111/j.15251497.2005.0118.x

Roberts C, Roome A, Algert C, Walsh S, Kurland M, Lawless K, Cartter ML. (1996, August). A meningococcal vaccination campaign on a university campus: vaccination rates and factors in nonparticipation. Am J Public Health, 86(8), 1155–1158. Retrieved September 28, 2009, from MEDLINE with Full Text database.

Salmon D, Sotir M, Pan W, Berg J, Omer S, Stokley S. (2009, February). Parental vaccine refusal in Wisconsin: a case-control study. WMJ: Official Publication of the State Medical Society of Wisconsin, 108(1), 17–23. Retrieved September 28, 2009, from MEDLINE with Full Text database.

Toffolon-Weiss M, Hagan K, Leston J, Peterson L, Provost E, Hennessy T. (2008, September). Alaska native parental attitudes on cervical cancer, HPV and the HPV vaccine. Int J Circumpol Hea, 67(4), 363–373. Retrieved September 28, 2009, from MEDLINE with Full Text database.

Vaccination: refuting the refusals. (2000, October 3). Can Med Assoc J, p. 801. Retrieved September 28, 2009, from Academic Search Premier database.

## Sample 3: MLA Style

Kendra's proposal shows how aspects of popular culture can be subject to scholarly analysis. Academic writers needn't always study Romantic poetry or the Monroe Doctrine. Here, a Hollywood film is the basis for a sophisticated paper. Do you see a distinction between the tradition of inquiry and the theoretical framework?

# Kendra Hunter, "'Box Office Poison': Misogyny in Luc Besson's Portrayal of Joan of Arc in *The Messenger*"

Joan of Arc was born in Domremy, France, in 1412, as a member of a peasant family. At the age of nineteen, she was successfully able to lead an entire army of men to victory. Joan claimed that she heard the voice of God, and that God had a personal mission for her: to save France. Initially, King Charles supported Joan by providing troops in the victorious battle to free Orléans. However, Joan's alliance with King Charles led to her betrayal and death. Eventually, she was sold to the English for 16,000 francs, charged with heresy and witchcraft, and burned at the stake. Joan of Arc has since become a familiar icon in Western culture—a figure mythologized in song, painting, literature, and film—although interpretations of her character vary. Luc Besson's *The Messenger* (1999) is among the more recent cinematic treatments of Joan.

Reviews of Besson's film have not been favourable. Brunette has criticized what he regards as the historical inaccuracies of the movie (para. 1). Similarly, Maxwell has charged that *The Messenger* "is founded on a lie": that "a true story of love and sacrifice ... is turned into a false [story] of hatred, bitterness, fury, and revenge" (52). In "Contrasting Visions of a Saint: Carl Dreyer's *The Passion of Joan of Arc* and Luc Besson's *The Messenger*," Scalia provides a more scholarly analysis of the film, contending that "Besson pursued a kind of nation-founding mythic tale of epic scope, one that necessarily sublimates the divine mission of Joan to the historical qualities of his spectacle" (para. 5). Meanwhile, in "Teaching Knighthood and the Late Medieval Battlefield using the Knights of *The Messenger*," Tsin studies the historical veracity of Besson's depiction of "the men who fought alongside Joan of Arc: the knights of the later stages of the Hundred Years' War" (para. 1). Taking another historical approach, Hobbins, in "The Cinematic Maid: Teaching Joan of Arc through Film," praises Besson for addressing "the central problem of Joan's voices more clearly and directly than any other film on the subject" (para. 17).

To date, then, commentary on Besson's portrayal of Joan has been primarily historical in nature, leaving other approaches to the film open for discussion. In an effort to fill this gap, the following paper examines misogyny in Luc Besson's *The Messenger*. My discussion of Besson's film is indebted to Susan Faludi's *Backlash: The Undeclared War against American Women*, which argues that film-makers in the twentieth century are producing movies that disparage independent women, making them appear weak or even psychotic (112-114). Faludi cites *Fatal Attraction* (1987), a film about a married man who has an affair with a single woman. When the affair takes place, the man's wife is out of town. When the time comes that the man must return to his wife, the single woman suffers a mental breakdown, becoming a sadistic killer. That is, the assertive woman, a woman who dares to assume male prerogatives, sexual or otherwise, becomes a monster. Drawing on Faludi's work, I will show that Besson's portrayal of Joan of Arc further exemplifies the misogynistic tendencies evident in twentieth-century film.

## Annotated Works Cited

Brunette, Peter. Review of *The Messenger: The Story of Joan of Arc*.<www.film. com/ film-review.1999>. Brunette criticizes the historical inaccuracies in the film.

Faludi, Susan. *Backlash: The Undeclared War Against American Women.* New
    York: Doubleday, 1991. Faludi, as noted above, believes that twentieth-
    century film shows a backlash against feminism.
Hobbins, Daniel. "The Cinematic Maid: Teaching Joan of Arc through Film."
    *Fiction and Film for French Historians: A Cultural Bulletin* 2.3 (2011). Web.
    <http://h-france.net/fffh/maybe-missed/cinematicmaid/>.
Maxwell, Ronald. "Review of *The Messenger*: Joan of Arc." *History Today*, 52-53.
    Print. Maxwell argues that Besson's portrayal "is founded on a lie": "a true
    story of love and sacrifice, of dedication and faith is turned to a false one
    of hatred, bitterness, fury, and revenge."
Scalia, Bill. "Contrasting Visions of a Saint: Carl Dreyer's *The Passion
    of Joan of Arc* and Luc Besson's *The Messenger*." *Literature/Film
    Quarterly* 2004:1412-1431. Web. <http://www.questia.com/library/
    journal/1P3-699892911/contrasting-visions-of-a-saint-carl-dreyer-s-the>.
*The Messenger: The Story of Joan of Arc.* Dir. Luc Besson. Columbia Pictures.
    1999. Film. Besson's creative interpretation of Joan's life and death.
Tsin, Matthieu Chan. "Teaching Knighthood and the Late Medieval Battlefield
    using the Knights of *The Messenger*." *Scientia Scholae* 7.1. Spring 2009. Web.
    <http://www.teamsmedieval.org/ofc/SP09/messenger.php>.

## Sample 4: APA Style

In the next sample, the research site is quite broad because it deals with the role
of Facebook in both Obama's 2008 presidential election and the Arab Spring of
2011. Yet the broad research site creates an opportunity for an interesting and
powerful thesis claim. In conversation with her instructor, Julia could make a
decision about the scope of her research site.

# Julia Roe, "Yes, Facebook Can:
# Political Engagement and Social Activism
# among Facebook Users"

Since the creation of Facebook in 2004, Facebook has become a vital form of communication. When Facebook began, accounts were limited to Harvard University
students. As it soared in popularity, the site expanded to more and more universities and was eventually made available to anyone with Internet access and a valid

e-mail address. The public reception has been overwhelmingly positive. According to the Facebook Press Room (2011), there are now over 500 million active users in more than 190 countries. Today this daily peer-to-peer communication site is at the forefront of social media. This paper examines the growing influence of Facebook on the political engagement and social activism of its users. First, in regard to political engagement, I will discuss the impact of Facebook on the 2008 U.S. presidential election. Second, addressing social activism, I will explore the role of Facebook in Middle Eastern revolutions during the "Arab Spring" of 2011.

There has been much written analyzing the influence of Facebook as a political power-player. For example, a Master's thesis titled *The Face of Social Networking: The Political Potential of Facebook and its Impact on Traditional Methods of Civic Engagement* (Wilkes, 2008) examines the correlation between online and offline political/civic involvement. Wilkes incorporates the Facebook activity surrounding the 2008 U.S. election into her discussion of how the social networking site directly engages individuals in politics. Correspondingly, in "From Networked Nominee to Networked Nation: Examining the Impact of Web 2.0 and Social Media on Political Participation and Civic Engagement in the 2008 Obama Campaign," Cogburn and Espinoza-Vasquez (2011) discuss the uses of Facebook in the Obama 2008 campaign. In "The Middle East's Generation Facebook" (Eltahawy, 2008), the potential of Facebook as a tool to spark an effective and widespread political revolution is explored in relation to the Arab Spring uprisings in Egypt. Similarly, in "On the Arab Street, Rage is Contagious," Haulslohner (2011) points out that the revolutions in Tunisia and Egypt were both fueled and organized by Facebook posts. Based on such research, I will argue that the 2008 U.S. presidential election and the Arab Spring revolutions reveal that Facebook has an unprecedented potential to incite and facilitate political engagement and social activism among the general public, giving Facebook users the power to both elect and overthrow a government.

### References

China, W. (2011). The Facebook revolution. *New African 503*, p. 24.

Cogburn, D. L., Espinoza-Vasquez, F. K. (2011). From networked nominee to networked nation: Examining the impact of Web 2.0 and social media on political participation and civic engagement in the 2008 Obama campaign. *Journal of Political Marketing 10*(1/2), pp. 189-213.

Donnelly-Smith, L. (Spring/Summer 2008). Political engagement in the age of Facebook: Student voices. *Peer Review 10* (2/3), pp. 37-39.

Eltahawy, M. (Fall, 2008). The Middle East's generation Facebook. *World Policy Journal 25*:3, pp. 69-77.

Haulslohner, A. (2011). On the Arab street, rage is contagious. *Time 177*:5, pp. 36-39.

Mattera, J. (2010). *Obama zombies.* New York: Threshold Editions.

McClure, D., & Dorris, M. (Winter 2009/2010). The Obama technology agenda: Open, transparent, and collaborative. *Public Manager 38*:4, pp. 36-39.

Pasek, J., More, E., & Romer, D. (2009). Realizing the social Internet? Online social networking meets offline civic engagement. *Journal of Information Technology & Politics 6*: 3/4, pp. 197-215.

Robertson, S. P., Vatrapu, R. K., & Medina, R. (Apr-Sep 2010). Online video "friends" social networking: Overlapping online public spheres in the 2008 U.S. presidential election. *Journal of Information Technology & Politics 7*:2/3, pp. 182-201.

Wilkes, M. (2008). *The face of social networking: The political potential of Facebook and its impact on traditional methods of civic engagement* (Master's thesis). Georgetown University, Washington, DC.

Woolley, J. K., Limperos, A. M., & Oliver, M. B. (2010, November/December). The 2008 presidential election, 2.0: A content analysis of user-generated political Facebook groups. *Mass Communication & Society 13*(5), 631-652.

## Sample 5: APA Style

Brandy's proposal is succinct. It consists of a single paragraph, yet also reveals evidence of considerable research. Block and label what you see here. Also note the phrase "high debt worry students," which Brandy cites from one of her sources. This phrase is an example of nominalization, a sentence-level feature of academic writing about which we'll have more to say later in this chapter and in Chapter 8.

## Brandy Palmer, "Higher Risks for Higher Education: Financial Debt and Stress Among Post-Secondary Students"

In the past decade, it has become increasingly difficult to get a secure job without first attending a post-secondary institution (PSI). Thus, a large number of students plan on attending a PSI immediately after graduation from high school. However, in recent years, post-secondary tuition in North America has been climbing at an alarming rate. Furthermore, costs of attending a PSI have shifted from the state to the student (Callender & Jackson, 2005, p. 511), increasing the amount of debt a student will have upon PSI graduation. As a result, students are becoming less likely to view PSIs as a valuable investment, and more likely to view them in "terms of unacceptable debt accrual" (Callender & Jackson, 2008, p. 406). Similarly, Cooke et al. (2004) found that "high debt worry students felt more tense, anxious ... [and] more unhappy" (p. 58). Both Conlon (2006) and Kim (2007) found that financial considerations were among the most important for students in Canada, the U.S., and Great Britain. In addition, it was found by Rickinson and Rutherford (1995) that "students who withdrew from university ... cited serious financial problems as a reason for leaving" (as cited in Jessop et al., 2005, p. 422). Accordingly, this paper examines financial debt and stress among post-secondary students. First, I will discuss debt among post-secondary students from a quantitative perspective, noting actual debt totals and the long-term economic effects of incurring such debt. Second, I will discuss student debt from a qualitative perspective, considering the psychological and physical impacts of financial stress. I will show that the possibility of incurring a large amount of debt, coupled with the negative effect of such debt on psychological and physical health, may make the decision to attend a post-secondary institution more stressful than ever before and may even restrict access for prospective students from a lower socio-economic demographic.

## References

Callender, C., & Jackson, J. (2005, October). Does the fear of debt deter students from higher education? *Journal of Social Policy, 34*(4), 509-540. Retrieved February 18, 2009, doi:10.101 7/S004727940500913X

Callender, C., & Jackson, J. (2008, August). Does the fear of debt constrain choice of university and subject of study? *Studies in Higher Education, 33*(4), 405-429. Retrieved February 17, 2009, doi:10.1080/03075070802211802

Conlon, M. (2006, July). The politics of access: Measuring the social returns on post-secondary education. *Higher Education Management & Policy, 18*(2), 1-9. Retrieved February 16, 2009, from Academic Search Premier database.

Cooke, R., Barkham, M., Audin, K., Bradley, M., & Davy, J. (2004, February). Student debt and its relation to student mental health. *Journal of*

*Further & Higher Education, 28*(1), 53-66. Retrieved February 17, 2009, doi:10.1080/0309877032000161814

Dowd, A. (2008, June). Dynamic interactions and intersubjectivity: Challenges to causal modeling in studies of college student debt. *Review of Educational Research, 78*(2), 232-259. Retrieved February 17, 2009, from Academic Search Premier database.

Gerrard, E., & Roberts, R. (2006, November). Student parents, hardship and debt: A qualitative study. *Journal of Further & Higher Education, 30*(4), 393-403. Retrieved February 18, 2009, doi:10.1080/03098770600965409

Jessop, D., Herberts, C., & Solomon, L. (2005, September). The impact of financial circumstances on student health. *British Journal of Health Psychology, 10*(3), 421-439. Retrieved February 18, 2009, doi:10.1348/135910705X25480

Kim, D. (2007, Spring). The effect of loans on students' degree attainment: Differences by student and institutional characteristics. *Harvard Educational Review, 77*(1), 64-100. Retrieved February 16, 2009, from Academic Search Premier database.

Norvilitis, J., Merwin, M., Osberg, T., Roehling, P., Young, P., & Kamas, M. (2006, June). Personality factors, money attitudes, financial knowledge, and credit-card debt in college students. *Journal of Applied Social Psychology, 36*(6), 1395-1413. doi:10.1111/j.0021-9029.2006.00065.x

Perna, L. (2008, November). Understanding high school students' willingness to borrow to pay college prices. *Research in Higher Education, 49*(7), 589-606. doi:10.1007/s11162-008-9095-6

Thomas, L. (2002, August). Student retention in higher education: The role of institutional habitus. *Journal of Education Policy, 17*(4), 423-442. Retrieved February 16, 2009, doi:10.1080/02680930210140257

Tumen, S., & Shulruf, B. (2008, November). The effect of student loan schemes on students returning to study. *Journal of Higher Education Policy & Management, 30*(4), 401-414. Retrieved February 17, 2009, doi:10.1080/13600800802383075

Williams, J. (2006). The pedagogy of debt. *College Literature, 33* (4), 155-169. Retrieved February 18, 2009, from Academic Search Premier database.

Williams, J. (2008, Fall). Student debt and the spirit of indenture. *Dissent (00123846), 55*(4), 73-78. Retrieved February 18, 2009, from Academic Search Premier database.

## Sample 6: APA Style

Here's another proposal that's influenced by personal experience. Hong Zhu herself surely faced challenges as an immigrant student. Further, as a parent, she likely attempted to support her own children as they faced such challenges. Hong Zhu could have written a personal essay on this topic. As a student in an academic writing class, however, she is careful to apply an extensive body of research to her writing. That said, in the introduction to Hong Zhu's paper, she has an opportunity to engage in self-disclosure (see Chapter 5).

---

# Hong Zhu, "Burden of Hope: Educational Challenges Faced by Canadian Immigrant Children"

Since the mid-nineteenth century, in particular, immigrants have made a significant contribution to the development of Canada (Citizenship and Immigration Canada, 2007). In the past century, more than 13.4 million immigrants have come to Canada. To date, the immigrant wave reached its peak during the 1990s. Accordingly, the 2001 census revealed that 18.4% of Canada's population was born outside of Canada (Statistics Canada, 2007). It is also reported that "immigration could become the only source for population growth by 2030" (CBC News). Among immigrants, children are a notable group. In the last few years, there has been an increase in the number of children under the age of 19 being brought into Canada (CBC News). Being of school age, these immigrant children have experienced much hardship and faced many challenges in their new country. This paper asks the following question: what are the educational challenges faced by Canadian immigrant children?

Study of Canadian immigrant children is not a new topic. In "Educational Experiences of Immigrant Students from the Former Soviet Union," Jazira (2005) has provided "a case study of an ethnic school in Toronto" (p. 181). Jazira points out some disadvantages of the Canadian school system and advocates for a model of ethnic schooling for immigrant children's education in Canada. From a similar point of view, Abada et al. (2009) examine "the ethnic differences in university education attainment among the children of Canadian immigrants" (p. 1). In addition, more and more specialists focus on the family factors influencing immigrant chidren. Li (2004) has published a paper entitled "Parental Expectations of Chinese Immigrants." Li revealed "a folk theory" about Canadian immigrant children's educational achievement. In another study, "Doing Well vs. Feeling Well," Qin (2008) compared "two groups of adolescents from Chinese immigrant families" to emphasize the importance of the parent-child relationship. Other researchers have reported that "very high educational aspirations" are shown among immigrant children (Anisef, Hou, & Ram; Krahn & Taylor; Worswick; as cited in Abada et al., 2009, p. 3). However, "high levels of educational attainment" are not achieved by all of them (p. 3). Building on this tradition of inquiry, I will show that the burden of cultural conflicts and high parental expectations are the primary challenges faced by Canadian immigrant children.

## References

Abada, T., Hou, F., & Ram, B. (2009). Ethnic differences in educational attainment among the children of Canadian immigrants. *Canadian Journal of Sociology, 34(1)*, 1-28. Retrieved September 22, 2009, from Academic Search Premier Database.

CBC News. (2007). Retrieved October 23, 2009, from http://www.cbc.ca/canada/story/2007/03/13/census-canada.html

Citizenship and Immigration Canada. (2007). Retrieved October 23, 2009, from http://www.cic.gc.ca

Dyson, L. (2005). The lives of recent Chinese immigrant children in Canadian society: Values, aspirations, and social experiences. *Canadian Ethnic Studies, 37(2)*, 49-66. Retrieved September 22, 2009, from Academic Search Premier Database.

Hao, L., & Bruns, M. (1998, July). Parent-child differences in educational expectations and the academic achievement of immigrant and Native students. *Sociology of Education, 7*(3), 175-198. Retrieved September 22, 2009, from www.jstor.org/stable/2673201

Jazira, A. (2005, June). Educational experiences of immigrant students from the former Soviet Union: A case study of an ethnic school in Toronto. *Educational Studies, 31(2)*, 181-195. Retrieved September 22, 2009, from Academic Search Premier Database.

Kobayashi, A., & Preston, V. (2007, August). Transnationalism through the life course: Hong Kong immigrants in Canada. *Asia Pacific Viewpoint, 48(2)*, 151-167. Retrieved September 22, 2009, from Academic Search Premier Database.

Ladky, M., & Peterson, S. (2008). Successful practices for immigrant parent involvement: An Ontario perspective. *Multicultural Perspectives, 10(2)*, 82-89. Retrieved September 22, 2009, from Academic Search Premier Database.

Li, J. (2004, July). Parental expectations of Chinese immigrants: A folk theory about children's school achievement. *Race, Ethnicity & Education, 7(2)*, 167-183. Retrieved February 22, 2008, from Academic Search Premier Database.

Ng, W., & Greer, A. (2004). Beyond Bible stories: The role of culture-specific myths/stories in the identity formation of nondominant immigrant children. *Religious Education, 99(2)*, 125-136. Retrieved September 22, 2009, from Academic Search Premier Database.

Qin, D. (2008). Doing well vs. feeling well: Understanding family dynamics and psychological adjustment of Chinese immigrant adolescents. *J Youth Adolescence. 37*, 22-35. Retrieved September 22, 2009, from Academic Search Premier Database.

Statistics Canada. (2008). Retrieved October 23, 2009, from www.statcan.gc.ca

Wakil, S., Siddique, C., & Wakil, F. (1981, November). Between two cultures: A study in socialization of children of immigrants. *Journal of Marriage and Family, 43(4)*, 929-940. Retrieved September 22, 2009, from Academic Search Premier Database.

Wason-Ellam, L. (2001, January). Living against the wind: Pathways chosen by Chinese immigrants. *Canadian Ethnic Studies, 33(1)*, 71-100. Retrieved September 22, 2009, from Academic Search Premier Database.

## Sample 7: APA Style

Susana's paper reflects an important trend in academic writing insofar as it deals with environmental concerns. Not only in the natural sciences but in the humanities and social sciences as well, scholars are addressing contemporary concerns about the relationship between economic development, the environment, and the sustainability of life on earth. The attention paid to this issue is comparable to the attention paid to gender and race in the 1970s, 1980s, and 1990s. Block and label.

# Susana Tang, "Angel or Devil?: The Environmental and Social Effects of China's Three Gorges Dam"

The Three Gorges Dam (TGD) on China's Yangtze River, the largest hydroelectric project in the world, was approved in 1992. Prior to approval, this project encountered many problems and delays. It was "infeasible in the 1960s, unaffordable in the 1970s, politically and technically opposed in the 1980s," but finally there was a decision to build it in the early 1990s (Jackson & Sleigh, 2000, p. 224). It took 17 years and cost at least $12 billion to build the Three Gorges Dam (Sullivan, 1995, p. 266). The project has influenced 20 million people upstream and 300 million downstream, and at least 1 million people needed to be relocated (Jackson & Sleigh, p. 224). The dam is over 1900 meters (1.2 miles) wide and 185 meters (607 feet) high (Sullivan, p. 266). The three main functions of the Three Gorges Dam are flood control, improved river transport, and the generation of electricity (Jackson & Sleigh, p. 227).

Over the past decades, many scholars have pointed out some harmful aspects of the TGD project. In "The Three Gorges Project: Dammed if They Do," Sullivan (1995) indicates that the TGD project has brought some disadvantages to the environmental, political, and social well-being of China (pp. 266-269). Furthermore, in "Resettlement for China's Three Gorges Dam: Socio-Economic Impact and Institutional Tensions," Jackson and Sleigh (2000) also claim the project has caused some economic, ecological, and social difficulties (pp. 225-241). Most scholars have focused on the anthropological problems, noting migration and resettlement features (Heggelund, 2006; Hwang, Xi, Cao et al, 2007; Yu & Xiang, 2006; Andrews-Speed & Ma, 2008). This paper will examine the varied effects of the Three Gorges Dam in China. First, I will discuss the environmental consequences of the TGD. Second, I will observe the impacts that the TGD has had on humans. My paper demonstrates that while the TGD has been promoted as an "angel" by Chinese authorities, many people, especially those directly affected by the dam, regard it as an environmental and social catastrophe.

## References

Andrews-Speed, P., & Ma, X. (2008, May). Energy production and social marginalisation in China. *Journal of Contemporary China, 17*(55), 247-272. Retrieved February 22, 2009, from Academic Search Premier database.

Heggelund, G. (2006, January). Resettlement programmes and environmental capacity in the Three Gorges Dam project. *Development & Change, 37*(1), 179-199. Retrieved February 22, 2009, from Academic Search Premier database.

Houghton, J. (2004). *Global warming: The complete briefing*. Toronto: Cambridge University Press.

Hwang, S., Xi, J., Cao, Y., Feng, X., & Qiao, X. (2007, September). Anticipation of migration and psychological stress and the Three Gorges Dam project, China. *Social Science & Medicine, 65*(5), 1012-1024. Retrieved February 22, 2009, from Academic Search Premier database.

Jackson, S., & Sleigh, A. (2000, June). Resettlement for China's Three Gorges Dam: Socio-economic impact and institutional tensions. *Communist & Post-Communist Studies, 33*(2), 223. Retrieved February 22, 2009, from Academic Search Premier database.

Jun, X., Chen, Y. (2001, December). Water problems and opportunities in the hydrological sciences in China. *Hydrological Sciences, 46(6)*. Retrieved March 27, 2009, from www.clw.csiro.au/revegih/file_for_download/Attached_to_update3.pdf

Pew Center on Global Climate Change (2007, May). *Coal and climate change facts*. Retrieved March 25, 2009, from www.pewclimate.org/global-warming-basics/coalfacts.cfm

Sullivan, L. (1995, September). The Three Gorges project: Dammed if they do?. *Current History, 94*(593), 266. Retrieved February 22, 2009, from Academic Search Premier database.

Svensson, B. (2005, August). Greenhouse gas emissions from hydroelectric reservoirs: A global perspective. *Global warming and hydroelectric reservoirs*, 25-37. Retrieved March 24, 2009, from www.rheoconsult.com/Exp/Rio2005.pdf

Thwin, M. A., Wong, G. Y. G., Christou, J. (Producers), & Chang, Y. (Director). (2007). *Up the Yangtze*. Canada: EyeSteel (Yangtze) Productions Inc. / National Film Board of Canada.

Yu, C., & Xiang, H. (2006, Spring). Power games and migrant adaptability in migration villages. *Chinese Sociology & Anthropology, 38*(3), 71-89. Retrieved February 22, 2009, from Academic Search Premier database.

## Sample 8: APA Style

Okay, all you sports fans, here's one for you!

---

# Barnabas Wanapia, "Beyond the Game: Fan Violence in European Football"

At a soccer game in March 1997, in a small Netherlands town called Bewerwijk, a 35-year-old Dutch man was beaten and stabbed to death, and other hooligans severely injured. This was a result of the rivalry arising from two different hooligan groups, approximately three thousand in total. In response to this murder, the Dutch authorities arrested and convicted the "main perpetrators" of the act. A similar event occurred on October 19, 1999, when Manchester United played against the Olympic Marseilles in Stade Velodrome in Marseilles. The United fans assembled at the stadium to watch their team play, and the Olympic Marseilles fans were also present to watch the match. The Manchester United fans were in the barricaded section of the stadium, while the Marseilles fans were elsewhere in the stadium. The Olympic Marseilles fans threw objects like batteries, beer bottles containing urine, plastic seats, and coins in the stadium as the match went on. The Manchester United fans became frustrated during the second half of the game when the Olympic Marseilles scored the winning goal. The Manchester United fans reacted to the actions of the Marseilles fans, and a fight broke out between a United fan and the Olympic Marseilles stewards. This led to injuries sustained by a well-known United hooligan, his gangs, and some stewards.

Soccer violence has attracted increasing scholarly attention. The sociological analysis has focused on the "causes of inter-group violence between football supporters" since the early 1970s. King (2001) studied the causes of fan violence or hooliganism. Other studies by Dunning et al. (1986) mainly focused on the pattern of fighting between rival groups. In "Tackling Football Hooliganism: A Quantitative Study of the Public Order, Policing and Psychology," Scott et al. (2008) contributed to the "science of crowd dynamics and psychology by examining the social psychological processes related ... to the final of the 2004 Union Européenne de Football Association (UEFA)." In "'The Way It Was': An Account of Soccer Violence in the 1980s," Gibbons et al. (2008) stated that football hooliganism, which became prevalent in the 1970s, was recognised in the 1960s as a significant contemporary social problem in Britain.

Drawing on the foregoing studies, my paper examines fan violence in soccer. First, I will discuss the causes and effects of fan violence. Second, I will discuss preventive measures. I will demonstrate that the causes of soccer violence are rooted in social relationships, media influence, and immediate environmental stimuli; however, effective preventive measures may draw on strategies and considerations associated with the developing knowledge of crowd control.

## References

Back, L., Crabbe, T., & Solomos, J. (1999, September). Beyond the racist/hooligan couplet: Race, social theory and football culture. *The British Journal of Sociology, 50*(3), 419-442. Retrieved September 26, 2009, from MEDLINE with Full Text database.

Brick, C. (2000, Spring). Taking offence: Modern moralities and the perception of the football fan. *Soccer & Society, 1*(1), 158. Retrieved September 26, 2009, from Academic Search Premier database.

Dunning, E., Murphy, P., & Williams, J. (1986, June). Spectator violence at football matches: Towards a sociological explanation. *British Journal of Sociology, 37*(2), 221. Retrieved September 26, 2009, from Academic Search Premier database.

Folkesson, P., Nyberg, C., Archer, T., & Norlander, T. (2002, July). Soccer referees' experience of threat and aggression: Effects of age, experience, and life orientation on outcome of coping strategy. *Aggressive Behavior, 28*(4), 317-327. Retrieved September 26, 2009, doi:10.1002/ab.90028

Gibbons, T., Dixon, K., & Braye, S. (2008, March). "The way it was": An account of soccer violence in the 1980s. *Soccer & Society, 9*(1), 28-41. Retrieved September 26, 2009, doi:10.1080/14660970701616704

Johnes, M. (2000, Summer). Hooligans and barrackers: Crowd disorder and soccer in South Wales, c. 1906-39. *Soccer & Society, 1*(2), 19. Retrieved September 26, 2009, from Academic Search Premier database.

Kerr, J., & De Kock, H. (2002, January). Aggression, violence, and the death of a Dutch soccer hooligan: A reversal theory explanation. *Aggressive Behavior, 28*(1), 1-10. Retrieved September 26, 2009, doi:10.1002/ab.90001

King, A. (2001, November). Violent pasts: Collective memory and football hooliganism. *Sociological Review, 49*(4), 568-585. Retrieved September 26, 2009, doi:10.1111/1467-954X.ep5487186

Mathias, P. (1991, April). Football fans: Fanatics or friends? *Journal of Community & Applied Social Psychology, 1*(1), 29-32. Retrieved September 26, 2009, doi:10.1002/casp.2450010105

Roadburg, A. (1980, June). Factors precipitating fan violence: A new comparison of professional soccer in Britain and North America. *British*

*Journal of Sociology, 31*(2), 265-276. Retrieved September 26, 2009, from Biomedical Reference Collection: Comprehensive database.

Stott, C., Adang, O., Livingstone, A., & Schreiber, M. (2008, May). Tackling football hooliganism: A quantitative study of public order, policing and crowd psychology. *Psychology, Public Policy, and Law, 14*(2), 115-141. Retrieved September 26, 2009, doi:10.1037/a0013419

Williams, J. (1991, April). When violence overshadows the spirit of sporting competition: Italian football fans and their sports clubs. *Journal of Community & Applied Social Psychology, 1*(1), 23-28. Retrieved September 26, 2009, doi:10.1002/casp.2450010104

If you have been asked to prepare a proposal and list of references for your own research project, consider the samples presented above as potential models. Each of these proposals has a different topic, yet, in some respects, they all "sound" alike because the writers are deploying a similar set of features. Through the recurring encounter with these features, you can detect the familiar register of academic discourse. Your own proposal should "sound" like the ones above.

## The Jenna Files

Notes to self:

- Okay, the proposal. The next big assignment. I like the idea that there are definite ingredients that should go into a proposal. It's like a recipe. You follow grandma's recipe, the kimchi turns out just like grandma's.
- For my topic—cyberbullying and teen girls' suicide—I'm thinking of including context, topic, specific forecasting, a tradition of inquiry, and thesis. For some reason, I'm looking forward to writing the tradition of inquiry. I have a lot of good sources, and I want to see them gathered together in one paragraph.

Jenna's proposal follows. The instructor's comments are indicated here by a number and a corresponding comment at the end of the box, and you'll notice they are quite comprehensive; however, in the context of an actual class, some of these comments could have been made in a conversation during office hours or after class.

## The Jenna Files

### The Tragedy of Technological Triumph:[1] Cyberbullying among Teenage Girls and Suicide[2]

On September 13, 2013,[3] Rebecca, a 12-year-old girl, committed suicide after 15 middle-school students repeatedly bullied her in person and online. Rebecca was bullied for over a year, and the bullies urged her though online websites and smart phone applications to kill herself. When Rebecca's mother, Tricia Norman, found out that Rebecca was being bullied, Norman {pulled her daughter out}[4] of school and closed down her Facebook account (Alvarez, 2013, p. 1-2).[5] However, according to Hinduja and Patchin (2011), adolescents value the Internet community websites very highly, and they cannot "live" without the Internet;[6] "two-thirds of youth go online every day for school work, to keep in touch with their friends, to learn about celebrities, to share their digital creations, or for many other reasons" (p. 23). Therefore, Rebecca could not stop[7] using social media, and she opened a new community website account. When Rebecca was once again bullied through the new website, she committed suicide (Alvarez, 2013, p. 3).

Accordingly,[8] this paper will present cyberbullying as a serious social problem, and explore the relationship between cyberbullying and suicide among teenage girls.[9] First, I will describe the characteristics of cyberbullying and compare them with traditional bullying. Second, I will explore the negative effects of cyberbullying and its effects on teenage girls. Third, I will examine why victims of cyberbullying try to solve their problems by themselves rather than reporting the incidents.[10]

Many researchers have claimed that[11] cyberbullying has social-psychological effects, such as inducing suicidal thoughts that lead to attempted and successful suicides.[12] Pirjo, Heini, and Rimpela[13] (2012) showed that for girls from 12 to 16 years old, the rate of being cyberbullied is almost twice as high as it is for boys in the same age group (p. 4).[14] Hinduja and Patchin (2010) reported on a survey of Internet use conducted on 1,963 randomly selected middle-school students. Students who had been victims of cyberbullying were more likely to attempt suicide than those who had not (p. 207). Thus, I argue that cyberbullying can lead to suicide among teenage girls.[15]

## References

Alvarez, L. (2013, September 13). Girl's suicide points to rise in apps used by cyberbullies. *The New York Times*. Retrieved from http://www.nytimes.com

Bauman, S., Toomey, R. B., & Walker, L. J. (2013). Associations among bullying, cyberbullying, and suicide in high school students. *Journal of Adolescence, 36*, 341-350.

Bhat, C. S., Chang, S., & Linscott, J. A. (2010). Addressing cyberbullying as a media literacy issue. *New Horizons in Education, 58*, 34-43.

Dooley, J. J., Pyzalski, J., & Cross, D. (2009). Cyberbullying versus face-to-face bullying. *Journal of Psychology, 217(4)*, 182-188. doi: 10.1027/0044-3409.271.4.182

Hinduja, S., & Patchin, J. W. (2010). Bullying, cyberbullying, and suicide. *Archives Of Suicide Research, 14*(3), 206-221. doi:10.1080/13811118.2010.4 94133

Hinduja, S., & Patchin, J. W. (2011). Overview of cyberbullying. White Paper. *White House Conference on Bullying Prevention*. Retrieved from Cyberbullying Research Centre.

Lindfors, P. L., Kaltiala-Heino, R., & Rimpelä, A. H. (2012). Cyberbullying among Finnish adolescents—a population-based study. *BMC Public Health, 12*(1), 1-5. doi:10.1186/1471-2458-12-1027

Schneider, S., O'Donnell, L., Stueve, A., & Coulter, R. W. (2012). Cyberbullying, school bullying, and psychological distress: A regional census of high school students. *American Journal of Public Health, 102*(1), 171-177. doi:10.2105/AJPH.2011.300308

Thom, K., Edwards, G., Nakarada-Kordic, I., McKenna, B., O'Brien, A., & Nairn, R. (2011). Suicide online: Portrayal of website-related suicide by the New Zealand media. *New Media & Society, 13*(8), 1355-1372. doi:10.1177/1461444811406521

**Instructor comments:**

1. The allusive phrase is very broad. Do you mean all technological triumphs are tragic? Should the allusive phrase be more specifically related to the explanatory phrase, i.e., topic?
2. I'm struggling to understand how to "chunk" the elements of your explanatory phrase or topic. Do you mean {Cyberbullying} among

{Teenage Girls and Suicide} or do you mean {Cyberbullying among Teenage Girls} and {Suicide}? Is there a better way to formulate the explanatory phrase by reconsidering the placement/use of prepositions and conjunctions? The best explanatory phrases clearly distinguish between abstraction and research site.

3. Good use of APA style dates.
4. Colloquialisms should be avoided in the genre of academic writing.
5. Check APA style for page abbreviations for multiple pages.
6. See the discussion of reported speech in chapter 6 of your textbook. Rather than using a semi-colon, use a colon to introduce an explanatory quotation after an independent clause.
7. Precision? Felt she could not stop?
8. In this case, do you really need the transition to introduce topic?
9. Your presentation of topic here is much clearer than in the second part of your two-part title. You could move this language up into your title.
10. Clear specific forecasting for now, but let's stay open to considering how many sections the paper will actually have. There may be an opportunity to join what are now forecast as Sections 2 and 3.
11. Carefully consider your choice of attributive verbs. See the discussion of attributive verbs in chapter 6 of *Designs for Disciplines*. "Claims" may imply that you are standing at a critical distance from these researchers. Do you want to hold them at arm's length or embrace their findings?
12. Successful? How do people affected by suicide actually talk about suicide? I have a friend who says her son "completed" suicide. She and others in her community of discourse prefer "completed" as opposed to "committed" or "successful." "Completed" doesn't carry any judgment. This point relates to the concept of genre.
13. Have a look at this entry in your References.
14. The summary of Lindors et al. doesn't support your guiding sentence in this paragraph. Think about the structure of this paragraph and the order in which you want to introduce your sources. The tradition of inquiry, as a whole, is a bit thin, but your list of references is impressive. Try to acknowledge more of your sources when presenting the tradition of inquiry. Also note that you can refer to your sources through integrated or non-integrated reference. See the discussion of reported speech in chapter 6.

> 15. This is a strong start on a thesis claim, but as you continue to work on your paper, it may be possible to improve the knowledge claim. One strategy is to reconsider your thesis in light of the sections forecasted for the core of your paper. Ideally, a thesis claim will address the central point of each major section.

# The Formality of Scholarly Style

Before moving more deeply into the discussion of academic writing, let's pause for a moment to consider the formality of scholarly discourse. The expressions used in academic writing sound different from the expressions that we are used to in our everyday lives, as we converse with friends and family members. For this reason, academic writing often sounds unnatural. Confronted with a page of academic prose, we might feel as though we have suddenly parachuted into an alien country. The dialect, idiom, or accent is not quite what we are accustomed to.

Standard dictionaries attach different meanings to the word *formal*. According to the *Oxford Dictionary*, "formal" can mean "prim," "stiff," or "perfunctory." It is associations like these that give academic formality a bad name. Reading published research articles gives the feeling that some authors take themselves and their subject too seriously.

On the other hand, there may be ways of justifying the formality of scholarly style. The *Oxford Dictionary* also defines "formal" as "precise" and "explicit." So when two people want to make sure that they understand each other, they write up a *formal* agreement. Academic writers, as people who deal with knowledge, share this desire for precision and explicitness. For them, formality may actually foster clarity. Viewed in this more positive light, mannerisms that strike us as elevated may reflect the needs of knowledge-making communities. In sum, we should avoid blanket judgments about formality in academic writing. The style of an individual researcher needs to be judged on its own merits, based on how effectively it handles knowledge, the commodity of academic communities.

The subsections that follow touch on some general aspects of style that academic instructors often comment on as they evaluate student writing. It is worth keeping these stylistic considerations in mind, from the proposal stage through to the finished paper.

## Grammatical Correctness

Your instructors will expect grammatical correctness. We are using the term "grammar" loosely, to include spelling, punctuation, subject–verb agreement, clear pronoun reference, effective transitions, and so on. While English instructors may pay special attention to grammatical correctness, it will also be a concern for instructors in other disciplines, even if they choose not to mark errors. There is, in fact, a presumption that the ability to write grammatically correct prose is a prerequisite for university-level courses. Therefore, proposals and papers should be carefully checked.

---

### Short Exercise

Identify grammatical problems in the following sentences:

1. In the introduction to *Travels in Western North America* Hopwood states that when Thompson was two, his father passed away, leaving him, his mother, and his younger brother.
2. The intentions of the founders of the school, were to "educate poor children in the principals of piety and virtue and thereby lay a foundation for a sober and Christian life" (2).
3. In March of 1995; Silken Laumann and her Canadian teammates faced hardship when Pan-Am officials, in Argentina, stripped them of their gold medals.
4. Laumann states that Victoria Rowing Club physician Dr. Richard Backus had recommended the drug after coming down with the cold shortly before the Pan-Am games.
5. Women in ancient civilizations were considered property and were used primarily to make babies to carry on the bloodline. The women of ancient Egypt were considered privileged because they had the same rights as men and were allowed to rule as men did.
6. To this day, the study of dreaming still remains a mystery as to what purpose dreams serve.... Many studies have been done that reveal the daily lives of people reflect in their dreaming periods at night.

---

## Colloquialisms

Informal speech is full of casual expressions and clichés, the meaning of which is readily understood ( for example, "a bird in the hand is worth two in the bush"). In the academic disciplines, however, colloquialisms will be regarded negatively by your instructor. The instructor will understand your meaning, but in the cliché above, a bird-in-the-hand versus birds-in-bushes are *figurative* expressions of a relationship between certainty and possibility, providing a warning to risk-takers. Yet the genre of academic discourse favours a *literal* expression of ideas, so colloquialisms should be replaced by more literal language.

---

### Short Exercise

Identify colloquialisms in the following passages and explain how such constructions create ambiguity:

1. Since the dawn of man ...
2. Since the beginnings of Canadian history ...
3. ... in 1975, the death penalty was banned completely on Canadian soil.
4. Throughout history, women have usually been considered secondary to men.
5. Why did Canada turn away from the death penalty while our neighbours still dish it out?
6. Toronto, 1962, saw Canada's last state-run execution.
7. A great deal of Thompson's life was directed by fate.
8. I will argue that Thompson was not necessarily a great hero nor a failure: he did make mistakes and struggled with pride, but most importantly, Thompson had a good heart.
9. To build a road across this land would consist of building bridges and removing thousands and thousands of trees.
10. Even though Esme Tuck and her family had made it to Canada seemingly no worse for the wear, their travel was far from over.
11. Phillips explores the ethical implications that came up in these totally different incidents.

---

## Complex Terminology

Most writing handbooks discourage complex terminology, which often goes by the name of "jargon" or "technical language." The assumption is that words or phrases readily understood by the general populace are better than words or phrases that are not (the simpler, the better). Academic writers, in particular, are criticized for their use of "professional slang." Malcolm Cowley, an advocate of standard English, makes the case:

> ... a vast majority [of academics] write in a language that has to be learned ... It has a private vocabulary which, in addition to strictly [discipline-specific] terms, includes new words for the commonest actions, feelings, and circumstances. It has the beginnings of a new grammar and syntax, much inferior to English grammar in force and precision. (as cited in *The Broadview Reader*, 1987, pp. 23–24)

From Cowley's perspective, complex terminology lacks clarity: academic writers use a "barbarous jargon" that "fuz[zes] up the obvious" (Cowley, as cited in *The Broadview Reader*, 1987, p. 23). The popular bias against what some view as academic snobbery is evident in a headline in the *Edmonton Journal*: "Professors who resort to jargon discredit society" (Simons, 1999, p. A8). Certainly, there are times when academic writing is needlessly obscure.

Simple language, however, is not always practical in academic writing. Contrary to Cowley's assertion, academic writers often challenge our *common* sense, deal with dense detail, and manage uncommonly complex and abstract ideas. This arduous work enables them to refine or revise our understanding of the world. Accordingly, this text takes a more tolerant view of complex terminology. "Big words" or discipline-specific jargon can be effective, even necessary, tools in academic writing. For example, a recent article we found on the Web is about "the rise of evidence-based health sciences librarianship." "Evidence-based health sciences librarianship" is a long noun phrase, which some might regard as wordy, but it actually compresses the description of a specialized practice into just a few words, making it easier to discuss aspects of that particular kind of library work. Without the compression that such dense noun phrases provide, the discussion would be mired in the repetition of "library work in the health sciences that is based on evidence." The first, more compact phrase is an example of nominalization, something that is very common in academic writing (look back on Brandy Palmer's proposal and the phrase "high debt worry students") (p. 85). The word *nominalization* comes from the Latin *nomen*, meaning name, so, in the most basic sense, nominalization means naming. When nominalization occurs in academic writing, prepositions, verbs, and other parts of speech are omitted, creating heavily modified nouns within long noun phrases. The density of such phrases allows scholars to move beyond description to an analysis and discussion of their results. Thus, nominalization has important advantages and is actually one of the most distinctive, telltale, and useful features of academic writing as a genre. As you continue your journey into the world of academic writing, you will encounter dense thickets of nouns that place heavy demands on readers, but these demands are a vital part of the academic landscape. In your own writing, however, remember that long noun phrases may call for definition when first used. Also remember that there is no need to rely on a thesaurus simply to replace plain vocabulary with uncommon vocabulary. Be as straightforward and clear as you can, but understand that in academic writing, straightforward clarity may involve complex terminology. Decisions about vocabulary involve ongoing judgment calls that need to be made on a case-by-case, sentence-by-sentence basis. Achieving clarity is hard work. For a further discussion of nominalization, see Chapter 8, "Freight-Train Nouns: The Density of Scientific Writing."

## Needlessly Complex Wording

### Short Exercise

Reduce these phrases to something simpler without changing the meaning:

| | |
|---|---|
| observational data | food item |
| individual food item categories | abundantly found food constituent |
| given the fact that | in this day and age |
| for the purpose of | in spite of the fact that |
| was of the opinion that | as a result of |

In the sentence in the box below, highlight the simple subject and the two main verbs.

> The move from a structuralist account in which capital is understood to structure social relationships in relatively homologous ways to a view of hegemony in which power relations are subject to repetition, convergence, and rearticulation brought the question of temporality into the thinking of structure, and marked a shift from a form of Althusserian theory that takes structural totalities as theoretical objects to one in which the insights into the contingent possibility of structure inaugurate a renewed conception of hegemony as bound up with the contingent sites and strategies of the rearticulation of power. (as cited in Simons, 1999, p. A8)

In essence, the sentence is telling us that a "move" "brought" something and "marked" something. However, the subject–predicate pattern is packed with phrases and clauses that obscure meaning.

## Wording That Is Not Complex Enough

Conversely, in the next example, an uncommon abstract noun (xenophobia) that is not heard in everyday speech makes the statement more concise even as it places greater demands on readers' vocabulary. The complex term is useful because it keeps the writing from getting bogged down in the repetition of the phrase "fear toward people who were different from him."

> This essay examines Ambrose Bierce's fear toward people who were different from him.
>
> [or, more effectively:]
>
> This essay examines xenophobia in the writings of Ambrose Bierce.

## Effectively Complex Wording

In the examples below, complex nouns such as "habituation," "aversive conditioning," and "dyslexia" are defined immediately or elsewhere in the paper.

Such complex terminology makes an effective and essential contribution to these papers.

---

First, I will explore the problems of black bear habituation. Second, I will examine how aversive conditioning can sometimes be used as a solution to the problem of habituation. Finally, I will apply these concepts to the circumstances in Fort Nelson, to determine if aversive conditioning would have been a viable alternative to extermination.

Dyslexia is a neurologically based learning disability that hinders language acquisition and processing.

I will argue that Luc Besson's *The Messenger* reflects a misogynistic backlash against twentieth-century feminism.

In relation to Monica Storrs' descriptions of landscape, it is worth noting that the terms "sublime" and "picturesque" were used throughout the nineteenth-century British exploration of Canada.

---

## Objectivity

Delving more deeply into the formal qualities of research articles, we can take a preliminary look at the scholarly concern for patterns of communication that ensure reliability. Whereas personal essays and letters tend to convey *subjective impressions* (that which is true for one person), research articles tend to seek *objective knowledge* (that which can be validated by repeated testing).

The distinct styles of the personal essay and the research article (which point to *apparent* distinctions between subjectivity and objectivity, between impressions and knowledge) are evident in passages from two essays on related subjects. Both passages describe an Aboriginal world view, explaining how Native peoples perceive nature and their relationship to it. In this sense, both passages essentially say the same thing or make the same point, yet they do so in very different ways.

The first passage is taken from a personal essay by Leah Idlout-Paulson, entitled "Wonderful Life" (1993):

I can be a cloud ... way up in the sky where I can see you first, then everyone and go everywhere with all kinds of colors: hanging low or high, in the North, South, West, or East.... But, when clouds are crying the people won't like it for me to cry for them; so I wish I was a big moon with a big, big, smiling face that everyone can see. But, the moon is always changing into different forms ... [and] I would only appear during the evening with a wide smiling face, so I wish I was a sun who is keeping warm and making everybody warm too at the same time. But, the people would always ask me to keep shining and keep them warm and when it is getting too hot for them, they would look for something to cover themselves from me or to hide from me where they can have more fun without me. So I wish I was a star, but I don't know which one.... So I wish I was a tree, but trees don't move around at all to go with the others. So I wish I was an animal ... (pp. 57–58)

Idlout-Paulson's essay was first published in *Inuit Today*, a monthly magazine devoted to Inuit culture.

The second passage, previously cited in the discussion of summarizing, is taken from a research article by Shelagh Grant (1989), entitled "Myths of the North in the Canadian Ethos":

There are many cultures and subcultures among the Indian and Inuit of northern Canada, but they share similar attitudes toward the land, derived in part from the long experience of survival in what many southerners consider a hostile environment. The image of the north as "homeland" is essentially a southern expression for the intensely spiritual concept of land held by northern natives.... Prior to European contact, everything within the Inuit's natural world had a spiritual connotation, a sanctity which must be respected. The infinite space and majestic grandeur of the Arctic "gave northern man a special awe for the might and majesty of the world, impressed upon him his own insignificance, and made him both mystically-inclined and humble" ... Any life form or inanimate object which had a sense of permanency was thought to have a spirit or soul, a belief which explains his profound respect for nature.[12] He was not a separate entity arriving on earth; he was always there, at one with, and a part of the natural world. (p. 18)

12. See *Northern Voices: Inuit Writing in English*, ed., Penny Petrone (Toronto: University of Toronto P, 1988) 202–203.

Shelagh Grant teaches history and Canadian studies at Trent University, and her article was published in *The Northern Review*, an academic journal.

The authorial voice in the first piece describes personal *feelings*: there is little or no distance between what is being written and the writer herself. Accordingly, Idlout-Paulson gives free expression to her emotions. As a personal essayist, she bares her soul, deriving content from her own felt experience of the world. By contrast, the authorial voice in the second piece is more detached and analytical. If Idlout-Paulson wants to describe how life is for her, Grant wants to describe how life is for other people. Thus, whereas Idlout-Paulson uses *I* frequently, the first-person pronoun does not appear at all in Grant's passage, which investigates phenomena external to the authorial self. We do not mean to suggest that *I* <u>never</u> appears in academic writing (see "Self-Disclosure" in Chapter 5), but the absence of *I*, in this case, contributes to the impersonal tone of Grant's writing. Some readers might even characterize the Grant excerpt as comparatively cool or dispassionate.

Nevertheless, Grant's impersonal way of writing serves the knowledge-making values of her discourse community. As an academic, Grant is seeking to convey an "objective" description of human experience, and her way of writing helps to satisfy this expectation. That is, Grant's style helps to create an impression of impartiality: she presents herself as an unbiased, logical expert, as someone who knows her subject through rigorous study. In addition, Grant inserts a superscript numeral (see the raised "[12]"), which, in context, refers the reader to an endnote, which in turn refers to an anthology entitled *Inuit Writing in English*. Grant cites this anthology to support the claims she is making, and it is probably safe to assume that several of the writing samples in the anthology bring us full circle, back to Idlout-Paulson's more personal approach. Grant employs personal narratives such as Idlout-Paulson's as *evidence* for academic claims.

For aspiring academic writers, the distinction between subjectivity and objectivity is a useful one, but it is also important to remember that this distinction is largely a matter of presentation. Indeed, although a professional academic writer like Shelagh Grant attempts to secure her claim to objective truth by heeding matters such as tone and evidence, her position is still very much a personal one. It is Grant herself, after all, who has decided what to focus on in her work, how to interpret the data before her, and how much to emphasize the significance of some data over the significance of others. Put another way, Grant's account of Northern myths in the Canadian ethos cannot help but reveal something about Grant herself, even though she may not overtly refer to herself in her own work. Grant's description of the "homeland" myth, for example, may indirectly reveal an authorial disenchantment with Euro-Canadian attitudes toward nature. Thus, in describing Native world views, Grant may be idealizing attitudes that provide a desirable alternative to her own cultural inheritance. Ultimately, then, Grant's academic objectivity might be regarded as an illusion sustained by particular stylistic gestures. The point we are making is not a criticism of Grant as an individual. It applies to all academic writing. When we try to tell about the world, we are also revealing something about ourselves.

In an effort to be more honest about the inherent subjectivity of all human perceptions, some academic writers have tried to put the writer back into the writing. "I," for example, does occur in academic articles, especially those from the humanities and social sciences. Some writers go a step further and embellish *I* by discussing their backgrounds and their relationships with their topics. Alice Carlick (1995), for example, in her essay on the importance of a girl's puberty rites in Tagish and Inland Tlingit society, briefly refers to her own personal investment in and experience of her research site: "As a First Nations person hearing and reading First Nations stories," Carlick writes, "I interpret such stories using both my personal experience and my academic training" (p. 34). In a follow-up comment, Carlick continues to situate herself in relation to her topic by elaborating on the nature of her academic training: "Because my studies at university have included literature as well as anthropology, I will combine both perspectives to discuss how Mrs. Sidney's story 'The Girl and the Grizzly' helps us understand social customs surrounding the training of young women" (p. 34). Paradoxically, then, for scholars such as Carlick, part of academic "objectivity" entails acknowledging one's subjectivity. In other instances, the autobiographical impulse in academic writing results in more lengthy moments of self-disclosure (see Chapter 5).

While clear-cut distinctions between objectivity and subjectivity are ultimately impossible to maintain, the *ideal* of objectivity still exerts a powerful force on academic writing. This is apparent when we examine the extent to which academic writers employ other "voices." Academics use other voices whenever they cite someone else's written or spoken words. The presence of other voices is an aspect of academic style that *seems* to allow for an impartial weighing of evidence, guarding against what the academic community would regard as the danger of excessive subjectivity.

## Ideas for Further Study

1. Check out the periodical shelves at your library or a periodical database that offers full-text articles. Read through an article or two for examples of scholarly wordings. Are such expressions used effectively?
2. Block and label the rhetorical features in the following proposal.

---

### Dallas Bartsch, "'Survival of the Fittest': Gender Imagery in Media Coverage of the Iditarod Sled Dog Race"

In late January 1925, a diphtheria epidemic broke out amongst the children of Nome, Alaska. Five lives were lost and the closest medicine was over 1,000 miles away, in Anchorage, Alaska. Although there were planes in Fairbanks, they had been dismantled for the winter. The only hope was to get the life-saving serum to the remaining victims by dogsled. A plan was made and with the help of twenty dog mushers who formed a relay from Nenana to Nome, the diphtheria medicine reached the stranded children in a record five days and seven hours. In 1973, Joe Redington founded the Iditarod Sled Dog Race in memory of the Alaska dogs who ran the life-saving relay. This race covers 1,151 miles, by dog team, from Anchorage to Nome.

The Iditarod Sled Dog Race is one of the few sports where both men and women compete against each other. Accordingly, this essay examines gender imagery in media coverage of the Iditarod Sled Dog Race. First, I will consider media coverage of the race from 1985 to 1990, years of great success for female competitors. Second, I will look at how the media portrayed female racers from 1991 to 2001. My primary sources include promotional videos, Internet interviews, and newspaper articles. Gender stereotyping by the media is a familiar practice in the sports industry. Pamela Creedon (1999) states that the media denies sportswomen the power and prestige that should be theirs. In other studies, Alexander (1994), Miller and Levy (1996), and Kolvula (1999) investigate gender conflicts and how the media depicts them. Building on these and other works, I will argue that the media has portrayed women in the Iditarod as having little if any value compared to the male competitors.

# References

*The Broadview Reader*. (1987). H. Rosengarten & J. Flick (Eds.). Peterborough: Broadview.

Carlick, A. (1995). The girl and the grizzly: Bringing traditional narratives into Yukon classrooms. *The Northern Review: A Multi-Disciplinary Journal of the Arts and Sciences of the North, 14,* 34–47.

Giltrow, J. (2002). *Academic writing: Writing and reading in the disciplines* (3rd ed.). Peterborough: Broadview.

Grant, S. (1989). Myths of the North in the Canadian ethos. *The Northern Review, 3/4,* 15–41.

Idlout-Paulson, L. (1993). Wonderful life. In R. Gedalof (Ed.), *Paper stays put: A collection of Inuit writing* (pp. 57–58). Edmonton: Hurtig.

Rosen, L. J., & Behrens, L. (1994). *The Allyn & Bacon handbook* (2nd ed.). Toronto: Allyn & Bacon.

Simons, P. (1999, January 10). Top scholars scoop bad writing award. *Edmonton Journal,* p. A8.

# CHAPTER 5

# Hello, Reader!

## Rhetorical Moves in Scholarly Introductions

> Introductions are known to be troublesome, and nearly all academic writers admit to having more difficulty with getting started on a piece of academic writing than they have with its continuation. The opening paragraphs somehow present the writer with an unnerving wealth of options: decisions have to be made about the amount and type of background knowledge to be included ... about the winsomeness of the appeal to the readership ... and about the directness of the approach.
>
> —John M. Swales,
> *Genre Analysis: English in Academic and Research Settings*

We've already noted that topic proposals and introductions share many of the same rhetorical features, so this chapter on scholarly introductions may seem repetitive; however, the beginning to a research paper carries such special challenges that we think it is wise to elaborate on introductory patterns. Indeed, the elaboration in this chapter will coincide with an opportunity to refine the topic proposal, and, thereby, create a solid introduction. As academic writers move from a proposal to an introduction, they have an opportunity to reconsider their opening "moves." For example, as we trace the growth of a paper from a proposal to an introduction, we may encounter such developments as the addition of an epigraph; an enriched rendering of context; the presentation of "self-disclosure," which situates topic in relation to a writer's experience; an enhanced account of theory or methods; and a more complex, nuanced thesis. Overall, an introduction reveals more time spent on research and reflection. Because the introduction is now formally a part of the paper itself, some of the conclusion-like rhetorical features that may appear in proposals will momentarily disappear only to reappear in the conclusion to the paper.

Further, in this chapter, we also show how introductory material is formatted within the paper itself, and this is where a consideration of "front matter" comes in. Rather than merely retracing the same steps, then, we provide an embellished discussion of opening knowledge-making features. Introductions take time, and we want to give them the time they deserve.

At the outset of the discussion, let's emphasize the distinction between the kind of attention-getting introductions that we encounter in, say, personal essays, and the more formal, knowledge-making introductions that we encounter in academic writing. The introductions to personal essays are *anecdotal* in the sense that they often tell a story, describe something, provide a quotation, and so on. Indeed, countless composition handbooks provide student writers with a neat set of strategies for beginning what are really pre-disciplinary essays. Such strategies are supposed to function as "hooks" that engage readers. On the other hand, the knowledge-making introductions of academic papers are *epistemic* in the sense that they are concerned with the conditions under which knowledge is produced. (The adjective "epistemic" comes from "epistemology," a branch of philosophy that deals with the conditions, sources, and justification of knowledge [Epistemology, 1995, p. 273].) Epistemic introductions tend to be more formal or serious than anecdotal introductions because the shift from private belief to disciplinary knowledge entails a host of very demanding expectations involving issues of definition, procedure, metadiscourse, objectivity, and evidence. Such demands tend to formalize academic writing (see Chapter 4). As John Swales (1990) observes in the epigraph above, this formalization of the writing process is nowhere more apparent than in scholarly introductions.

The bulk of discussion material in this chapter provides an explanation of *rhetorical features* (*coherence structures*). Mindful of Swales's (1990) observation that introductory "textual elements ... occur in suitably robust preferred orders" (p. 145), we have presented these features in a logical order, but also wish to acknowledge the possibility of variations. Moreover, few if any research papers contain all of the coherence structures presented here. Accordingly, it would be helpful to regard the various elements as offering a set of possibilities rather than prescriptive necessities. While academic introductions require a rigorous approach to knowledge-making, writers are still faced with choices about how to present their material. These choices may sometimes be influenced by personal preference, but more often they are determined by topic and by traditional disciplinary practices (Swales, 1990, pp. 137–166).

# Front Matter

The phrase "front matter" refers to the preliminary greetings that researchers extend to their readers. The precise configuration of front matter is usually determined by the different stylistic conventions that prevail in different disciplines.

"Hello, Reader!"

## Two-Part Titles

Although the precise rhetorical configuration of two-part titles varies, a two-part format is common in academic writing across the disciplines, particularly in the humanities and social sciences. Loosely speaking, of course, *any* title with two parts is a two-part title. This text, however, recommends a specific structure consisting of an *allusive phrase* followed by an *explanatory phrase.* Allusive phrases indirectly refer to the topic at issue and may consist of a brief quotation, a pertinent noun phrase, some key words, and so on. Explanatory phrases, on the other hand, succinctly articulate *topic*, providing both the prestige abstraction(s) and the research site.

---

George C. Nitzburg and Barry A. Farber

(*Allusive Phrase*)
Putting Up Emotional (Facebook) Walls?:
(*Explanatory Phrase*)
{Attachment Status} and {Emerging Adults' Experiences of
Social Networking Sites}
{*Prestige Abstraction*}          {*Research Site*}

---

---

Amy Snow Landa and Carl Elliot

(*Allusive Phrase*)
From Community to Commodity:
(*Explanatory Phrase*)
{The Ethics} of {Pharma-Funded Social Networking Sites for Physicians}
{*Prestige Abstraction*} {*Research Site*}

---

J. Spencer Clark

(*Allusive Phrase*)
Encounters with Historical Agency:
(*Explanatory Phrase*)
{The Value} of {Non-Fiction Graphic Novels in the Classroom}
{*Prestige Abstraction*} {*Research Site*}

---

Deborah Jermyn and Janet McCabe

(*Allusive Phrase*)
Sea of Love:
(*Explanatory Phrase*)
{Place, Desire} and {the Beaches of Romantic Comedy}
{*Prestige Abstractions*} {*Research Site*}

---

Kristin M. Barton

(*Allusive Phrase*)
Why We Watch Them Dance and Sing:
(*Explanatory Phrase*)
{The Uses and Gratifications} of {Talent-Based Reality Television}
{*Prestige Abstractions*} {*Research Site*}

Olivier Driessens

(*Allusive Phrase*)
The Celebritization of Society and Culture:
(*Explanatory Phrase*)
Understanding the {Structural Dynamics} of {Celebrity Culture}
{*Prestige* Abstraction} {*Research Site*}

In those cases where two-part titles depart from the pattern described above, any number of configurations may be present. On occasion, as in the example below, one will encounter a two-part title that "spreads" topic (research site and abstraction) throughout the first and second parts.

Jeffrey S. Hopkins

{West Edmonton Mall:}
{*Research Site*}
{Landscape of Myths and Elsewhereness}
{*Prestige Abstractions*}

In the next example, powerful abstractions appear in the allusive phrase, and the explanatory phrase consists primarily of the research site.

Samuel T. Gladding and Jose Villalba

(*Allusive Phrase*)
{Imitation, Impersonation, and Transformation:}
{*Prestige Abstractions*}
(*Explanatory Phrase*)
{Using Male Role Models in Films} to Promote Maturity
{*Research Site*}

Alternatively, as in the next examples, one may encounter an allusive phrase followed by a partial articulation of topic in the explanatory phrase. In these cases, the explanatory phrase gives us the research site only.

Kerry Abel

(*Allusive Phrase*)
Of Two Minds:
(*Explanatory Phrase*)
{Dene Response to the Mackenzie Missions, 1858–1902}
{*Research Site only*}

Chase Wesley Raymond

(*Allusive Phrase*)
Negotiating Entitlement to Language:
(*Explanatory Phrase*)
{Calling 911 Without English}
{*Research Site only*}

While practices vary, the precise configuration of an allusive phrase followed by an explanatory phrase offers an effective method of constructing scholarly titles in the humanities and social sciences. The pattern we recommend is analogous to the larger patterns of inquiry and clarification that characterize academic research: allusive phrases present evocative or puzzling details ("The Devil Sings the Blues"), while explanatory phrases "process" such details through generalization and abstraction ("Heavy Metal, Gothic Fiction, and 'Postmodern' Discourse"). Carefully configured two-part titles carry considerable rhetorical force.

In the natural sciences, and perhaps in some of the more empirical branches of the social sciences, there may be a preference for one-part titles that simply give topic (see Chapter 8).

## Title Pages

In the social sciences, instructors will often expect students to follow APA style, which calls for a title page. A sample APA title page follows, for a paper written by Shari Harrison (2001). Please refer to the most recent edition of the

*Publication Manual of the American Psychological Association*, a writing handbook, or one of the many websites that deal with formatting and documentation
for further instructions on formatting the title page.

---

Making the Grade                                                           1



 Making the Grade: Creating a Successful Learning Environment
        for Post-Secondary Students with Learning Disabilities



                        Shari Harrison



              University of Northern British Columbia

---

## Abstracts

Abstracts (not to be confused with prestige abstractions) are another feature
that appears more commonly in the social and natural sciences than in the
humanities. Abstracts provide a brief summary of the ensuing research, highlighting key features such as topic, methods or theoretical frame (where applicable), thesis, and main points. Abstracts do not contain documentation, tables,
and other supplementary features of the article. In APA style, abstracts appear
on a separate page, after the title page and before the first page of text. The page
on which the abstract is presented has the shortened title and page number as
a header and is entitled "Abstract."

**Abstract**

This article explores policies and practices that support the creation of a successful learning environment for postsecondary students with learning disabilities. I argue that instructors and institutions can more effectively meet the needs of all students by re-evaluating traditional instructional procedures. By using new pedagogical knowledge and understanding, instructors can begin to focus on the experience of learning from the student's perspective. The philosophy of valuing the learner's experience of learning is intertwined with the phenomenological approach to curriculum theory, an approach which focuses on individual perceptions and experiences of education and learning. Instructors undertaking this paradigm shift toward learner-centred learning may diversify learning assessment procedures without sacrificing assessment standards. Moreover, learning-strategy instruction may also assist students with learning disabilities. In sum, incorporating learner-centred instruction and learning strategies into classrooms can help make postsecondary education more responsive to social needs.

## First Page of Text

In APA style, the first page of text follows the title page and the abstract. Note how the first page of the text of Harrison's article (2001) continues the header and reiterates the full title:

Making the Grade: Creating a Successful Learning Environment
for Post-Secondary Students with Learning Disabilities

"Northern Lights College provides and promotes opportunities for life-long learning. Northern Lights College will provide accessible, responsive and diverse learning opportunities to enhance the quality of life for the community it serves" (Northern Lights College Calendar, 2001, p. 3). So reads the Northern Lights College Mission Statement, an educational ideal that is echoed in colleges and universities across the country. Creating an accessible and responsive environment for all students, and especially those students with learning disabilities, isn't as simple as it may sound though....

MLA style is used mainly in English and philosophy. In MLA style, which does not call for a title page or abstract, the first page of text is what greets the reader. Author, instructor, course, and date are presented top left. A header, consisting of the author's last name, a space, and a page number, appears right-aligned in the header. The full title is centred under the date. All elements are double-spaced. For further instructions on formatting MLA style papers, refer to the latest edition of the *MLA Handbook for Writers of Research Papers*. See the example that follows:

---

Vokaty 1

Helen Vokaty
Professor Beaulne
English 105
3 Apr. 1999

"In Transaction with Nature": *Into the Wild* as Quest, Odyssey, and Ordeal

In "Canadian Exploration as Literature," T. D. MacLulich argues that exploration writing can fall into one of three categories: quest, odyssey, and/or ordeal. The various patterns are often guided by the narrator's shaping of the adventure, a concept that MacLulich refers to as "emplotment" (86). According to MacLulich, an adventure can be retold as a quest, in which the central theme is the successful attainment of a specific goal (87). An odyssey, on the other hand, places less emphasis on the attainment of a particular goal, and more on the "incidental details of the journey" (88). Finally, an ordeal entails great hardship and focuses on survival, often ending in tragedy (87). MacLulich states that "the three forms [of exploration writing] are not necessarily mutually exclusive, but may exist in combination" (88).

---

## Epigraphs

Using an epigraph may contribute to the sophistication of your paper. Epigraphs are quotations that are usually placed immediately after the title and before the introduction. They are usually supplemented by an attributive noun phrase.

> ## Robin Ridington,
> ## "'When Poison Gas Come Down Like a Fog':
> ## A Native Community's Response
> ## to Cultural Disaster"
>
> Just like you blowing something, sounds like that.
> And they knew it right away, something happened down there.
> And pretty soon, just like a fog come down.
> Come down the hill.
> > —Angus Davis, Blueberry Band
>
> The Blueberry Reserve is a community of Cree and Beaver Indians about 72 kilo-metres north of Fort St. John, British Columbia....
>
> *Source:* Ridington (1990, p. 206)

## Features That Appear in Introductory Paragraphs

The following elements should be considered as you move beyond the front matter. Try to make informed choices about which features you will include, based on the requirements of individual topics and disciplinary conventions. Ideally, the features that you incorporate will be recognized by informed readers as familiar knowledge-making gestures.

### Establishing a Context

It is common for academic writers in the humanities and social sciences to begin their papers by presenting background information or illustrative mater-ial that establishes a context for topic. When researchers provide context for their work, they "step back a pace or two" (Northey, Knight, & Draper, 2012, p. 84) and ease into topic. Context "sets the stage" for knowledge-making activities.

In pre-disciplinary composition classes, strategies for establishing a con-text are usually described as ways of "hooking" readers. Such classes empha-size catching the attention of a reader, as though readers are easily distracted people who must be enticed. The assumption is rooted in the competitive

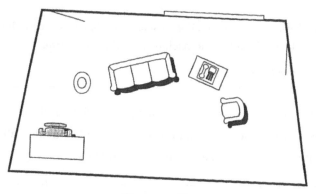

Stage setting

realities of popular journalism, where writers address a mass audience with a short attention span. The rationale for establishing a context in academic writing is somewhat different in that the social conditions of the genre involve a more limited audience with a professional interest in discipline-based topics. Accordingly, scholarly discourse usually exhibits openings that are somewhat less flamboyant or dramatic. Since academic writers assume that their readers are like-minded people who share an interest in disciplinary investigation, perhaps introductory contexts for research papers do not try quite as hard as those in journalism to engage the audience at an emotional level. To the uninitiated reader, the result might be uninviting, but academic readers are driven by interests that supersede entertainment value. The following excerpt simply begins with historical details:

## Greg Gillespie, "'I Was Well Pleased with Our Sport among the Buffalo': Big-Game Hunters, Travel Writing, and Cultural Imperialism in the British North American West, 1847–72"

During the mid-nineteenth century, big-game hunters from Great Britain traveled to the British North American West and cast their imperial eyes across the landscape. These aristocratic men traveled thousands of miles for sport, exploration, and adventure, and recorded their experiences in their travel narratives. They used their books, arranged and reproduced for readerships in England, to inscribe cultural meaning on the little-known territory. Big-game hunters used their travel writings to construct the West as a familiar, resource-rich land that appeared ready-made for the encroaching imperial enterprise.

*Source:* Gillespie (2002, p. 555)

This next example of introductory context—which literally refers to a stage setting—does demonstrate a flair for the dramatic (not coincidentally, perhaps, the paper appears in a journal entitled *Modern Drama*):

## Richard Paul Knowles, "Post-, 'Grapes,' Nuts and Flakes: 'Coach's Corner' as Post-Colonial Performance"

We're still trapped in Canada: we're the ventriloquist's dummy on the British and American knee. When the voices come in from all these other places, it's very hard to forge our own.
—Urjo Kareda

In "The Dummy," a short scene in the Rich Salutin/Theatre Passe Muraille collective creation "1837: The Farmer's Revolt," two actors playing a ventriloquist and his dummy address the crowd onstage and off in an allegorical representation of post-colonial mimicry.[2] As the scene opens, the (pre-)Canadian colonial dummy speaks only in the voice (literally) of "John Bull—your imperial ventriloquist," mouths platitudes and promises to cut trees and fight Yankees for England while being (literally) manipulated and having his pockets picked by the imperial puppet master. Towards the end of the scene, however, ignoring arguments that on his own he will be helpless, "a pitiable colonial," he stands independently and speaks in his own voice for the first time, rallying the crowd and introducing William Lyon Mackenzie, the radical political reformer and leader of the only class revolt in English Canada's history.

The scene is simple enough, except in its veiled critique (within the context of a nationalist collective creation) of the power structures of the traditional theatre in Canada, in which colonial actors, constructed as workers, use British accents to mouth the words and mimic the manners of British, or more recently, American playwrights and directors. I introduce it here, however, as a starting point for the analysis of a different kind of post-colonial performance, one that takes place not in the theatre, but in the intermissions between the first and second periods of telecast hockey games on the Canadian Broadcasting Corporation (CBC)....

*Source:* Knowles (1995, p. 123)

In other cases, academic writers may omit background or illustrative material entirely and demonstrate a more immediate focus on the challenges presented by the topic (MacDonald, 1994, pp. 47–48). As in the following examples, openings that get right down to business may *define a key term*, provide an outright announcement of *topic*, or present a *tradition of inquiry* (which identifies previous research related to the topic).

The first two papers begin with definitions:

## C. M. Tam et al., "Feng Shui and Its Impacts on Land and Property Developments"

"Feng Shui," literally meaning "wind" and "water," is ancient Chinese geomancy. It is abstract, invisible, untouchable, and intangible—as the wind, hard to see, and as water, difficult to be grasped. Thus it is considered mysterious.

*Source:* Tam et al. (1999, p. 152)

## Scott MacAulay, "The Smokestack Leaned Toward Capitalism: An Examination of the Middle Way Program of the Antigonish Movement"

The Antigonish Movement is the name given to a program of populist adult education and co-operative development that emerged in eastern Nova Scotia in the late 1920s. The intellectual and organizational center of the Movement was the Extension Department of St. Francis Xavier University in the town of Antigonish. The Movement represents the start of a long tradition of local development in this part of Canada that argues that people and communities in the region can and should take responsibility for local economic development.

*Source:* MacAulay (2002, p. 43)

The next paper begins with topic:

## Pamela Hyde, "Managing Bodies— Managing Relationships: The Popular Media and the Social Construction of Women's Bodies and Social Roles from the 1930s to the 1950s"

This paper, based on a discourse analysis of the New Zealand *Woman's Weekly* from the 1930s to the 1950s, [examines] the ways in which women's bodies and social roles have been historically constructed and reconstructed in accordance with changing social circumstances and expectations during the prewar, wartime, and postwar period. It discusses the ways in which power operated as pleasurable and desirable codes of self-surveillance and improvement, and shows that these codes were inextricably linked with gender relations.

*Source:* Hyde (2000, pp. 157–158)

The next two examples present traditions of inquiry:

## Tony Arruda, "'You Would Have Had Your Pick': Youth, Gender, and Jobs in Williams Lake, British Columbia, 1945–75"

In 1990, Canadian historians Patricia Rooke and Rudy Schnell described the field of Canadian history of childhood and youth as a "truly marginal subspecialty" of Canadian historical scholarship dominated by studies of the child-saving movement, juvenile immigration, and juvenile delinquency, and offering up only a small volume of dissertations.[1] Not much has changed in the intervening years. In this paper I attempt to address two further observations of the field....

*Source:* Arruda (1998, p. 225)

> ### Joan Valery and Patricia O'Connor, "The Nature and Amount of Support College-Age Adolescents Request and Receive from Parents"
>
> Many researchers have suggested that children are able to increase their capacity to deal with aversive stressors through the use of social support (Cause, Reed, Landesman, & Gonzales, 1990; Cutrona, 1990; Sandler, Miller, Short, & Wolchik, 1989; Thoits, 1986; Wills, Vaccaro, & McNamara, 1992).
>
> *Source:* Valery & O'Connor (1997, p. 323)

These blunter, down-to-business openings are particularly common in the sciences, where a greater emphasis is placed on brevity and where disciplinary processes can be compactly defined (see Chapter 8).

## Acknowledging a Tradition of Inquiry

As researchers, academic writers are under an obligation to situate their own work in relation to other voices in the research community. Thus, early on in a paper, academics often refer to previous studies that bear some relationship to the current investigation (Swales, 1990, pp. 140–142; Hyland, 1999). Janet Giltrow (2002) aptly describes this move as acknowledging "a tradition of inquiry" (p. 243). The closeness of the connection between the current study and previous studies may vary. Sometimes, for example, previous researchers may have anticipated the precise topic (both the research site and the prestige abstraction) under immediate investigation. In these cases, whether the current researcher wants to refute or build on the previous studies, she must acknowledge her predecessors. On other occasions, a researcher will bring a new abstraction to a research site that has typically been studied from other perspectives. Even in situations like this, however, previous work should be acknowledged. Thus, traditions of inquiry "map" particular domains of knowledge (Giltrow, 2002, p. 263). John Swales (1990) draws an "ecological analogy," explaining that a writer's acknowledgement of previous studies situates her topic within an "ecosystem" of knowledge-making activities (pp. 140–142).

Presenting a tradition of inquiry calls on the summary skills of the primary writer. Once again, moreover, the primary writer will have choices to make. Indeed, previous studies can be summarized through what we have chosen to call *integrated reference* or *non-integrated reference*. (For a more comprehensive discussion of modes of reference, and for previous research relating to this distinction, see Chapter 6.) In what we have called integrated reference, previous researchers are named in an attributive expression before the citation. In non-integrated reference, the names of previous researchers appear in a citation only. See the examples below.

---

## A Limited Tradition of Inquiry
## Presented through Integrated Reference

**Pamela den Ouden, "'My Uttermost Valleys': Patriarchal Fear of the Feminine in Robert Service's Poetry and Prose"**

Margaret Atwood points out that Service "habitually personifies the North as a savage but fascinating female" (18).

*Source:* den Ouden (1998, p. 113)

---

## Tradition of Inquiry Presented through
## Integrated Reference, with Extensive Summary
## of the First Source

**Eva St. Jean, "Swedes on the Move: Politics, Culture, and Work among Swedish Immigrants in British Columbia, 1900–1950"**

In an article on masculinity among farmers in northern Sweden, ethnologist Ella Johansson shows that Swedish men idealized and depended on women in a manner that differed from what occurred in countries where men measured their masculinity through their control over women. Johansson suggests that Swedes from farming communities admired women's work ethic and that women played a significant role in moulding their sons' characters, by helping them develop qualities that were central to young men's self-image as they crossed from being youngsters to manhood. Johansson suggests that since unmarried men were seen as youngsters regardless of age, the mother's role in the development of the male character was duplicated by the fiancée, and that only through marriage could men advance to the higher social position as fully mature men.[137]

**Note**

137. Ella Johansson, "Beautiful Men, Fine Women and Good Work People: Gender and Skill in Northern Sweden, 1850–1950," Gender & History 1.2 (Summer 1989): 200–212. Angus McLaren notes a similar reluctance to accept unmarried men as a fully integrated part of society in Europe, where some social scientists even considered single men as social threat. McLaren, *The Trials of Masculinity*, 55.

*Source:* St. Jean (2004, pp. 262–263)

# A More Extensive Tradition of Inquiry Presented through Integrated Reference

### Cheryl Kirschner, "Desperate Measures: Commercial Interests and the Murders at St. John's Fort"

Over the past decade, scholars have discussed the causes and effects of the murders at St. John's Fort. According to Robin Ridington, in "Changes of Mind: Dunne-za Resistance to Empire," the native people claim that the murders were "justified retaliation" for the mysterious death of a native hunter who had requested to leave the post in order to return to his band.[3] Conversely, in *Delayed Frontier: The Peace River Country to 1909*, David Leonard writes: " the perpetrators were reported to have been Beaver Indians who were angry at the pending closure of the post ..."[4] In "Early Fur-Trade History in the Peace River District of British Columbia, 1794–1824," Finola Finlay focuses on the effect of the murders: "The murders at St. John's have been cited by all authorities as the cause of the closure of [the Peace River] forts."[5]

*Source:* Kirschner (1998, p. 1)

---

## A Tradition of Inquiry
## Presented through Non-Integrated Reference

**David Hamer, "Wildfire's Influence on Yellow Hedysarum Digging Habitat and its Use by Grizzly Bears in Banff National Park, Alberta"**

Hedysarum roots (*Hedysarum alpinum* and *H. sulphurescens*) are a primary food of grizzly bears in the Front Ranges of the Canadian Rocky Mountains. Although they have low digestibility and thus may be overrepresented when diet is determined by means of faecal analysis (Hewitt and Robbins 1996), hedysarum roots likely dominate the annual diet of some Front Range grizzly bears (*Ursus arctos*) in some years. Hedysarum roots are dug from April through early June before green vegetation is widely available, in August if buffaloberry (*Shepherdia canadensis*) fruits are sparse or slow to ripen, and in September through November after fruit-fall (Russell et al. 1979; Wielgus 1986; Hamer and Herrero 1987*a*; Hamer et al. 1991). If the buffaloberry crop fails, roots can dominate the diet from August until the bears hibernate in late October or November (Pearson 1975; Russell et al. 1979; Hamer and Herrero 1987*a*).

*Source:* Hamer (1999, p. 1513)

---

Non-integrated reference is a "short-hand" means of presenting a tradition of inquiry and is typical of how traditions of inquiry appear in scientific writing.

---

## An Extensive Tradition of Inquiry
## Presented through a Mix of Integrated and
## Non-Integrated Reference

**J. E. Martin and S. M. Janosik, "The Use of Legal Terminology in Student Conduct Codes: A Content Analysis"**

Research on campus discipline has taken many forms. Dutton, Smith, and Zarle (1969) have examined the role of the college administrator in student discipline. Lancaster, Cooper, and Hartman (1993) have offered their own insights into the role of campus disciplinary officers and the environment in which they work. The effects of litigation on the judicial affairs function have been studied (Ostroth, Armstrong, & Campbell, 1978; Steele, Johnson, & Rickard, 1984; Palmer, Penney,

Gehring, & Neiger, 1997). The student offender has been studied by many authors (Janosik, Davis, & Spencer, 1985; Janosik, Dinn, & Spencer, 1986; Kern & Rentz, 1991; Tidsdale & Brown, 1965; Trace, Foster, Perkins, & Hillman, 1979). Dannells (1990, 1991) studies changes in judicial policies and procedures longitudinally. Fitch and Murry (2001) studied the effectiveness of student judicial systems in doctoral-granting universities. Judicial decision-making and sanctioning have also been studied (Janosik, 1995; Janosik & Riehl, 2000).

*Source:* Martin & Janosik (2004, p. 38)

## Describing a Knowledge Deficit

On occasion, academic writers discover a "new" research site (something that has received little if any scholarly attention); alternatively, they may discover that fresh abstractions reinvigorate "old" research sites. In these cases, researchers find unoccupied or relatively unpopulated niches for their own knowledge-making activities (Swales, 1990, p. 142; Giltrow, 2002, pp. 264–265). These blank spaces present a special opportunity for researchers to make an original contribution to knowledge. Some of the most significant research often involves branching out into new territory. In order to affirm that a knowledge gap exists, researchers will sometimes sketch out *neighbouring* knowledge domains. In circumstances like this, a tradition of inquiry is followed by the identification of what Giltrow (2002) calls a "knowledge deficit" (pp. 262–269).

So far, the knowledge deficits we've discussed involve unoccupied territory:

## The Simple Articulation of a Knowledge Deficit

### G. J. Nowacki and M. D. Abrams, "The Demise of Fire and 'Mesophication' of Forests in the Eastern United States"

Many studies have individually documented fire regime change and subsequent shifts in vegetation over time (Heinselman 1973, Clark 1990, Abrams and Nowacki 1992, Wolf 2004). However, a broadscale synthesis, projection, and discussion of fire-regime change across the Eastern United States is currently lacking. Similarly, discussions regarding the ecological consequences of long-term fire suppression have been largely restricted to local levels. Here, using geospatial analyses of past and current fire regimes, we estimate the extent and magnitude of fire regime change throughout the East. We focus on the vast oak-pine and tallgrass prairie-savanna formations in the Eastern United States to illustrate and discuss the biotic and abiotic ramifications of fire regime change and, in the process, to document the near-universal "mesophication" of fire-dependent communities.

*Source:* Nowacki & Abrams (2008, p. 124)

# The Articulation of a Knowledge Deficit with Extensive Supplementary Endnotes

**J. N. Boeving, "The Right to Be Present before Military Commissions and Federal Courts: Protecting National Security in an Age of Classified Information"**

One right which has received little attention in legal scholarship, however, is the right of an accused to be present during trial. The lack of scholarly discourse stems primarily from the perception that the existence of the right is largely settled, even if its precise contours may not be.[11] It is well established that there are certain instances where a defendant must be present, and other instances where his presence is not fundamentally required for the proper administration of justice. A secondary reason for the lack of scholarly discourse is that the right to be present is not textually provided for in the Constitution. Rather, it is entwined with the right of confrontation,[12] and thus is often inadvertently overlooked.[13]

**Notes:**

11. See, e.g., Lewis v. United States, 146 U.S. 370, 372 (1892) ("A leading principle that pervades the entire law of criminal procedure is that, after indictment found, nothing shall be done in the absence of the prisoner.") *See generally* FED R. CRIM. P. 43.

12. See Brett H. McGurk, *Prosecutorial Comment on a Defendant's Presence at Trial: Will* Griffin *Play in a Sixth Amendment Arena?* 31 UWLA L REVC 207, 228 (2000) ("Nevertheless, the Supreme Court has held that one of the most basic rights guaranteed by the latter clause—the Confrontation Clause—is the right of the accused to be present in the courtroom at every stage of trial.").

13. See, e.g., Akhil Reed Amar, *Sixth Amendment First Principles,* 84 GEO. LJ. 641 (1996). In his description of the rights contained in the Sixth Amendment, Amar does not identify a discrete right to be present. Instead, he explains that it seems subsumed in the right of confrontation. *See id.* at 689 (explaining that the Confrontation Clause is intended to allow the defendant to hear a witness's story, which assumes that the defendant is present to hear).

*Source:* Boeving (2007, p. 467)

# A Tradition of Inquiry in a Neighbouring Knowledge Domain, Followed by a Knowledge Deficit

**J. Ryan, "Experiencing Urban Schooling: The Adjustment of Native Students to the Demands of a Post-Secondary Education Program"**

While numerous studies have addressed the Native urban experience (Bud, 1986; Leibow, 1989; Shoemaker, 1988; Graves, 1970; Mucha, 1983, 1984; McCaskill, 1970, 1981; Clatworthy and Hull, 1983; Dosman, 1972; Moronis, 1982), the issue of temporary student migration to cities on the part of Native people seeking to expand their educational horizons, and the subsequent impact on their capacity to apply themselves to their studies, has received scant attention.

*Source:* Ryan (1995, p. 212)

# Another Tradition of Inquiry in a Neighbouring Knowledge Domain Followed by a Knowledge Deficit

**Andrea Lawson and Gregory Fouts, "Mental Illness in Disney Animated Films"**

The effect on adults of the media's portrayal of mental illness and persons with mental illness has been extensively researched (1-6). The portrayals have been found to be overwhelmingly negative (5, 7, 8) and have been associated with adults' possessing negative attitudes and behaviours regarding mental illness and persons with a mental illness (2, 4, 5). However, little research has examined such representations in children's media and the possible effects on children.

*Source:* Lawson & Fouts (2004, p. 311)

figuratively speaking, the academic writer moves into a blank space on the knowledge map. This is an ambitious undertaking. There is another kind of knowledge deficit that may be easier to address. In this case, academic writers may simply identify "unconfirmed" territory that is characterized by debate or signs of inconclusiveness. Here, previous scholars have made forays into a knowledge domain, but the academic community appears to be working with competing maps that provide different views of the same landscape. Such differences of opinion may be implicit in the summary comments that accompany a tradition of inquiry; however, the difference of opinion can be highlighted in a comment that explicitly acknowledges signs of inconclusiveness.

The example that follows describes competing views about the philosophical orientation of an early 20th-century Canadian writer, Frederick Philip Grove. These competing views create a knowledge deficit that takes the form of a debate, and the author of the article, Rudolf Bader, steps into this debate. Notice, too, how high the stakes are. Academic debate becomes an occasion for intense drama that consists of "spectacular revelations" (!) and firm assertions of revisionary "starting point[s]." In this passage, you'll also see a reference to Janet Giltrow, not in her role as a leading authority on academic writing, but as a literary critic. This is a sign of how broad academic careers can be.

## A Tradition of Inquiry That Depicts Two Competing Schools of Thought

### Rudolf Bader, "Frederick Philip Grove and Naturalism Reconsidered"

In 1932, Robert Ayre compared Grove with the great American master of literary naturalism, Theodore Dreiser: "If the analogy be not pressed too closely, he might be called the Theodore Dreiser of Canada; these two austere spirits, these two men with the clumsy tongues, have much in common."[1] The obituary tribute to Grove written by Northrop Frye for *The Canadian Forum* took up Ayre's reference to Dreiser.[2] Ronald Sutherland doubts whether Grove ever had the opportunity or the inclination to read such American authors as Crane, Dreiser, Norris, and others,[3] but he agrees that Grove was a naturalistic writer, pointing out the "naturalistic emphasis upon the futility of individual self-reliance"[4] ... Thus, with relatively slight variations, the early Grove critics accepted the naturalistic label for Grove.

... It was George Woodcock who first realized that the question of Grove's indebtedness to naturalism was dependent on his European background, at least to a certain extent; and [that] the two significant literary movements in Europe [at the time] were those of naturalism and symbolism.[5] Douglas Spettigue also tried to differentiate more carefully in his assessment of Grove's allegiance to naturalism.[6] He finds that there is a difference between the early Grove and the late Grove, and that most of Grove's novels can be called tragic rather than naturalistic. Spettigue shows how Grove, especially in his late novels, tried to follow an ethical orientation.

However, even before Spettigue's spectacular revelations, the interpretation of Grove's novels in the light of naturalism was met by an opposing view. In an article in *Canadian Literature*, Frank Birbalsingh, in 1970, asserted that Grove's characters did not respond passively but followed personal values.... Birbalsingh finds that Grove, unlike the major American naturalist writers, did not have a Marxist background, his views being more open rather than narrowly political, and he concludes that Grove was neither a socialist nor a naturalist, but an existentialist.

Grove himself had something to say about naturalism. In an essay on "Realism in Literature" (1929), in which he divides some outstanding works from world literature into two major categories ("Realistic" versus "Romantic") ... he reminds his Canadian readers of the original meaning of the term "naturalist": "We are used to thinking that the word naturalist denotes, in English, something entirely different from what it connotes in French. That is an error. A naturalist, in English, means a scientist; but no more emphatically so than in French."[14] In an article on Grove and his audience, Janet Giltrow obviously refers to this scientific naturalism when she writes: "Before the twentieth century, the naturalist's art in America had traditional connections with a European audience."[15] And it seems that Grove was still very much the scientist when he set forth into literature.... The reviews of his first published work in English show this.... It seems obvious then that any assessment of Grove's naturalism would be incomplete without giving due consideration to the original, scientific meaning of the term. The observant eye of the scientist must remain the starting point for any interpretation of Grove's view of the world.

*Source:* Bader (1985, pp. 222–224)

## Topic

Readers of this text will now be familiar with a rigorous approach to articulating and identifying topic (see Chapter 2). As previously noted, we encourage students to think of topic as a rhetorical feature that consists of a research site (an *area* of investigation) plus a prestige abstraction (an *idea* or concept that is recognized as important in academic culture). Moreover, we have shown that academic proposals and introductions often explicitly announce (or flag) topic through metadiscursive verbs such as "examine," "explore," "focus on," and so on. Given the fundamental importance of topic, we have provided more examples of how it may surface in published research.

In the three excerpts below, the topic formula should be readily evident:

"This paper attempts to explore ... shifts in affective and ideological meaning between Barbara Gowdy's short story 'We So Seldom Look on Love' and Lynne Stopkewich's 1996 film adaptation *Kissed.*" (Parpart, 2002, p. 52)

"Focusing on black-white couples, this exploratory study examines ... dominant and marginalized discourses in interracial relationships ..." (Killian, 2002, p. 604)

"... we investigated the extent to which the higher prevalence of specific reading disability among boys was an artifact of gender bias." (Share & Silva, 2003, p. 5)

In the two passages that follow, the research site is easy to discern, but it might be harder to settle on an abstraction.

"This article will focus on two BBC reality series, *999* and *Children's Hospital,* and will examine why these series are popular with British audiences, in particular, focusing on the 'entertainment potential' (Kilborn, 1994, p. 425)." (Hill, 2000, p. 194)

"... the present study explored how feminist family science teachers conceptualize teaching, translate theory into classroom practice, and handle challenging situations." (Blaisure & Koivunen, 2003, p. 22)

The metadiscourse of topic can also be associated with nouns like "purpose," "aim," or "objective." Thus, when some instructors call for introductions that contain a "statement of purpose," they may simply be attaching a different label to topic. The samples that follow present this pattern in published research:

"The aim in this article is to historicize and conceptualize [possible changes] in visual culture, and to suggest plausible explanations for the proliferation of reality TV in the digital era." (Fetveit, 1999)

"The purpose of this study was to determine the nature and amount of parental support older adolescents request and receive from parents." (Valery & O'Connor, 1997)

"The objective of this paper is to explore whether Feng Shui would affect property values." (Tam et al., 1999, p. 152)

In the above instances, topic sounds very much like the kind of generalized structural forecast that is described below. Thus, in some papers, topic may be rolled into a broad comment about structure, but we advise student writers to make fine distinctions between topic and structural forecasts.

Finally, since we are dealing with the various presentations of topic, it is worth noting that there may be occasions where topic (aboutness) and thesis (argument) appear interwoven within a single sentence, as in the next example:

"This article examines these narratives in order to understand how they construct an 'Oprah' persona whose life story as it is appropriated in popular biographies resonates with and reinforces the ideology of the American Dream, implying the accessibility of this dream to black Americans despite the structural, economic, and political obstacles to achievement and survival in a racist society." (Cloud, 1996, p. 116)

Once again, however, we advise student researchers to make careful distinctions among introductory rhetorical features and to announce topic and thesis separately.

## Structural Forecasts

Structural "forecasts" relate to matters of organization (Giltrow, 2002, p. 236). That is, such statements anticipate the structure of a paper by providing advance notice about how material will be presented to readers. According to Giltrow, "forecasts play an important role in helping readers manage the contents of their mental desktops.... [For example,] [t]hey guide readers in determining when one section is finished and another is beginning ..." (p. 238). We wish to point out that such comments can be fairly general or quite specific. *General forecasting*, as we use the phrase, merely provides a broad sense of direction and may, as noted above, be virtually identical to topic. What we choose to call *specific forecasting*, on the other hand, is a more distinctive and perhaps more useful feature, functioning like a relatively detailed, step-by-step outline. Frequently, specific forecasting is accompanied by adverbs that designate chronology ("First," "Second," "Third," and so on).

---

## General Forecasting

### S. Grant, "Myths of the North in the Canadian Ethos"

To fully understand [the overarching, national myth of the north], one must first identify the many lesser myths which gave special meaning to the north and eventually combined to form the vague but all-encompassing core myth.

*Source:* Grant (1989, p. 15)

---

## Specific Forecasting

### H. Hobbs, "Victim Participation in International Criminal Proceedings: Problems and Potential Solutions in Implementing an Effective and Vital Component of Justice"

This Article first considers the question of "who is a victim" in international law. It then examines victim participation generally, evaluating its potential benefits and the modalities of participation in three specific jurisdictions (two international and one national). Next, it moves on to explore many of the difficulties involved in institutionalizing victim participation in international criminal proceedings. It analyzes how the admissibility of victims may affect fundamental fair-trial rights, such as equality of arms and undue delay, how the sheer number of victims in international crimes exacerbates issues of fraud and subversion and the divergent interests of the prosecution and victim's counsel, and how poor structural implementation still hinders effective victim participation. This Article also proposes three solutions to these issues. It argues that informing the admissibility structure, collectivizing victim participation, and limiting preparations to moral and collective awards offer the best way forward for systemic development of the International Criminal Court (ICC) and future ad hoc international tribunals.

*Source:* Hobbs (2014, p. 3)

## Self-Disclosure

It is increasingly common in academic writing, particularly in the humanities and in some areas of the social sciences, for writers to situate themselves in relation to their topic. In these instances, academic writers move beyond what Janet Giltrow (2002) refers to as the merely "discursive 'I'" (pp. 233–236), which often appears in first-person metadiscursive announcements of such features as topic, thesis, and forecasting ( for example, *I examine; I argue; First, I discuss*). Even the modest appearance of *I* in constructions like these may surprise students, some of whom arrive at college and university with the sense that *I* should be avoided entirely in academic writing. Obviously, however, this is not a universally accepted rule.

In fact, in recent years, *I* or *We*—pronouns that designate authors—have made even bolder appearances in academic writing. In these cases, we learn a little more about that *I* who examines, argues, or discusses. In these more intensely personal moments, readers encounter *self-disclosure*, a personal gesture that acknowledges the "constructedness" of all knowledge. This tendency to reveal the self as the generator of knowledge has been associated with feminism, an intellectual perspective that has a political investment in disputing the notion of absolute objectivity. In this text, we suggest that it is possible to trace an ascending scale of self-disclosure that charts increasingly bolder appearances of the writing self. We begin with the merely discursive *I*, then move toward a more autobiographical *I* that engages in more self-disclosure, providing more details about the writer. This greater self-disclosure was traditionally associated with personal essays but has recently claimed a space in academic writing.

In the first sample, personal pronouns flag topic and thesis:

# The Merely Discursive *I*

**Franca Iacovetta, "Gossip, Contest, and Power in the Making of Suburban Bad Girls: Toronto, 1945–60"**

*My* exploration of the various forces that converged in the making of postwar suburban Toronto bad girls confirms the wisdom of Foucault's famous axiom, that knowledge is power, and the Gramscian concept of hegemony central to many Marxist and feminist analyses of moral regulation. *My* analysis has also obviously benefited enormously from the recent spate of excellent feminist works on female transgression and the courts, and on women and social-welfare systems more generally.... *I have tried to suggest* how parents, especially mothers, but also caseworkers, empowered themselves in battles to intimidate, supervise, control, or punish deviant teenage girls. [italics added]

*Source:* Iacovetta (1999, p. 621)

In the next two samples, personal pronouns signal writing selves that have first-hand experience of the topic. Here, the "eyes" are witnesses to the research site.

# The *I* as Witness: Sample 1

## Jacqueline Hookimaw-Witt, "Any Changes Since Residential School?"

The statement about Native people that "these people need education" is usually made when *our* situation in Canadian society is presented; and it is used as a suggestion as to how *our* problems should be solved. *I heard* this statement from the non-Native health director in *my community* of Attawapiskat when *I was there* to do research for my master's thesis. *I also worked in the Safe House*, which is the home to which solvent abusers were brought as an alternative to a jail cell. The form of solvent abuse in Attawapiskat is sniffing gasoline, and it has infested a large portion of *our* youths.... [T]he health director set the stage for how to solve the problem, namely, by education of the youths. [italics added]

*Source:* Hookimaw-Witt (1998, p. 159)

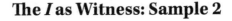

# The *I* as Witness: Sample 2

### David W. Friesen and Jeff Orr, "New Paths, Old Ways: Exploring the Places of Influence on the Role Identity"

*We are both* non-Aboriginal and former faculty members with the Aboriginal teacher education program from which the participants graduated. Long after joining southern teacher education institutions, *we continued* to hear stories about our former students and their influence as Aboriginal educators on northern education. *We began* to propose ways to document their influences without evaluating them or comparing them with non-Aboriginal teachers. *We wondered* what it was about their teacher identity that enabled them to influence positively students, schools, and communities. *We wished* to find out what Aboriginality means for their teaching by gaining insight into the notion of Aboriginal teacher role identity. *Our initial contact with the graduates* to propose this project was greeted with overwhelming support. [italics added]

*Source:* Friesen & Orr (1998, pp. 188–189)

In the next example, the writers express an even more intimate relationship with their research site, acknowledging their own emotional engagement:

# The *I* as Emotionally Engaged Researcher

### Susanna Egan and Gabriele Helms, "The Many Tongues of Mothertalk: Life Stories of Mary Kiyoshi Kiyooka"

*We ourselves* come to Mary Kiyooka's life stories as outsiders, but undoubtedly read them for their resonance with *our own experiences. As women of two generations, and as immigrants from England and Germany respectively, we respond* to Mary Kiyooka's experience of immigration from Japan to Canada. *We respond* to Kiyooka's involvement with his mother's text, recognizing its power to explain his identity as both Canadian and Japanese. *We respond* to the challenges of translation and the grounding of Kiyooka's sensibilities in two languages. *We respond* to Marlatt's editorial involvement derived from her sense of responsibility to Mary and Roy Kiyooka and part of her longstanding commitment to oral and community histories. *We also read Mothertalk* in light of very significant help from those whose readings have preceded our own. [italics added]

*Source:* Egan & Helms (1999, p. 49)

In our final examples, the writers present autobiographical details:

# The Autobiographical *I*: Sample 1

**Lorraine York, "'What It Took and Took/To Be a Man': Teaching Timothy Findley and the Construction of Masculinities"**

Now,
it is their brokenness
you long to touch, the parts
they left behind or lost
as they learned too soon
too many years ago
what it took and took
to be a man.

This essay will be a journey through *my own thinking* about this complex field of study: masculinities, social institutions (such as, in *my* case, the university) and power, a journey that began with *my teaching* of a course on Timothy Findley and the construction of masculinities. Beginning *my narrative* of this journey with Crozier's lines [a reference to the epigraph] is *important to me*, I sense, because they present a woman in the act of speaking about masculinities—*a role that I have had to assume in the classroom and, to a lesser extent, with my teaching colleagues*. [italics added]

*Source:* York (1999, p. 15)

## The Autobiographical *I*: Sample 2

**Robyn R. Warhol and Diane Price Herndl,** *Feminisms: An Anthology of Literary Criticism and Theory*

*"We" are Robyn and Diane; we speak as white, middle-class heterosexual American feminist academics in our early thirties* (to cover a number of the categories feminist criticism has lately been emphasizing as significant to one's reading and speaking position: race, class, sexual orientation, nationality, political positioning, education-level, and age). *Colleagues at the University of Vermont since 1989, we too have found that we share passionate interests in fiction, feminism and quilt-making.*

Source: Warhol & Herndl (1997, p. ix)

While self-disclosure represents an important new trend in academic writing, it would be misleading to say that the use of *I* has been sanctioned by all academics. To the contrary, the "avoid I" advice that students sometimes bring to post-secondary studies reflects real tensions in academic culture. Clearly, *I* is more acceptable in the humanities than in the natural sciences, leaving the social sciences as a kind of ambivalent middle ground. Here is what Northey, Knight, and Draper (2012) have to say about *I* in *Making Sense: Geography and Environmental Sciences: A Student's Guide to Research and Writing* (5th ed.):

A formal essay is not a personal outpouring, as in a personal letter or e-mail to someone close to you. Therefore you should keep it from becoming I-centred. It's acceptable to use the occasional first-person pronoun if the assignment calls for your opinions—as long as they are backed by evidence. But you should avoid the *I think* or *in my view* approach when the fact or argument speaks for itself. Still, if the choice is between using *I* and creating a tangle of passive constructions, it is almost always better to choose *I*. (Hint: when you do use *I*, it will be less noticeable if you place it in the middle of the sentence rather than the beginning.) (p. 10)

In sum, *I* has "HANDLE WITH CARE" stamped all over it. Accordingly, students should consult with individual instructors about the use of *I*.

## Methods

Since we have already divided the narrative structure of humanities and social sciences articles into an introduction, a core, and a conclusion, we'll treat "methods" as an introductory rhetorical feature. Alternatively, we could think of a methods section as a bridge between the introduction and the core.

In the humanities and social sciences, a methods section may be advisable when scholars engage in special types of knowledge-making activities. For example, methods sections may convey information about archival materials (primary sources) that are not available to the broader disciplinary audience. Similarly, if social scientists use questionnaires as a research tool, information about the questionnaire would likely be provided in a methods section. Thus, methods sections are generally advisable when researchers adopt distinctive knowledge-making strategies.

The traditional rationale for including a methods section is that this feature enables a disciplinary audience to evaluate the reliability of knowledge claims. Hypothetically, at least, by setting out their methods, scholars hold their activities up for inspection, permitting colleagues to evaluate whatever claims or findings are being presented. Accordingly, we advise students to think of a methods section as commenting on basic questions about who or what was studied, where and when the study was conducted, how it was conducted, and why certain choices were made. The length of methods sections varies, from a paragraph (or part of a paragraph) to several paragraphs. A methods section in the humanities and social sciences might be regarded as a fairly brief yet comprehensive story about how knowledge was made, and it may be an advisable rhetorical feature in student papers, depending on the topic. In Jenna's research, for example, there is an opportunity for original research (a questionnaire) that would call for a methods section (see Chapter 8).

Despite their story-like function, however, methods sections often defy standard notions of good writing, tending to present what Swales (1990) describes as "bald" narratives characterized by choppy sentences, heavy doses of statistical information, and agentless or passive-voice constructions. These tendencies are more pronounced in the natural sciences, but it is possible to catch glimpses of them in the so-called "softer" disciplines.

Undergraduate writers in the social sciences may have special opportunities to use a methods section if they are dealing with archival material—unpublished documents that are housed in, say, a local museum. In these cases, methods sections typically convey certain information about the source:

- *Identification:* Identify and contextualize your source as specifically as possible.
- *Selection Rationale:* Explain the rationale for relying on the material.
- *Appearance:* For unpublished archival materials, academic writers sometimes describe the physical appearance or features of the text (length, formatting, etc.).
- *Content Summary:* Briefly summarize content.
- *Analytical Procedure:* Explain, in detail, *how* you conducted a *content analysis.*

As you're reading methods sections, it will be possible to block and label the features identified above. It's also worth noting that methods sections in the social sciences often spend considerable time describing an analytical procedure. This is where content analysis comes into play. In presenting content analysis in a methods section, academic writers describe the *quantification* of an interpretive perspective. Content analysis is all about organizational schemes, about how content in the primary source was divided up and counted. Interestingly, the presentation of content analysis in the social sciences has a lot in common with the kind of "close reading" that occurs in literary criticism. Indeed, literary critics, like social scientists, often sift through and track image patterns. In literary criticism, however, this interpretive activity is usually taken for granted and not described in a methods section. Here again, then, we see differences in disciplinary cultures. In the social sciences, there is a desire to place controls on subjectivity by describing interpretive processes. In the humanities, on the other hand, subjectivity is given freer rein.

Next, we present sample methods sections from a variety of papers. The first sample is from Andrea Lawson and Greg Fouts's "Mental Illness in Disney Animated Films" from the *Canadian Journal of Psychiatry*.

# Andrea Lawson and Greg Fouts, "Mental Illness in Disney Animated Films"

## Method

TWDC [The Walt Disney Corporation] produced 40 full-length animated feature films between 1937 and 2001. These films are defined as having a duration of at least 40 to 45 minutes and as having been released into theatres (26). All such films were included in the study, except for those without one consistent story line from start to finish ( for example, *Fantasia, Fantasia 2000, Make Mine Music*, and *Melody Time*), primarily education films ( for example, *Saludos Amigos*), and those not available on video during the coding period ( for example, *Atlantis*). Thus, we analyzed a total of 34 films for content.

## Coding Manual

We developed a coding manual to systematize the content analysis. The manual contained the variables coded, the operational definitions, the criteria for coding, and examples. During the manual development, we conducted several practice codings of the variables using non-Disney TV cartoons. We did this to ensure clarity of the variable definitions, the examples, and the coding options. Several practice rounds and manual refinements were required to attain an acceptable level of intercoder agreement for each variable.

Below we describe the coding of each film. First, we coded film and character information, that is, film title, the year produced, and the name and sex of principal characters. Principal characters were defined as those around whom the film's action primarily revolved, those whose actions significantly influenced the plot, or those who were present on-screen for a significant portion of the film. Second, we coded mental illness as portrayed by the principal character, that is, all verbalizations about a principal character referring to mental illness, including verbalizations about a principal character by others or self-references by the principal character. An examination of the research literature (6, 23) reveals 64 words referring to mental illness (for example, "crazy," "lunatic," and "nuts") and 37 phrases (for example, "out of one's mind" and "not in touch with reality"). The words and phrases were cast into a table with a number assigned to each. A coder recorded the number of the word or phrase and the frequency with which it occurred in the film. Third, we coded mental illness as portrayed by minor characters, to obtain a complete coding of all references to mental illness. We coded minor characters (including inanimate objects and groups), using a procedure identical to that used for principal characters. Here, however, minor characters were coded in total, rather than individually. For example, if a teacup character was referred to as "loony" and another minor character as "crazy," we recorded 2 instances of mental illness.

To ensure accuracy and interpretability of the data, we did not code comments about a particular situation (such as a "crazy" situation) and negations of a word or phrase (for example, "You're not crazy"). Included in coding were comments about a character's thoughts, ideas, actions, or clothing (such as "What's with the crazy getup?"), as well as written words (for example, "Looney Bin" appearing on a building). We included thoughts, ideas, actions, and clothing because these refer directly to a character's state of mind. Other characters, or the characters themselves, viewed these traits as irrational, illogical, inferior, unpredictable, and (or) lacking control. This coding is consistent with the use of mental illness words to refer to negative and potentially frightening characteristics of people.

## Coder Training and Reliability

One researcher was the primary coder and coded all 34 films. To determine intercoder reliability, a second coder was trained. Training consisted of the reliability coder studying the manual, practising with the researcher, and practising with independent coding, using a sample of non-Disney TV cartoons. Training continued until both coders agreed on the interpretation of each variable and its criteria for coding. Once training was complete, the films were charted independently without further discussion.

*Source:* Lawson & Fouts (2004, pp. 311–312)

In the sample above, notice the extensive description of coding practices. The procedure associated with content analysis is described in careful detail. Our next sample is from Janice E. Martin and Steven M. Janosik's "The Use of Legal Terminology in Student Conduct Codes: A Content Analysis."

# Janice E. Martin and Steven M. Janosik, "The Use of Legal Terminology in Student Conduct Codes: A Content Analysis"

## Method

A content analysis was used to answer the research questions. Such an analysis is conducted through a sequential process that describes various forms of communications (Merriam, 1998). Descriptive categories, based on the purpose of the research, are created as a framework to help sort the data. Then, after a sample is drawn, data are collected and analyzed, and results are interpreted. Researchers use a set protocol to collect and code the data and count units of analysis. In this study, all of the documents were retrieved from institutional Web sites. Further, in an effort to ensure comparable documents, each document selected had to contain three sections for analysis. The three sections, as recommended by Stoner and Cerminara (1990), were a preamble, a conduct code, and judicial procedures.

## Sampling

To answer the research questions posed in this study, a total of 20 4-year, not-for-profit institutions were chosen using stratified random sampling. To select the public–private sample, all 4-year, not-for-profit institutions were identified by institutional type and placed randomly in a list. Starting from the top of the list, the first institution named was checked to see if an appropriate Web-based document was available online. If it was, the institution's document was added to the sample. If not, the researchers proceeded to the next institution on the list until five public institutions were identified. A similar process was used to identify small 4-year not-for-profit institutions (less than 5000 FTE students) and large 4-year not-for-profit institutions (greater than 15,000 FTE students).

## Data Collection

Once the four groups of institutions were identified, three copies of their respective codes were printed. One copy was kept in original condition, the second copy was used to color code legal words and phrases, and the third copy was cut so that the data and surrounding text could be regrouped with similar examples from other institutions.

To help with the identification of legal words and phrases, Stoner's model code and the recommendations made by Stoner and Cerminara (1990), Pavela (2000), Stoner (2000), and Gehring (2001) were reviewed. A list of legalistic words and phrases and non-legalistic language was compiled and used as evaluative keys.

To help with coding, a color-coded highlighting system was used in the data collection process. Words and phrases that were representative of legalistic language were highlighted in yellow. Non-legalistic language was highlighted in green. Examples of words and phrases in each of the two categories, based on the literature previously mentioned, are shown in Table 1.

*Source:* Martin & Janosik (2004, pp. 38–40)

---

The following sample presents excerpts from a methods section for a paper entitled "Attitudes toward Oil and Gas Development among Forest Recreationists." Note the use of subheadings within the section and how "Procedures" provides details about a questionnaire:

---

# Edward E. Langenau, Jr. et al., "Attitudes toward Oil and Gas Development among Forest Recreationists"

## Methods

### Study Area

Research on the attitudes of forest visitors toward oil and gas development was done on the Pigeon River Country State Forest (PRCSF). At the time of the study, the forest comprised about 83,000 acres of public land in Otsego, Cheboygan, and Montmorency counties of Michigan, about 200 miles northeast of Lansing....

### Subjects

A sample of recreationists visiting the forest between March 1, 1981 and February 28, 1982, were participants in this study. About 38 percent of all people visiting the PRCSF during the year were included in the sample. Individuals that were cutting firewood for noncommercial use were included, although this may not always have been recreation. Individuals working for an oil or logging company on the forest were included only if contacted while recreating on their own time.

### Procedures

A recreational use survey was conducted on 152 sample days between March 1, 1981 and February 28, 1982 (Ryel et al., 1982). Field workers left 1,569 postcards with vehicle occupants or on vehicle windshields on sample days. These pre-paid and pre-addressed postcards asked for names and addresses of all people in the vehicle. About 62 percent of the postcards were returned. A sample of 596 vehicles was drawn from those contacted during recreational surveys. Names and addresses of individuals in sample vehicles were taken from postcards. Telephone calls were then made to registered vehicle owners if a postcard had not been received. Names and addresses of all vehicle occupants were requested.

A mail questionnaire was developed to measure attitudes toward oil and gas development in the forest. This was pre-tested and modified after interviews in the field. Questionnaires were mailed to two sets of visitors (those contacted between March 1, 1981 and August 31, 1981, and those contacted between September 1, 1981 and February 28, 1982). Two follow-up forms were mailed to visitors who did not initially respond. The cover letters specified that children under 12 years of age need not return forms.

Questionnaire items were written and data analyzed according to the model previously discussed to include visitor characteristics, recreational behaviour, values, beliefs, and attitudes. Relationships were tested at an alpha level of 0.01.

*Source:* Langenau et al. (1984, pp. 164, 165)

The next methods section, from an article entitled "Images of Society in Klondike Gold Rush Narratives," refers to oral interviews and archival documents. In this case, however, the account of procedures is not very detailed. Moreover, the statement of methods was incorporated into an introductory paragraph that was not preceded by a methods subheading:

## Julie Cruikshank, "Images of Society in Klondike Gold Rush Narratives: Skookum Jim and the Discovery of Gold"

The oral accounts come from two native women with whom I have been recording life histories for a number of years: Mrs. Kitty Smith, born about 1890, and Mrs. Angela Sidney, born in 1902. Each incorporates references to the gold rush into her life story (Cruikshank et al. 1990).[3] Parallel accounts have been recorded with native elders who are no longer living (see Skookum Jim Friendship Centre),[4] but I refer here specifically to Mrs. Sidney's and Mrs. Smith's accounts because we have discussed them so fully. The written accounts come from books and from archival documents—private and published journals, lawyers' records, newspapers—located while I was trying to put the oral narratives into some broader historical context.

*Source:* Cruikshank (1992, p. 22)

The final sample is from a student paper about media reports on the building of a large earth-filled dam. Here, the use of archival material is described in greater detail:

## Laurie Dressler, "Harnessing the Peace: Environmental and Economic Themes Amid Public Responses to the Construction of the Bennett Dam, 1957–1968"

### Methods

The information gathered to describe public responses to the building of the Bennett Dam is taken from articles and editorial comments in the *Alaska Highway News*, 1957–1968. The North Peace Museum maintains a catalogued archive of newspapers from March 16, 1944 to December 24, 1975. Articles pertaining to the dam are recorded in the catalogue; however, editorial comments and Letters to the Editor are not. Thus, in order to ensure the thoroughness of my own research, it was necessary to review each of the *Alaska Highway News* weekly publications, page by page, between 1957 and 1968. The back issues of the newspapers have been kept in very good condition in cardboard boxes, one year per box, and shelved according to the year of publication. Further responses by local residents are taken from *This Was Our Valley*, written by Shirlee Smith Matheson and Earl K. Pollon. I will also be drawing information from the Fort Chipewyan Way of Life Study, which addresses the impact on economic and environmental issues downstream of the dam on the Peace-Athabasca Delta, once the waterflow of the Peace River was reduced.

*Source:* Dressler (n.d.)

## Theoretical Framework

Theoretical frameworks are a common feature of scholarly writing in the humanities and social sciences. One way of thinking about theory is to regard it as a lens through which a researcher *views* her work. This definition is loyal to the semantic roots of *theory*—a Greek word that means *to see*. In effect, therefore, academic writers who adopt theoretical frames choose to see the world through someone else's eyes. This opportunity to see differently holds a special appeal in the humanities and social sciences, where the serious business of knowledge-making may sometimes appear to be a little too subjective. Indeed, theoretical frames seem to come between the researcher and her work, thereby placing an apparent check on subjectivity. Such a check may, however, be more apparent than real, for there is clearly a good deal of individual discretion involved in the choice and application of theoretical frames.

These frames simply offer a scaffolding that enables scholars to construct knowledge in new and sometimes surprising ways. Indeed, theory, as an intellectual support system, often fosters a departure from common habits of perception. This departure from established norms makes theory valuable yet potentially controversial. One of the telltale characteristics of theoretical frameworks is that they involve systems of ideas that can be shuffled around and applied to different areas of investigation, yielding new insights. Because of this, theory can serve as a genuinely interdisciplinary and groundbreaking force in academic writing.

Theoretical frames, then, are portable, ready-made structures that provide a way of building on a research site and prestige abstraction. Theories, in this sense, are different from *traditions of inquiry* because they tend to exist independently of *topics*. Indeed, theories usually make big assertions. Consider Marxist or feminist theories about the influence of class and gender on human reality. Studies that comprise a tradition of inquiry, on the other hand, have a much closer connection to topic, often dwelling extensively on the particular research site under investigation. Imagine your research activity on the vast scale of a mental galaxy. Theory is the sun, a powerhouse that emits light and energy. Topic is the earth, where we are standing. Studies that function as a tradition of inquiry are like the moon, which remains within the gravitational pull of topic.

In presenting theoretical frames, academic writers frequently borrow ideas from other people, often famous scholars who have become shining stars in the halls of academia. However, not all theoretical frameworks are flagged by big names. On occasion, theory is introduced simply as a consciously adopted assumption. In either case, though, the inclusion of a theoretical framework is not generally something that a researcher must justify. Instead, the value of theory is tacitly understood, so disciplinary audiences tend to accept the announcement and imposition of theory as a rhetorical strategy, unless, perhaps, a particular set of theoretical ideas is out of vogue.

There is also an important distinction to be made between theoretical frameworks and *thesis claims*. Whereas thesis claims must be justified or demonstrated through argument and evidence, theory helps *to shape* argument and evidence. A theoretical framework is a thought-apparatus that will influence *thesis*; it should not be confused with the thesis itself, the specific knowledge claim that the primary writer makes in his or her own words.

Finally, it is worth noting that theory is often a rhetorical feature that recurs *throughout* research articles: typically, readers will encounter a sustained imposition and explanation of theory in an introduction; lighter returns to theory throughout core paragraphs; and a heavy reinstatement of theory in a conclusion. On rare occasions, the presentation of theoretical concepts may be delayed, so that theory does not make an appearance until relatively late in a paper.

In the example that follows, notice how theory is associated with some big names:

## Robert M. Seiler and Tamara P. Seiler, "The Social Construction of the Canadian Cowboy: Calgary Exhibition and Stampede Posters, 1952–1972"

The approach we have taken builds on the work of socio-semiotics theorists, including Roland Barthes, Stuart Hall, Mikhail Bakhtin, Pierre Bourdieu and Michel de Certeau. It sees popular culture as a site of struggle, focusing on the popular tactics used to evade or subvert the forces of dominance[6]. Analysts who take this approach argue that ordinary people use the resources the elites (who control the cultural industries) provide to produce popular culture. In contrast to the mass cultural model, which conceptualizes artifacts in terms of unified meaning, the popular cultural model conceptualizes cultural artifacts as polysemic, open to a variety of quite different, even contradictory, readings. Some support the ideological meanings of cultural elites; others clearly oppose those meanings.

*Source:* Seiler & Seiler (2008, p. 294)

In the next example, watch for thesis (argument or knowledge-claim) emerging from theory:

## D. A. West, "Re-searching the North in Canada: An Introduction to the Canadian Northern Discourse"

The geographical region known commonly as the North in Canada has been, and continues to be, produced by a discourse of power which emanates from the strategic deployment of a grid of knowledge. In other words, the North in Canada is more than simply a geophysical region. It is also and concurrently a region of the mind. In this sense, it appears to be very much like Edward Said's Orient.

In his much-discussed study of *Orientalism*, Said argues that the Orient was constituted as an "other" to the West. Through the deployment of the strategies of power/knowledge by the Orientalist, the Orient was produced and collected in an archive of knowledge that creates and re-creates the conditions of its existence.

I propose to introduce the conditions by which the North can be understood, first as an "other" to Europe, and secondly as an "other" to Canada. In short, I will argue that the North continues to be produced by a discourse of power, and is contained within an archive of knowledge that is continually created and re-created through re-search.

*Source:* West (1991, p. 109)

In this final sample, the primary writer borrows a set of theoretical ideas, even as he indicates a readiness to use others. This mixing and matching reinforces the flexibility of theory:

## Robert E. Terrill, "Spectacular Repression: Sanitizing the Batman"

This work [on Batman] remains predominantly within a Jungian framework, both because doing so facilitates framing this critique as an extension of the earlier Jungian analysis (Terrill, 1993) and because Jung offers a particularly rich vocabulary for discussing the presentation of archetypal images in contemporary public discourse. However, as the argument develops it borrows from other theoretical vocabularies, particularly toward augmenting Jung's rather sketchy discussion of homosexuality as it relates to the presentation of archetypes.

*Source:* Terrill (2000, p. 495)

## Defining Key Terms

We have already noted that some papers begin with a definition of key terms, providing a more down-to-business version of context. Alternatively, definitions of key terms could come later in an introduction. This is the case in Mayes's paper below. The definitions appear in the third paragraph of the full paper.

## Andrew D. H. Mayes, "Deuteronomistic Ideology and the Theology of the Old Testament"

An important part of our task is a clarification of terms.... In 1976, P. D. Miller discussed the implications for Israelite religion of the view that no human thought is immune to the ideologizing influences of its social context. Miller notes that 'ideology' may mean, in a neutral way, 'a description of the way things are in a society, the values, ideas and conceptions of a society which cause it to do or act as it does'. But it commonly has a pejorative sense: it is a partial view of the way things are, a view which is a function of the conditions of the person who holds it; the ideas expressed are to be interpreted in the light of those conditions and are not to be taken at face value. Two quotations emphasize this partial nature of ideology:

> An ideology is a selective interpretation of the state of affairs in society made by those who share some particular conception of what it ought to be ...
>
> [An ideology is] that composite myth by which a society or group identifies itself, not only for itself but also for other societies and groups. An ideology posits the group's goals and the justification of these goals in terms of which the group deals with other groups and with conflicts within the group; it defines and interprets the situation; it aims to overcome indifference to the common good; it reduces excessive emphasis on individual action. It makes possible group action.

*Source:* Mayes (1999, pp. 58–59)

## Posing a Research Question

Frequently, introductions to research papers will pose one or more questions. These questions typically indicate the investigative concerns of the paper. If it is possible to identify a primary research question, the answer to that question is very often the thesis of the paper.

### Janice E. Martin and Steven M. Janosik, "The Use of Legal Terminology in Student Conduct Codes: A Content Analysis"

The following research questions were used to guide this study:

1. What type of language is being used in selected not-for-profit, 4-year college and university student conduct codes?
2. If legal terminology is present, which words and phrases are most common?

3. How does the use of legal terminology vary between private and public, 4-year, not-for-profit institutions?
4. How does the use of legal terminology vary between small and large 4-year, not-for-profit institutions?

*Source:* Martin & Janosik (2004, p. 38)

## Stating a Thesis

A thesis expresses the overarching knowledge claim that a writer is attempting to substantiate. Whereas the research site and prestige abstraction form the topic, the thesis is the *argument* that emerges from the topic. Emerging from the topic (and, perhaps, from a theoretical framework), the thesis comprises an individual writer's knowledge-making message to the academic community. While structural forecasts, for example, explain how a paper is organized, a thesis statement explains the position that a paper takes. Myers (1985) explains that "all researchers are faced with decisions about the level of claim they might wish to make. The higher the level of claim, the more likely that it will involve contradicting large bodies of the relevant literature ..." (as cited in Swales, 1990, p. 117).

In the humanities and social sciences, a thesis frequently appears at or near the end of the introductory section of a paper. In some cases, readers may be able to highlight a single sentence that best conveys the writer's overarching knowledge claim. Sentences such as this mark important moments in the knowledge-making process and so they are often flagged by their own brand of *metadiscourse*—by metadiscursive verbs such as *argue, demonstrate, indicate, show, illustrate,* and so on. Alternatively, readers may find it difficult to isolate a single sentence as the best version of thesis. In cases like this, several things could be going on. For example, the thesis may not be in the introduction! In other instances, the thesis may be spread throughout several sentences or even an entire paragraph.

---

## An Introductory Paragraph
## in Which Readers May Find It Difficult to
## Foreground a Single Sentence as Thesis

**Richard C. Davis, "Thrice-Told Tales: The Exploration Writing of John Franklin"**

Subtly but consistently, as one moves from journal through fair copy to narrative, one encounters an image of native people that grows gradually more disparaging and condemning. The narrative casts Indian and Inuit in the role of predatory antagonist to civilization and portrays them as the chaotic, irrational enemy of order, a disapprobation that is considerably intensified from what appears in the journal. I must emphasize that the differences are not extreme: Franklin's desire to avoid subjective evaluations prevents any dramatic alterations. Nevertheless, it seems fair to say that many of the indigenous North Americans who appear in the narrative are portrayed as savages opposed to such European virtues as industry, trust, and reason.

*Source:* Davis (1989, p. 16)

---

In Davis's paper, perhaps several of the sentences vie for our attention as the one that best states the thesis.

In the following paper, the thesis is again spread throughout the paragraph, but this time, metadiscourse emphasizes the first sentence as an attempt to crystallize the argument. We've underlined the key sentence. In the second example, metadiscourse crystallizes the thesis at the end of the paragraph. Again, we've underlined the key passage.

---

## An Introductory Paragraph
## in Which a Single Sentence Is Foregrounded as
## Thesis through Metadiscourse

**Dana L. Cloud, "Hegemony or Concordance?: The Rhetoric of Tokenism in 'Oprah' Winfrey's Rags-to-Riches Biography"**

This article argues that the content, pervasiveness, and popularity of the "Oprah" narratives warrant the recognition of a "terministic screen" or genre of discourse called tokenist biography, defined as biological narratives that authorize a person from a marginalized or oppressed group to speak as a culture hero on the condition that the person's life story be framed in liberal-capitalist terms. Like Clarence Thomas during his Supreme Court confirmation hearings (see Morrison, 1992), "Oprah" is constructed in the biographical narratives that frame her rise to stardom in the late 1980s as a black person who, refusing identification with the politics of Black liberation, "proves" that the American Dream is possible for all Black Americans.

*Source:* Cloud (1996, pp. 116–117)

# A Thesis Sentence Embedded in an Introductory Paragraph That Contains Other Rhetorical Features

### Annette Hill, "Fearful and Safe: Audience Response to British Reality Programming"

This article will focus on two BBC reality series, *999* and *Children's Hospital*, and will examine why these series are popular with British audiences, in particular, focusing on the "entertainment potential" (Kilborn, 1994, p. 425) of programs that depict victims of accidents and life-threatening illnesses. Audience response to these series is linked to public trust in the BBC and program makers, and an "aesthetics of attraction" (Corner, 1995, p. 29), in which viewers experience fear and relief as the victims of a life-threatening accident or illness are saved by brave and hardworking emergency services and medical staff. The construction of a caring society in reality programs screened on a public service channel may not be an accurate reflection of healthcare in Britain, but the findings in this study indicate that audiences are attracted to life-affirming factual programs.

*Source:* Hill (2000, p. 194)

For clarity, we advise student writers in the humanities and social sciences to provide compact thesis statements at the end of an introduction (comparable to the last sample above), unless they have a compelling reason to avoid this strategy. Because a thesis is such an important rhetorical feature, it may be worth repeating, but such repetition is sometimes most effective when it occurs at strategic points in the core of a paper. Another alternative would be to delay the presentation of the thesis until the conclusion. However, this pattern is more common in the natural sciences, where papers begin with a *hypothesis* (see Chapter 8).

## Statement of Relevance

As previously noted, statements of relevance situate knowledge claims in a larger social and/or historical context, and in doing so they speak to the broader significance or meaning of academic research. In this sense, a statement of relevance often has moral implications—it frequently deals with what *should* or *ought to be* done to improve a situation (Giltrow, 2002, pp. 15, 314). As noted in the previous chapter, statements of relevance often appear in proposals. In a completed paper, statements of relevance may also appear in introductions but are perhaps more common in conclusions, where academic writers are particularly inclined to remind the disciplinary audience about the overarching importance of the research (see "Providing a Statement of Relevance," Chapter 7).

Here's an example of a statement of relevance in an introduction:

---

## Catherine Parsons, "Observer as the Observed: Objectification of Self in *The Swan*'s Mirror Scenes"

Broadcast on Fox in 2004, the reality television series *The Swan* utilized extensive plastic surgery, cosmetic dental work, nutrition counselling, fitness training, and psychotherapy to transform self-professed "ugly" women into pageant-ready "beauties." At the beginning of each episode the women stand before a mirror and describe "the body flaws that ... handicapped their emotional well-being through self-hate, failed heterosexual relationships, and neglect" (Weber & Tice, 2009, para. 15). During the next three months the women live away from their homes and families in utilitarian apartments devoid of all mirrors and reflective surfaces. It is not until the show's climactic reveal scene that *Swan* contestants, and indeed the audience, are privy to their "new" selves. Two women are featured in each weekly episode. The one who makes the most dramatic transformation, as deemed by the judges, moves on to the *Swan* pageant where she will compete for the title of "the Swan."

*The Swan* aired for two seasons in 2004: the first March through April, the second October through December. Despite its brief air-time, *The Swan* has garnered considerable attention. Weber and Tice (2009) considered *The Swan* a "media touch-stone .... worthy of scholarly attention" (paras. 10-11). In 2004, *The Swan* made repeated news in national newspapers and entertainment magazines, including *USA Today* and *People* (para. 9). Now, five years after its cancellation, it "is still broadcast, talked about, referenced, and parodied" (para. 10). While *The Swan* has been referenced widely in scholarly discussions of makeovers, pageantry, race, class, postfeminism, and consumerism, critics have not explicitly considered the importance of the mirror as facilitator of *The Swan* contestant's self-objectifying gaze.

Accordingly, this essay will examine the self-objectification manifested in *The Swan*'s mirror scenes. To accomplish this, I will first examine the contestant's pre-makeover critiques as they look in their mirrors. Second, I will consider the absence of mirrors during contestants' three-month transformations. Third, I will analyze contestants' reactions to their mirror-images in the dramatic reveal scenes. In this paper, I argue that *The Swan* does not alleviate the contestant's self-loathing; the show's cathartic reveal scene disturbingly reifies self-objectification as it fleetingly aligns her mirror-image with the approval of the social and cultural looking glass. Ultimately, therefore, *The Swan* fails to appease the self-objectification that induces women's bodily shame when their outward appearance is misaligned with the ideal sustained by the male gaze. It is not until the social and cultural looking glass appreciates the array of beauty present in this world that we can truly transcend self-objectification and its detrimental effects.

*Source:* Parsons (2009, pp. 2–3)

## The Flow of Introductory Rhetorical Features

Before leaving the discussion of introductions, we want to emphasize the importance of "flow," which, in this context, refers not to a general concept of graceful transitions but to an appropriate sequence of discipline-specific gestures. While a proposal provides a first opportunity to achieve a smooth sequence of opening rhetorical features, work on an introduction gives an opportunity to improve the flow through revision. John Swales (1990) diagrams what he describes as common initial rhetorical "moves" in scholarly writing (p.

141). We've done something similar below, but our flow charts reflect the terminology and concepts used in this book, and our own experience of recurring structural patterns in introductions.

We invite you to consider these patterns as guidelines that are subject to flexible adaptation, as "pieces" can be assembled in different ways—bits of the puzzle can be shifted, added, or deleted. As noted, the process of assembly is guided by logic, but the process also involves some discretion. The flow charts below, for example, tend to begin with background information and conclude with a thesis, but there is considerable variability among the intervening features. The sequence of moves, which visually and conceptually marks stages in the formation of knowledge, must ultimately be arranged within sentences and paragraphs. "Topic," for example, is often articulated within a single sentence, whereas "context" or a "theoretical framework" may occupy paragraphs of their own.

Below are some examples of variations.

---

### A Pattern That Relies Heavily on a Tradition of Inquiry

Background Information → Tradition of Inquiry → Topic → Specific Forecasting → Thesis

---

### A Pattern That Acknowledges a Tradition of Inquiry *and* Addresses a Knowledge Deficit

Background Information → Tradition of Inquiry → Knowledge Deficit → Topic → Specific Forecasting → Thesis

---

A logical sequence is at work here: tradition of inquiry—knowledge deficit—topic. This flow or movement could be paraphrased as follows: here's what's been done; here's what hasn't been done; the current study fills the gap.

## A Pattern with a Theoretical Frame

Background Information → Tradition of Inquiry → Knowledge Deficit → Topic → Theoretical Framework → Thesis

Whether theoretical frameworks are presented before or after the announcement of topic, theoretical frames often require a fair bit of space, running for a paragraph or more.

## A Pattern with a Methods Section

Background Information → Tradition of Inquiry → Topic → Specific Forecasting → Thesis → Methods

### The Jenna Files

Notes to self:

- I've made some changes to my proposal in an effort to turn it into a solid introduction to my paper. My instructor made a lot of comments on the proposal, and I tried to consider each of those during the rewriting. In a conversation after class, he added that I could develop my own questionnaire and that my survey could be described in a methods section and used in core paragraphs. Sounds good, but I might not have time.
- A lightbulb just turned on in my head! As I'm writing my introduction, I realize that paraphrasing isn't about changing the original words to different words. It is really about understanding the whole concept of what the author is trying to say and then rewriting it in my own way.

Here's Jenna's introduction. What changes has she made in revising the proposal? Instructor comments are again indicated by a number and a corresponding comment at the end of the box.

## The Jenna Files

### "That Dead Girl": Cyberbullying and Suicide among Teenage Girls ✓

On September 13, 2013, Rebecca, a 12-year-old girl, completed✓ suicide after 15 middle-school students repeatedly bullied her in person and online. Rebecca was bullied for over a year, and the bullies urged her though online websites and smart phone applications to kill herself. In response, Rebecca changed her online identity to "That Dead Girl" (Speere, 2013, para. 2). When Rebecca's mother, Tricia Norman, found out that Rebecca was being bullied, Norman withdrew✓ her daughter from school and closed down her Facebook account (Alvarez, 2013, pp. 1-2). However, according to Hinduja and Patchin (2011), adolescents value the Internet community websites very highly, and they cannot "live" without the Internet: "two-thirds of youth go online every day for school work, to keep in touch with their friends, to learn about celebrities, to share their digital creations, or for many other reasons" (p. 23). Therefore, Rebecca felt she could not stop using social media and opened a new community website account. When Rebecca was once again bullied through the new website, she resorted to✓ suicide (Alvarez, 2013, p. 3).

This paper will present cyberbullying as a serious social problem, exploring the relationship between cyberbullying and suicide among teenage girls. First, I will describe the characteristics of cyberbullying in comparison to traditional bullying. Second, I will examine why victims of cyberbullying try to solve their problems by themselves rather than reporting the incidents. Third, I will explore the negative effects of cyberbullying on teenage girls, which may culminate in suicide.

There is a growing body of research on cyberbullying. Pirjo, Heini, and Rimpela (2012) showed that for girls from 12 to 16 years old, the rate of being cyberbullied was almost twice as high as for boys in the same age group (p. 4). According to Bauman, Toomey, and Walker (2013), cyberbullying is more likely to lead to "reciprocal behavior" than traditional bullying, where physical power differentials more often determine perpetrator and victim (p. 347). Further, Bhat, Chang, and Linscott (2010) note that 30-40% of teens who are cyberbullied do not seek help and that when cyberbullied teens do seek help they most often turn to friends rather than adults (p. 36). Ultimately, research has shown that cyberbullying has detrimental social-psychological effects, such as inducing suicidal thoughts that lead to attempted and completed suicides. For example, Hinduja and Patchin (2010) reported on a survey of Internet use conducted on 1,963 randomly selected middle-school students. Students who had been victims of cyberbullying were more likely to attempt suicide than those who had not (p. 207). Hinduja and Patchin observed that girls, in particular, are at a greater risk of suicide.✓ Thus, I argue that cyberbullying is a unique social phenomenon whose "virtualness" further isolates victims and often leads to suicide among teenage girls.✓[1]

> **Instructor comment:**
>
> 1.  Nice work on the revisions, Jenna. The introduction is a significant improvement on the proposal. Let's stay open to changes to specific forecasting.

# Ideas for Further Study

1.  We encourage you to increase your familiarity with the rhetorical features we've been discussing by watching for the appearance of such features in the academic essays that comprise your expanding research notebook.

2.  For further practice, block and label rhetorical features that appear in the sample introductions below. We think you'll be able to easily identify familiar coherence structures. Also be aware of the flow of such features, for example, context → tradition of inquiry → knowledge deficit → specific forecasting → thesis → methods. Note that the following samples present a mix of introductions written by students and by professional scholars. The student work has a lot in common with the published articles. In fact, on the basis of content alone, it may be difficult to distinguish the student papers.

    This first sample was published in *Symbolic Interaction*. We're again intrigued by how an event in popular culture can be reframed through the lens of scholarly inquiry. At a personal level, many people may *feel* some uneasiness about social expectations associated with events such as bridal showers. Yet such ambivalence can be hard to define and understand in the context of ordinary life. In the introduction that follows, Beth Montemurro unpacks the nuances of social pressure, shedding light on everyday life through academic study.

# Sample Introduction 1

## Beth Montemurro, "'You Go 'Cause You Have To': The Bridal Shower as a Ritual of Obligation"

Quiet, anxious conversation fills the room. About twenty women sit at beautifully decorated tables. Some of the women sip mimosas from champagne flutes. Several flower arrangements in glass vases tied with pastel blue ribbons grace the centre of each table. In the corner, next to the table with the fountain of champagne punch, sits a smaller table for gifts. At this point, it already overflows with elaborately wrapped packages, most in white paper, trimmed with ribbons, bows, and flowers.... Such is the atmosphere of one bridal shower ... [a tradition-laden ritual scripted by planning guides and advice manuals].

A ritual is a dramatic enactment of the norms and moral sentiments of a society. According to Kertzer (1998), rituals give meaning to the world by "linking the past to the present and to the future" (pp. 9-10).... As events or activities that are repeated over time, rituals hold special cultural and symbolic meanings, not only to those who are directly involved, but also to members of the culture in which a ritual takes place. Victor Turner (1974) argues ... that "[in ritual] people are introduced to want to do what they must do. In this sense, ritual action is akin to a sublimation process.... [S]ymbolic behaviour actually creates society for pragmatic purposes" (p. 56). Although considerable research has been conducted on wedding rituals (Currie, 1993; Daly, 2005; Dickinson, 2007; Holcomb, 2005; Ingraham, 1999; Wilson, 2005; Zhou, 2003; etc.), little sociological research has focused on pre-wedding rituals such as the bridal shower. In an effort to fill that gap, this paper focuses on bridal showers as rituals of obligation. I argue that when women are invited to attend a bridal shower, regardless of their individual wishes or attitudes toward the union, social expectations *obligate* them to attend, celebrate, and partially subsidize the transition into marriage. Indeed, failure to do so would violate the rules of the community and subsequently be considered deviant and subject to sanctions.

*Source:* Adapted from Montemurro (2002, pp. 67–68)

As you can see below, from the number of authors, this introduction is from a collaboratively authored paper, written by students and the instructor in an intermediate academic writing course. Three students were responsible for writing the introduction, which was then subject to ongoing revision as it was incorporated into the larger paper. Do you see a distinction between the tradition of inquiry and the theoretical framework? Is there a discernible thesis? Block and label.

---

# Sample Introduction 2

**Steve Roe and students of Northern Lights College,\* "'If the Story Could Be Heard':[1] Colonial Discourse and the Surrender of Indian Reserve 172"**

> Heaven, according to Charlie Yahey [a Beaver Dreamer], is like Where Happiness Dwells. It is a place where people come together and greet their relatives they have not seen for an entire year.
>
> —Robin Ridington, *Trail to Heaven.*

This article is dedicated to the people of the Doig and Blueberry Bands.

Archaeological studies indicate that Aboriginal peoples inhabited Northeastern British Columbia more than 10,000 years BP.[2] The history of the Beaver people[3] reaches back into these bygone millennia. Traditional Beaver culture revolved around the seasons: hunting and berry picking during the summer and trapping during the winter. According to Hugh Brody, such activities combined to create an annual system that comprised a whole: each part made a unique contribution to the entire unit.[4] In the eighteenth and nineteenth centuries, an expanding fur trade economy began to deplete food resources. The situation reached a crisis point by the end of the nineteenth century when the Klondike gold rush brought unprecedented pressure to bear on the Aboriginal people of the region. Responding to encroachments on their territory, the Beaver people established a blockade that interrupted the flow of prospectors.[5] Treaty 8, signed partly in response to such tensions, recognized all entitlement to reserve lands for Native groups in Northern Alberta, Northeastern British Columbia, and the Northwest Territories.

On 11 April 1916, pursuant to Treaty 8, members of the Fort St. John Beaver Band chose 18,168 acres of rolling prairie, seven miles north of Fort St. John, as their reserve. Traditionally referred to as "Suu Na Chii K' Chi Ge" (the Place Where Happiness Dwells), the territory newly designated as Indian Reserve 172 (I.R. 172) had long served as an important summer gathering place for the Beaver people.[6] By the end of the First World War, however, White settlers began to lobby for the sale of I.R. 172. Political pressure for a sale mounted in the early 1940s when it became apparent that returning Second World War veterans would need land to settle. Finally, on 22 September 1945, the Fort St. John Beaver Band purportedly executed a surrender of I.R. 172 to the Government of Canada, "to sell or lease."[7]

The subsequent history of I.R. 172 is fraught with political and legal turmoil. In 1948 the reserve was sold to the Department of Veterans' Affairs for considerably less than its appraised value. Shortly thereafter, in 1949, oil and gas deposits were discovered on I.R. 172, and profits from these discoveries eventually accrued to the newly established settlers. In the early 1950s, the Fort St. John Beaver Band consented to the purchase of two smaller reserves north of town. Some families moved to the Doig River (I.R. 206), while other families relocated along the Blueberry River (I.R. 205). Thirty years later, in September 1978, chiefs from both the Doig and Blueberry communities began joint legal action against the Government of Canada, claiming damages for the improvident surrender and improper transfer of I.R. 172.[8] The plaintiffs' case was dismissed at the Federal Court Trial Division in 1987, and the dismissal was later upheld by a split decision at the Federal Court of Appeal in 1992.[9] The band appealed again, and in 1995 the Supreme Court of Canada found that the Crown breached its fiduciary obligation by selling the band's mineral rights and making no effort to correct its error.[10] By 1997 the plaintiffs had negotiated an out-of-court settlement for $147 million as restitution for oil and gas royalties.[11]

This paper examines colonial discourse in relation to the surrender of I.R. 172, focusing on governmental correspondence and newspaper journalism from 1933 to 1946. To be clear, we are *not* in a position to address Aboriginal perspectives on the surrender, nor do we wish to pursue legal questions as to whether the Crown's fiduciary responsibilities were fulfilled;[12] rather, we aim to comment on colonial habits of mind in the area and period at issue. First, we analyze governmental correspondence in the decade that preceded the surrender of I.R. 172, from 1933 to 1944. Second, we discuss governmental records during the period of the surrender itself, in the summer and fall of 1945. Third, we comment on newspaper journalism immediately before and after the surrender, from 1944 to 1946.

Substantial literature on the language of colonialism, both in British Columbia and throughout Canada, provides a theoretical framework for our understanding of settler attitudes towards I.R. 172. While previous studies acknowledge tensions in the provincial and national rhetoric dealing with Aboriginal peoples, there is widespread agreement that colonial discourse throughout the history of Indian-White relations in North America has been based on racist assumptions about Aboriginal inferiority, whereby Native "savagery" is the presumed antithesis to European "civilization."[13] The scholarship further identifies interrelated subthemes or image clusters that orbit around the central assumption of Aboriginal inferiority, constituting a network of discursive patterns that supported and normalized racism. The array of overlapping subthemes includes assumptions about Aboriginal destitution, bureaucratic paternalism, and the march of progress. Hugh Brody, dealing specifically with the Beaver of Northeastern British Columbia, explains that conceptions of Aboriginal destitution reflected a belief that Native peoples did not have any real culture, that they were poverty-stricken, diseased, and on the verge of extinction. According to Brody, not only were the hunters perceived as poor, but they were also thought to be "too ignorant even to appreciate the fact."[14] Bureaucratic paternalism was perceived as a humanely Canadian (i.e., non-American) solution to the "Indian Problem." Particularly apparent in the operation of residential schools, bureaucratic paternalism was founded on mistaken assumptions that Euro-Canadian managerial strategies (implemented through policies, laws, and institutions) would ensure fair treatment of Aboriginal peoples while bettering their living conditions. Elizabeth Furniss observes that Native peoples were often reconfigured as childlike Wards of the state, as "people to be patronized and protected."[15] Assumptions about the march of progress, meanwhile, linked the highest and best use of the land with agricultural and industrial development. Accordingly, the notion of progress was frequently associated with heroic images of White settlers occupying and taming "empty," "wasted" lands. Cole Harris explains that, "by the mid-nineteenth century[,] the very concepts of progress and development had acquired a particular momentum that served to reinforce the momentum of colonialism itself." Harris points out that "the idea of progress was also an attitude towards land, because progress was seen to be manifest in the growing European ability to dominate nature. In this light, people whose marks on the land were slight and whose lives were tuned to the rhythms of nature were obviously unprogressive and backward."[16] Clearly, all of these rhetorical positions affirmed what Furniss refers to as the perceived "morality of the colonial process."[17]

Drawing on the work of Brody, Furniss, Harris, and others, we show that the colonial discourse surrounding the event at issue exemplifies ideological constructions that have typified the rhetoric of racism in Canada. Indeed, in Northeastern British Columbia during the first half of the twentieth century, settlers and government officials used assumptions about Aboriginal destitution, bureaucratic paternalism, and the march of progress to control and limit the Aboriginal rights of the Dane-zaa First Nations, ultimately securing a transfer of the 18,000 acres that comprised I.R. 172.

**Notes:**

\*   This paper was collaboratively researched and written as a group project in an interdisciplinary course on academic writing. The student authors are Shelley Ergang, Sarah Filmer, Robert French, Pat Jansen, Jarveen Jhand, Aviva Jones, Julie Hindbo, Raffaella Loro, Karen MacIsaac, Jonathan Meyer, Alison Newth, and Karen Wiltse.

1.   From a comment by Leslie Pinder, Personal Interview, 15 February 2001.

2.   D. Alexander, J. Driver, and K. R. Fladmark, "The PaleoIndian Component at Charlie Lake Cave (HbRf 39), British Columbia," *American Antiquity* 53, 2 (1988): 371-84.

3.   The Beaver people of the Peace region are among the Athapaskan-speaking Aboriginals of the Western Subarctic. The Athapaskan Beaver refer to themselves as "Dane-zaa," a term that has appeared with variant English spellings in academic literature ("Dunne-za," etc.). In the seventeenth and eighteenth centuries, the Dane-zaa occasionally experienced territorial conflicts with Algonkian-speaking Cree peoples, who came to the area as hunters, trappers, and employees of the Hudson's Bay Company. By the early twentieth century, long after the cessation of such conflict, Cree families established close communal ties with Dane-zaa peoples living along the north banks of the Peace River. This group, although of mixed heritage, came to be known as the "Fort St. John Beaver Band" or "St. John Indians." Such usage is retained here to designate the Dane-zaa and Cree who hunted and trapped just north of Fort St. John prior to 1945.

4.   Hugh Brody, *Maps and Dreams: Indians and the British Columbia Frontier* (Vancouver: Douglas and McIntyre, 1981), 63.

5.   Diana Foster, *Treaty 8: A Shameful Chapter in Canadian History*, unpublished essay, 1998, Northern Lights College library holdings.

6.   Robin Ridington, "Cultures in Conflict: The Problem of Discourse," *Canadian Literature* (*Special Issue: Native Writers and Canadian Writing*) (1992): 273-89. See p. 284.

7.   Ibid., 285.

8.   Ibid., 286.

9.   *Apsassin* v. *Canada*, Supreme Court of Canada, *Dominion Law Reports* 100 (1995): 506.

10.   Ibid.

11.   Tania Wilson, "First Nations Win $147m in Lawsuit," *The Northerner*, 17 March 1988, 22.

12.   The question of fiduciary responsibility has been addressed by David C. Knoll, "Improvident Surrenders and the Crown's Fiduciary Obligations: *Blueberry Indian Band v. Canada*," *The Advocate* 54,5 (September 1996): 715-23. See also Paul J. Salembier, "Crown Fiduciary Duty, Indian Title, and the Lost Treasure of IR 172: The Legacy of *Apsassin* v. *The Queen*," *Canadian Native Law Reporter* 3 (1996): 1-24.

13.   See, for example, Hugh Brody's ground-breaking work in *Maps and Dreams*, 49-61. See also Ridington, "Cultures in Conflict," 285. Among more recent works, see Cole Harris, *Making Native Space: Colonialism, Resistance, and Reserves in British Columbia*

(Vancouver: UBC Press, 2002). Drawing upon Edward Said, Harris explains that "the culture of empire ... turns [on] a fundamental distinction between Europe and the rest of the world; that difference was codified and classified along a line from savagery to civilization" (50). See also Elizabeth Furniss, *The Burden of History: Colonialism and the Frontier Myth in a Rural Canadian Community* (Vancouver: UBC Press, 1999). Again relying on Said, Furniss notes that "the forms of knowledge produced [by colonizing nations] continually represent colonized peoples as inherently different from, and inferior to, the colonizing populations" (12; cf. 17, 18). Recent studies of Canadian residential schools confirm the foundational premises of colonial discourse. See Elizabeth Furniss, *Victims of Benevolence: The Dark Legacy of the Williams Lake Residential School* (Vancouver: Arsenal Pulp Press, 1992), 15. See also J. R. Miller, *Shingwauk's Vision: A History of Native Residential Schools* (Toronto: University of Toronto Press, 1996). Miller writes that "Indian culture was [seen as] defective because it was different.... The essence of the missionary indictment was that Natives were morally and intellectually degenerate" (185-6). Finally, see John S. Milloy, *A National Crime: The Canadian Government and the Residential School System, 1879 to 1986* (Winnipeg: University of Manitoba Press, 1999), 3-6.

14. Brody, *Maps and Dreams*, 53.
15. Furniss, *The Burden of History*, 18.
16. Harris, *Making Native Space*, 52-3.
17. Furniss, *The Burden of History*, 69.

*Source:* Roe et al. (2003, pp. 115–120)

Next is another student paper. Tammy's work is particularly noteworthy because the introductory rhetorical features are very clear.

# Sample Introduction 3

### Tammy Kostiuk, "Running Scared: Scapegoating in Newspaper Coverage of the Kelly Ellard Trial"

The last of eight people involved in the beating and death of Reena Virk, seventeen year old Kelly Ellard stood accused of Virk's murder in April 2000. Reena Virk, a fourteen year old Asian girl, was savagely beaten and drowned on Nov. 19, 1997, in a small town near Victoria, British Columbia, by a group of her peers—six girls and one boy. Five of the girls were later convicted of assault and subsequently appeared as witnesses for the Crown at Ellard's trial. The one male, Warren Glowatzki, was tried and convicted of second degree murder and during his trial he testified that he had been present when Virk was killed but that Ellard had committed the murder. The fact that Kelly Marie Ellard was fifteen at the time Virk was killed *and* white *and* female contributed to interest in her trial, which made daily headlines in newspapers around the world.

The tragic story of Reena Virk has received some scholarly attention. Feminists Bhandar (2000), Jiwani (1997), and Batacharya (2002) have all written about unacknowledged racism in Canadian society and its effect on the murder of Reena Virk and the trial of Kelly Ellard. Bhandar contends that the Ellard trial exemplifies the reluctance of Canada's legal community to address the "existence of pervasive, systemic racism in Canada" (p. 4). Jiwani argues that Virk's inability to conform to the sameness of a "white patriarchal culture" (p. 3) played an integral role in her death and "the erasure of race" (p. 1). Batacharya contends that dominant white feminism and its intersection with "racism, sexism, classism, ableism, and heterosexism" (p. 3) were factors in the murder and she addresses the significance of the absence of these issues in the media.

To date, however, little has been said about how the media portrayed Kelly Ellard. Accordingly, this paper focuses on scapegoating in newspaper coverage of the Kelly Ellard trial—but not, it is important to note, on the legal issue of her guilt or innocence. First, I will explain how Girard (1986) addresses the concept of scapegoating. Next, I will apply Girard's work to newspaper coverage of Ellard's trial. I will argue that the guilt or innocence of Kelly Ellard was never the real issue in media coverage of her trial; rather, the coverage sought a quick and easy resolution to a perceived social crisis by scapegoating Ellard. Indeed, this article will illustrate that Ellard was a victim of *media* persecution—not for the crime she was accused of but for what she represented.

*Source:* Kostiuk (n.d.)

In the introduction that follows, we really like Christy Gerlinsky's theoretical framework. Theoretical frameworks, you'll recall, are portable, and can be shifted from topic to topic. Accordingly, Christy's work presents opportunities for others to study landscape depiction in other texts.

## Sample Introduction 4

**Christy Gerlinsky, "Streamers in the Sky: The Picturesque and the Sublime in the Diary of Monica Storrs"**

Later the rays turned into search light beams of milky light, and then these began to curve into strange shapes, like a very slowly moving snake curling around the Northern horizon, and fading into faint rose and green, like a rainbow seen in the dark.[1]

—Monica Storrs

W. L. Morton's edited version of Monica Storrs' diary, *God's Galloping Girl: The Peace River Diaries of Monica Storrs,* provides an account of the years 1929–1931, in which Storrs emigrated to Canada as a missionary, travelled across the country, and finally settled in the Peace River region of northeastern British Columbia. Storrs was reared as a gentlewoman in Britain, and Christian beliefs were deeply instilled in her character. She came to the Peace River region at a time of new settlement, to serve in the Sunday schools, and to help both the Girl Guides and Boy Scout groups. Storrs herself did not have an easy childhood. Morton explains that at the age of two, Storrs was stricken with tuberculosis of the spine, which left her bedridden until the age of twelve, when she had to learn to walk again. The suffering experienced by Storrs as a child may explain her strong desire to work with children of the Peace River.[2] Except for Morton's own research, Storrs' experience in the Peace has received little scholarly attention. In an effort to fill this gap, I examine how Monica Storrs constructs place in her diary, particularly in relation to the sublime and picturesque.

In "The Aesthetic Map of the North, 1845-1859," I. S. MacLaren says that "the discovery of the North entailed a ... process of identification that combined human expectation and fact, illusion and empirical reality," meaning that the explorers used "metaphors" accepted in their own culture to measure the Canadian north, as well as the other places they travelled to.[3] According to MacLaren, such metaphors were used by explorers to relate an uncharted and unknown land to a familiar setting. This process of identification is a characteristic of human intelligence, facilitating the emotional need for home and familiarity. Even beyond one's natural home, there is an instinct to construct the new setting in relation to a setting that is already well known.[4] Similarly, in "Retaining Captaincy of the Soul: Response to Nature in the First Franklin Expedition," MacLaren suggests that the way an individual perceives nature is dependent upon the way their culture sees nature.[5] MacLaren's ideas can be traced back to J. Wreford Watson's "The Role of Illusion in North American Geography: A Note on the Geography of North American Settlement," which tells us that "mental impressions" often "condition" responses to place; thus, "lack of facts, misconceptions, and preconceptions" all lead to guesses and assumptions, which precede true findings.[6]

In relation to Storrs' construction of place, it is worth noting that the terms "sublime" and "picturesque" were used throughout the time of British exploration to describe the Canadian landscape. MacLaren notes that the sublime refers to wide open spaces which cannot be defined and stretch beyond the horizon; these spaces appear to be threatening, places that would not sustain human habitation but yield impressions and grandeur ultimately associated with God. Some examples of the sublime are mountain peaks or the far-stretching ocean. Natural wonders such as tornadoes, thunderstorms, and blizzards are also defined as being sublime.[7] The picturesque, on the other hand, involves a more inviting, pastoral setting, often with peaceful rivers, hazy mountains, and clusters of leafy trees backed by a sunset. Virtually all of the English countryside was conceived as picturesque.[8]

In the Introduction to Storrs' diary, Morton comments: "The wonder is how Monica went on serenely between the faith by which she lived and the reality in which she moved."[9] Perhaps the answer to this puzzle can be found in Storrs' culturally conditioned construction of place. I will demonstrate that Monica Storrs used the sublime and picturesque to familiarize her surroundings and create serenity for herself. In short, Monica Storrs employed British habits of landscape appreciation to make the Peace River region seem more like her own home.

*Source:* Gerlinsky (2002)

Kari's introduction, which includes a methods section, shows how first-year students can make use of primary sources to engage in original research. Watch for Kari's description of content analysis.

# Sample Introduction 5

### Kari MacTavish, "'Iron Maiden': Repressive Beauty in Women's Magazines"

This paper focuses on the way beauty is depicted through advertisements in popular women's magazines that are aimed at a readership of women between the ages of 18 and 25. In *The Beauty Myth: How Images of Beauty Are Used Against Women*, Wolf (1991) claims that women in our society are liberated; however, we are still ruled by a stereotypical image of beauty (p. 10). Wolf suggests that images of women are becoming progressively more repressive, cruel, and burdensome (p. 10). With the expansion of technology, women have become increasingly exposed to ideal images (p. 14), which are taking over their lives and causing them to be "vulnerable to outside approval" (p. 14). Ciano notes that every picture in advertising is retouched (as cited in Wolf, 1991, p. 82). In addition, Wolf observes that women's faces and their bodies are retouched using computer imaging, which creates a stereotypical, artificial image of women (p. 83). She states that advertisements in women's magazines reflect what women perceive to be desirable to men. Moreover, the ideal image is carefully constructed by advertisers (p. 73). Advertising is effective because it lowers women's self-esteem (p. 276), which causes women to spend more time and money to achieve the ideal image. Drawing on the foregoing theoretical concept, this paper argues that although Wolf's theory has been revised by third wave feminists, it is still applicable to contemporary society. Indeed, I will show that advertisements in women's magazines don't feature the products, but instead sell stereotypical images of women, images that are artificial, unattainable, highly sexualized, racially discriminatory, and therefore potentially destructive to women's self-esteem. Ultimately, such images may lead to neurosis, fragility, and insecurity.

## Methods

The data for this analysis was taken from four popular magazines, *Marie Claire*, *Elle*, *Cosmopolitan*, and *Shape*, which are aimed at a readership of women between the ages of 18 and 25. The magazines were purchased from my local grocery store in Dawson Creek, British Columbia, in February 2008, and were used to examine the images that are portrayed through advertisements in popular magazines. The analysis examined all of the full page advertisements in each of the selected magazines. The magazines open with numerous advertisements, which are virtually all for either beauty products or for fashion; however, the advertisements near the end of the magazines were for products unrelated to fashion or beauty. The advertisements for fashion and beauty products use images of women to sell their products, whereas only a fraction of the miscellaneous advertisements showcase women. In *Shape*, a fitness magazine, the majority of the advertisements are for diet programs, gyms, healthy foods, and exercise equipment, and there is not such an emphasis on beauty as there is on achieving a perfect, muscular physique.

After an examination of the layout of the advertisements in the magazines, the advertisements were extracted and classified into three major groups: advertisements for beauty products (skincare, makeup, body lotion, and hair products), advertisements for fashion (clothing, accessories, and jewellery), and miscellaneous advertisements. These three groups were then divided into

subgroups according to facial images and body images. Originally, I anticipated discussing the advertisements within these groupings and sub-group-
ings. However, further analysis revealed that many of the characteristics of
each of the original groups applied to all of the advertisements.

*Source:* MacTavish (n.d.)

3. Reading well-written abstracts can help you learn how to write a good
   abstract. Many article databases (e.g., Academic Search Premier or Pro-
   Quest) provide article, dissertation, and thesis abstracts. As a sample search
   at one of these sites, try the following keywords: *feminist* and *American* and
   *literature*. As you read through abstracts in the results list, note rhetorical
   features. Next, try a search of your own, using search terms that interest
   you. Use keywords from several disciplines. Read some of the abstracts. Are
   there noticeable differences between abstracts in the sciences and abstracts
   in the social sciences? Between English and the sciences?
4. Building on your proposal, think more about the shape of the introduction
   to your paper.

# References

Abel, K. (1989). Of two minds: Dene response to the Mackenzie missions, 1858–
1902. In K. S. Coates & W. R. Morrison (Eds.), *Interpreting Canada's North:
Selected readings* (pp. 77–93). Toronto: Copp Clark.

Arruda, T. F. (1998). "You would have had your pick": Youth, gender, and jobs in
Williams Lake, British Columbia, 1945–75. In R. Sandwell (Ed.), *Beyond the city
limits: Rural history in British Columbia* (pp. 225–234). Vancouver: UBC Press.

Bader, R. (1985). Frederick Philip Grove and naturalism reconsidered. In Robert
Kroetsch (Ed.), *Gaining Ground* (pp. 222–333). Edmonton: NeWest Press.

Blaisure, K. R., & Koivunen, J. M. (2003). Family science faculty members' experiences with teaching from a feminist perspective. *Family Relations, 52*(1), 22–32.

Boeving, J. N. (2007). The right to be present before military commissions and
federal courts: Protecting national security in an age of classified information.
*Harvard Journal of Law and Public Policy, 30*(2), 463–577.

Cloud, D. L. (1996). Hegemony or concordance?: The rhetoric of tokenism in "Oprah"
Winfrey's rags-to-riches biography. *Critical Studies in Mass Communication,
13*(2), 115–137.

Cruikshank, J. (1992, Winter). Images of society in Klondike gold rush narratives. *Ethnohistory, 39*(1), 20–41.

Davis, R. (1989). Thrice-told tales: The exploration writing of John Franklin. In J. Carlsen & B. Streijffert (Eds.), *The Canadian North: Essays in culture and literature* (pp. 15–26). Lund: Lund University Press.

den Ouden, P. (1998, Winter). "My uttermost valleys": Patriarchal fear of the feminine in Robert Service's poetry and prose. *The Northern Review: A Multidisciplinary Journal of the Arts and Sciences of the North, 19,* 113–121.

Dressler, Laurie. *Harnessing the Peace: Environmental and economic themes amid public responses to the construction of the Bennett Dam, 1957–1968.* Unpublished paper.

Egan, S., & Helms, G. (1999, Winter). The many tongues of mothertalk: Life stories of Mary Kiyoshi Kiyooka. *Canadian Literature, 163,* 47–77.

Epistemology. (1995). In R. Audi (Ed.), *Cambridge dictionary of philosophy* (2nd ed.), p. 273. Cambridge: Cambridge University Press.

Fetveit, A. (1999). Reality T.V. in the digital era: A paradox in visual culture? *Media, Culture, and Society, 21*(6), 787–804.

Friesen, D. W., & Orr, J. (1998). New paths, old ways: Exploring the places of influence on the role identity. *The Canadian Journal of Native Education, 22*(2), 188–200.

Gerlinsky, C. (2002). *Streamers in the sky: The picturesque and the sublime in the diary of Monica Storrs.* Unpublished paper.

Gillespie, G. (2002). "I was well pleased with our sport among the buffalo": Big-game hunters, travel writing, and cultural imperialism in the British North American west, 1847–72. *The Canadian Historical Review, 83*(4), 555–584.

Giltrow, J. (2002). *Academic writing: Writing and reading in the disciplines* (3rd ed.). Peterborough: Broadview Press.

Grant, S. (1989). Myths of the North in the Canadian ethos. *The Northern Review: A Multidisciplinary Journal of the Arts and Sciences of the North, 3/4,* 15–41.

Hamer, D. (1999). Wildfire's influence on yellow hedysarum digging habitat and its use by grizzly bears in Banff National Park, Alberta. *Canadian Journal of Zoology, 77*(10), 1513–1520.

Harrison, S. (2001). *Making the grade: Creating a successful learning environment for post-secondary students with learning disabilities.* Unpublished paper.

Hill, A. (2000, May). Fearful and safe: Audience response to British reality programming. *Television and New Media, 1*(2), 193–213.

Hobbs, H. (2014). Victim participation in international criminal proceedings: Problems and potential solutions in implementing an effective and vital component of justice. *Texas International Law Journal, 49*(1), 1–33.

Hookimaw-Witt, J. (1998). Any changes since residential school? *The Canadian Journal of Native Education, 22*(2), 159–170.

Hopkins, J. S. (1990). West Edmonton Mall: Landscape of myths and elsewhereness. *Canadian Geographer, 34*(1), 2–17.

Hyde, P. (2000, August). Managing bodies—managing relationships: The popular media and the social construction of women's bodies and social roles from the 1930s to the 1950s. *Journal of Sociology, 36*(12), 157–169.

Hyland, K. (1999). Academic attribution: Citation and the construction of disciplinary knowledge. *Applied Linguistics 20*(3), 341–367.

Iacovetta, F. (1999, December). Gossip, contest, and power in the making of suburban bad girls: Toronto, 1945–60. *Canadian Historical Review, 80*(4), 585–623.

Killian, K. D. (2002). Dominant and marginalized discourses in interracial couples' narratives: Implications for family therapists. *Family Process, 41*(4), 603–618.

Kirschner, C. (1998). *Desperate measures: Commercial Interests and the murders at St. John's Fort.* Unpublished paper.

Knowles, R. P. (1995). Post-, "grapes," nuts and flakes: "Coach's corner" as post-colonial performance. *Modern Drama, 38*(1), 123–130.

Kostiuk, Tammy. *Running scared: Scapegoating in newspaper coverage of the Kelly Ellard trial.* Unpublished paper.

Langenau, Edward Jr., et al. (1984). Attitudes toward oil and gas development among forest recreationists. *Journal of Leisure Research, 16*(2), 161–177.

Lawson, A., & Fouts, G. (2004). Mental illness in Disney animated films. *Canadian Journal of Psychiatry, 49*(5), 310–314.

MacAulay, S. (2002). The smokestack leaned toward capitalism: An examination of the Middle Way Program of the Antigonish Movement. *Journal of Canadian Studies 37*(1), 43–67.

MacDonald, S. P. (1994). *Professional and academic writing in the humanities and social sciences.* Carbondale: Southern Illinois University Press.

MacLaren, I. S. (1984). Retaining captaincy of the soul: Response to nature in the first Franklin expedition. *Essays in Canadian Writing, 28*, 57–92.

MacLulich, T. D. (1979). Canadian exploration as literature. *Canadian Literature, 81*, 72–85.

MacTavish, Kari. *"Iron maiden": Repressive beauty in women's magazines.* Unpublished paper.

Martin, J. E., & Janosik, S. M. (2004). The use of legal terminology in student conduct codes: A content analysis. *Journal of Student Affairs Research and Practice, 42*(1), 36–50.

Mayes, A. D. H. (1999). Deuteronomistic ideology and the theology of the Old Testament. *Journal for the Study of the Old Testament, 24*(82), 57–82. doi: 10.1177/030908929902408204

Montemurro, Beth. (2002). "You go 'cause you have to": The bridal shower as a ritual of obligation. *Symbolic Interaction, 25*(1), 67–92.

Northey, M., Knight, D. B., & Draper, D. (2012). *Making sense: Geography and environmental sciences: A student's guide to research and writing* (5th ed.) Toronto: Oxford University Press.

Nowacki, G. J., & Abrams, M. D. (2008). The demise of fire and "Mesophication" of forests in the eastern United States. *BioScience, 58*(2), 123–138.

Parpart, L. (2002). Adapting emotions: Notes on the transformation of affect and ideology from "We so seldom look on love" to *Kissed. Essays on Canadian Writing, 76*, 51–82.

Parsons, C. (2009). *Observer as the observed: Objectification of self in* The Swan's *mirror scenes.* Unpublished manuscript, Northern Lights College, Dawson Creek, Canada.

Ridington, R. (1990). "When poison gas come down like a fog": A Native community's response to cultural disaster. In R. Ridington, *Little bit know something: Stories in a language of anthropology* (pp. 206–224). Iowa City: University of Iowa Press.

Roe, S., Ergang, S., Filmer, S., French, R., Jansen, P., Jhand, J., . . . Wiltse, K. (2003). "If the story could be heard": Colonial discourse and the surrender of Indian Reserve 172. *BC Studies, 138/139*, 115–136.

Ryan, J. (1995). Experiencing urban schooling: The adjustment of Native students to the demands of a post-secondary education program. *The Canadian Journal of Native Studies, 15*(2), 211–229.

Seiler, R. M., & Seiler, T. P. (2008). The social construction of the Canadian cowboy: Calgary exhibition and stampede posters, 1952–1972. In M. Ferhan, *Icon, Brand, Myth: The Calgary Stampede* (pp. 293–394). Seattle: University of Washington Press.

Share, D. L., & Silva, P. A. (2003). Gender bias in IQ-discrepancy and post-discrepancy definitions of reading disability. *Journal of Learning Disabilities, 36*(1), 4–14.

St. Jean, E. (2004). *Swedes on the move: Politics, culture, and work among Swedish immigrants in British Columbia, 1900–1950* (Doctoral dissertation). University of Victoria, Victoria, BC. Retrieved from https://dspace.library.uvic.ca/bitstream/handle/1828/481/st_jean_2004.pdf?sequence=1

Swales, J. (1990). *Genre analysis: English in academic and research settings.* Cambridge: Cambridge University Press.

Tam, C. M., et al. (1999, December). Feng shui and its impacts on land and property developments. *Journal of Urban Planning and Development, 125*(4), 152–163.

Terrill, R. E. (2000, December). Spectacular repression: Sanitizing the Batman. *Critical Studies in Media Communication, 17*(4), 493–509.

Valery, J. H., & O'Connor, P. (1997, Summer). The nature and amount of support college-age adolescents request and receive from parents. *Adolescence, 32*(126), 323–337.

York, L. (1999). "What it took and took/to be a man": Teaching Timothy Findley and the construction of masculinities. *Journal of Canadian Studies, 33*(4), 15–30.

Warhol, R. R., & Herndl, D. P. (1997). *Feminisms: An anthology of literary criticism and theory*, p. ix. New Brunswick, NJ: Rutgers University Press.

West, D. A. (1991, Summer). Re-searching the North in Canada: An introduction to the Canadian northern discourse. *Journal of Canadian Studies, 26*(2), 108–119.

# CHAPTER 6

# Hills and Valleys:
## The Big Country of Core Paragraphs

> I thank you for your voices, thank you,
> Your most sweet voices.
>
> —Shakespeare

In general, the middle section or core of a research paper in the humanities and social sciences develops a thesis. In core paragraphs, writers often begin to draw extensively on their sources to present "low-level" details as evidence (Giltrow, 2002, p. 86). In this process, your research notebook will be a vital resource. At this point in the semester, your research notebook should consist of many pages of notes you made as you read your preliminary sources—articles, books, web pages. Ambitious readers may have paraphrased and summarized material, but in many cases the content of your research notebook will consist mostly of quotations (see Chapter 3). You will also be at a stage where it should be possible to begin sorting the low-level details in your research notebook into major categories that will eventually correspond to major sections in the core of your paper. As you proceed, you can begin to subdivide material *within* major sections, identifying more specific clusters of low-level details that will comprise the bulk of individual core paragraphs. Ultimately, the process of sorting and arranging leads to drafting. Such writing requires careful forethought, involving another set of rhetorical considerations that addresses not only broad organizational patterns, but the finer nuances of managing and presenting reported speech. Accordingly, this chapter deals with the skills that you will need to develop your thesis claim. An appropriate metaphor for the whole process of thesis development might be diving. We are now in a position to go deep.

# Methods of Development

Texts and syllabi for traditional composition classes often stress "methods of development," not to be confused with the methods sections that appear in some articles. Throughout a term, students may be asked to write a descriptive essay, a narrative essay, a process analysis essay, a definition essay, a comparative essay, an argumentative essay, and so on. Lists of these methods of development or "rhetorical modes" vary little from handbook to handbook, or from anthology to anthology. In Clouse's *Patterns for a Purpose* (1995), a handbook and anthology combined, argumentation is not regarded as a separate rhetorical mode; the editor claims that it is part of all the others. In any event, the modes themselves are foregrounded as central principles that guide writing. In Waldman and Norton's *Canadian Content* (2012), another anthology, the list looks something like this:

- Narration: telling of a sequence of events; an all-pervasive pattern
- Description: telling the characteristics of something
- Exemplification: using examples
- Process (or Chronological) Analysis: outlines the steps to complete a task
- Classification and Division: classification involves taking discrete items and putting them into a larger category; division entails breaking discrete items out of a larger category
- Comparison and Contrast: comparison deals with likenesses and contrast deals with differences

- Causal Analysis: one situation or event is presented as the cause or as the effect of another
- Definition: explains what something means or what something is
- Argument and Persuasion: explaining and convincing the reader of the writer's opinion. (p. 7)

These methods of development can be used as organizational starting points. Once you have written a proposal and drafted an introduction, you could begin to think about a method (or methods) of development that will enable you to validate your thesis. At this stage, it would probably be best to think about methods of development in relation to the core as a whole, but sooner or later you may find that certain sections or even particular paragraphs need their own developmental structure.

Thinking about the overall arrangement of the core, you could ask yourself questions like this: Does the thesis require the presentation of major examples? Does it obligate me to compare two or more things? Should I be describing or narrating a series of events? Finding simple answers to these questions may be difficult because it is likely that any given paper will do many of these things. Accordingly, isolating one or two rhetorical modes as the main methods of development for the whole paper or for major sections of the paper may be a somewhat subjective exercise. Chances are, numerous other modes will be at work in the overall structure of your paper, and some readers may regard these other modes as more dominant than the one(s) you focused on. Even so, the organizational modes that you consciously acknowledge and try to refine should help you to communicate with others. That, after all, is the purpose: in terms of overall structure, methods of development reflect general patterns that help us to think coherently about a given subject.

The activity of identifying methods of development can play itself out in your work on the research notebook. As you sort details into big groupings, methods of development should become apparent. Whether by instinct or intention, you will find yourself narrating, describing, exemplifying, comparing and contrasting, and defining.

Jumping ahead to the structure of completed papers, we can often see methods of development working effectively. As an example, take Tony Arruda's

"'You Would Have Had Your Pick': Youth, Gender, and Jobs in Williams Lake, British Columbia, 1945–1975" (1998). Arruda uses comparison and contrast as a dominant organizational principle that structures his entire essay, although chronology also plays a role in how he arranges his material. Arruda's thesis, contrary to his allusive phrase, is that during the study period, young people did *not* have their "pick" of part-time jobs in Williams Lake. Arruda argues that gender predetermined job opportunities: young men could work in relatively high-paying industrial jobs, but young women were limited to poor-paying jobs as office and domestic helpers. The thesis itself calls for an argument based on comparisons. This is how the comparison plays itself out, section by section, paragraph by paragraph throughout the 19-page paper:

## Arruda's Paper

### Introduction

Paragraphs 1–4: knowledge deficit; context; general forecasting; methods; topic (note that in this particular paper, Arruda delays an explicit announcement of his thesis until the conclusion)

### Core

#### Section 1: Girls and Boys Growing Up in the 40s and 50s

Paragraphs 5–8: Girls

Paragraphs 9–10: Boys
}  BLOCK CONTRAST

Paragraph 11: Girl/Boy

Millie and Norman
}  POINT-BY-POINT CONTRAST

#### Section 2: Girls and Boys Growing Up in the 60s and 70s

Paragraphs 12–14: Girls

Paragraphs 15–18: Boys
}  BLOCK CONTRAST

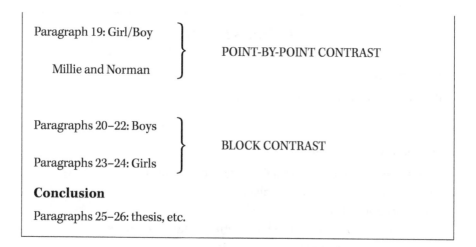

This kind of organization does not happen by accident. Clearly, Arruda had a plan or blueprint that was based on a fairly distinctive method of development. Your own thesis may not call for comparison and contrast, but you should have an understanding of your own overall organizational principles.

Here is another example of comparison and contrast. In "Masculinity and Marginality in *Rob Roy* and *Braveheart*," James Keller (1997) argues that *Rob Roy* and *Braveheart* are homophobic movies that disparage gay men while celebrating heterosexual men. Keller's use of comparison and contrast operates at multiple levels. Overall, at a "block" level of comparison, Keller finds thematic similarities in *Rob Roy* and *Braveheart*. He discusses *Rob Roy* in the first 10 paragraphs of the core. Then he gives a more compressed treatment of *Braveheart*, discussing this movie in the last five paragraphs of the core. Furthermore, within this overarching block structure, Keller effectively uses "point-by-point" contrast to highlight differences between the antagonists and protagonists in the respective movies. According to Keller, the antagonists are the untrustworthy homosexual villains while the protagonists are the noble heterosexual heroes. Here's how an outline looks:

# Keller's Paper

## Introduction

Para. 1–2: context; theoretical framework; thesis

## Core

### Section 1: Discussion of *Rob Roy*

Para. 3: opening comments on and summary of the movie

Para. 4–7: Archie as homosexual villain

Para. 8–10: Rob as heterosexual hero

Para. 11: an even finer point-by-point contrast of Rob and Archie

Para. 12: summary comments on the movie

### Section 2: Discussion of *Braveheart*

Para. 13: opening comments on the movie

Para. 14: Prince Edward as homosexual villain

Para. 15–16: William Wallace as heterosexual hero

Para. 17: summary comments on the movie

## Conclusion

Para. 18: recapping thesis; statement of relevance

---

Here's another one. In "Popular Images of the North in Literature and Film," Frank Norris (1992) argues that popular entertainment genres do not represent the North in realistic ways and probably never will. In Section 1 of his paper, Norris describes the content of 19th-century literature about the North, including newspaper articles and dime novels. In Section 2, Norris explains how such 19th-century literature influenced Hollywood movies beginning with the silent films of the 1920s. In Section 3 of the core, Norris analyzes the content of movies from 1920 till the present. Norris's research site is very broad, broader than we would recommend for a 10–12-page student paper, and, not surprisingly perhaps, he uses multiple methods of development. Section 1 is mostly descriptive. Section 2 presents cause and effect. Section 3 uses exemplification, discussing movies in chronological order.

## Norris's Paper

### Introduction

Para. 1: context; research questions (this is another paper in which an explicit announcement of the thesis is delayed until the conclusion)

### Core

#### Section 1: Discussion of Literature That Precedes the Films

Para. 2–11: dime novels, newspaper articles, etc.

#### Section 2: Influence of the Literature on the Forthcoming Films

Para. 12–18: the literature influences the movies

#### Section 3: Discussion of Movies from 1920 Until the Present

Para. 19–37: the movies have not been very realistic

### Conclusion

Para. 38–39: thesis; statement of relevance, etc.

In yet another paper, entitled "Portraits of Criminals on Bruce Springsteen's *Nebraska*: The Enigmatic Criminal, the Sympathetic Criminal, and the Criminal as Brother," Samuel J. Levine (2005) argues that Springsteen's artistry "leads us to reexamine the way we look at criminals and perhaps rethink some of the ways we look at criminal justice in the United States." Section 1 of the core deals with "the enigmatic criminal." Section 2, "the sympathetic criminal." Section 3, "the criminal as brother."

## Levine's Paper

### Introduction

Para. 1–3: context; thesis

### Core

#### Section 1: The Enigmatic Criminal: "Nebraska"

Para. 4–6: discussion of the enigmatic criminal

**Section 2: The Sympathetic Criminal**

Para. 7: introductory paragraph for this section
Para. 8–10: "Atlantic City"
Para. 11–16: "Johnny 99"
Para. 17–20: "State Trooper"

**Section 3: The Criminal as Brother**

Para. 21–28: "Highway Patrolman"

**Conclusion**

Para. 29: recapping thesis; statement of relevance

---

Levine uses division and exemplification to develop his thesis. As we can clearly see, Springsteen's re-envisioned criminals are divided into three groups. Further, each type is discussed through sample songs.

In "Thrice-Told Tales: The Exploration Writing of John Franklin," Richard C. Davis (1989) analyzes images of Aboriginal peoples in three successive versions about Franklin's second land expedition to the Canadian North. Davis argues that as a reader progresses through the journal, fair copy, and published versions of Franklin's trip, images of Aboriginal peoples become progressively more "disparaging and condemning." Like Arruda, Davis uses comparison and contrast, but Davis's paper also makes excellent use of chronology, description, and exemplification.

---

# Davis's Paper

### Introduction

Para. 1–3: context; theoretical framework; topic; thesis

### Core

(Davis does not use subheadings in the core of his paper)
Para. 4–6: images of the Dogrib in the journal and then in the published version
Para. 7-12: an extended discussion of images of the Loucheux in the journal, fair copy, and published version
Para. 13: transitional paragraph

Para. 14–19: an extended discussion of images of the Inuit as Franklin progresses from the journal, to the fair copy, to the published version of the story.

**Conclusion**

Para. 20: recapping of thesis

The organizational structure of Davis's essay is particularly impressive because comparison and contrast is so well supported by other methods of development, such as chronology.

# Structure of Core Paragraphs

So far in this chapter, we've surveyed methods of development and how they can be used to enhance the *overall* organization of the core. Now we will look at common macrostructural patterns of individual core paragraphs, patterns that allow you to situate your voice amid the voices of your sources. What's at stake here is determining an appropriate "space" for your own voice, even as you present the thoughts and ideas (voices) of others.

For starters, we'd again like to refer to the groundbreaking work of Janet Giltrow (2002) by imagining academic paragraphs in geographical or spatial terms, as a "landscape" of peaks and valleys (p. 77). Academic paragraphs frequently begin on a peak or viewing platform that presents what we will call a *guiding sentence*. In a guiding sentence, academic writers speak in their own voice. Here, having mulled over their research, they present assertions or claims that function as main points in the course of their argument. Guiding sentences represent the *informed* views of the writer, and in this sense, perhaps, they can ultimately be traced back to sources. Nevertheless, at this high level of generalization, academic writers tend to make stand-alone observations that momentarily float free from any documentation. Like advance scouts, guiding sentences chart a route forward. Other textbooks use the phrase "topic sentence" to identify what we have called guiding sentences. However, we have attached a special meaning to the concept of topic, so we have reserved that term for its designated purpose.

After the presentation of a guiding sentence, which may be supplemented by some follow-up generalizations, core paragraphs tend to descend very quickly into a "valley" of *low-level details* (Giltrow, 2002, p. 77). These valleys are usually filled with dense thickets of *reported speech*. Here, along the valley floor, writers embrace their sources, presenting evidence for guiding sentences by quoting, paraphrasing, or summarizing other voices. Some paragraphs end on the valley floor, with low-level detail, so that readers must await the next paragraph before once again ascending to higher ground. Alternatively, paragraphs may climb back up on their own and offer *retrospective* or *transitional sentences*. Retrospective sentences recap and emphasize opening generalizations, while transitional sentences anticipate terrain in the next paragraph. In academic paragraphs, then, we encounter a grand landscape of varying elevations—an impressive terrain of peaks and valleys. This is the distinctive country of academic writing. Such geography places demands on writers and readers. From the rarified air of high-level generalization and abstraction to the dense valleys of reported speech, academic paragraphs make for arduous travelling.

Maps and photographs can provide visual analogies for paragraph topography. A topographical map, for example, shows the varying elevation of landforms, which can be seen as corresponding to varying heights in core paragraphs. Consider the bird's-eye view of a peak-and-valley landscape shown in the first diagram below. The lines join points of the same elevation. The correspondence to core paragraphs in academic writing becomes clearer in the second diagram, which provides a cross-section perspective of the landscape elevation.

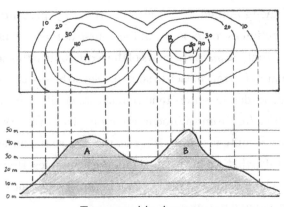

Topographical maps

Photographs can also be used to represent the varying elevations of core paragraphs. The first photograph below is analogous to a paragraph that starts "high," with a guiding sentence, and ends "low," in a valley of detail.

High-low topography

The next photograph is analogous to a paragraph that again starts "high," descends into a valley of detail, and then rises at the end to provide a closing sentence that could be retrospective or transitional. In academic writing, we think that most high-level closing sentences tend to be retrospective in that they review the ground just covered. Academic writers are in no hurry—much as a mountaineer glances back to view the sheer beauty of the peak and valley just traversed, a concluding sentence often recaps the points just made.

High-low-high topography

The high-low and high-low-high topographies are not the only possible patterns, but these two patterns are so prevalent that we'd like to dwell on them for now, as we move to some sample paragraphs. The basic rhetorical features under discussion have been blocked in Sample 1. Identify these patterns in the other samples that follow.

---

# Sample 1

**Nancy Theberge, "A Feminist Analysis of Responses to Sports Violence: Media Coverage of the 1987 World Junior Hockey Championship"**

Although interpretations locating the problem in the culture and social organization of the sport were in the minority among the views of sportswriters, the comments of one writer stood out as an exception. *Vancouver Sun* sports columnist James Lawton wrote a series of impassioned pieces condemning the incident and all who took part. On January 5 Lawton wrote that the event was a crude and brutal betrayal of reason and "any sense that Canadian hockey might finally strip itself of the illusion that masculinity and thuggery are in some way inextricably mixed."[18] On January 7 he stated that the crime of the incident "is not the rather pathetic failure of [the players] to keep control of their feelings. It is the systematic corruption of the idea of sport that goes into the training of so many of those players."[19] On the 16th he wrote of "the normality of the jungle" that characterizes hockey, and said that the "episode made nonsense of the concept of sport." Lawton's column on this day was titled "Jelinek Totally Wrong," a reference to the minister's decision to appeal the suspension of the Canadian team by the IHF. He argued that the decision was "morally bankrupt" and "the point that should be hammered now is that there were alternatives to such full-blooded involvement in the brawl." He concluded this column by urging an international review of the game.[20] Throughout his pieces, Lawton criticized those who defended the actions of the Canadian players on any grounds. More significantly, his analysis placed the event in a larger context by directing attention to the need for fundamental change in the sport.

*(Margin annotations: Guiding Sentence; Low-Level Details; Retrospective Closing Sentences)*

*Source:* Theberge (1989, pp. 247–256)

As you block and label Arruda's paragraph, decide whether it ends high or low. What would be the telltale signs of a paragraph that ends low?

---

# Sample 2

**Tony Arruda, "'You Would Have Had Your Pick': Youth, Gender, and Jobs in Williams Lake, British Columbia, 1945–75"**

In response to the general question, "What sorts of part-time jobs were there for girls after school?" women who entered their teens in the 1940's or early 1950's invariably cited a very limited range of options: "the drug store," "the grocery store," or "Mackenzie's department store." Relatively few girls actually worked outside their homes or family-run enterprises. Camille Summerland recalled she was the only girl in a class with over a dozen girls who worked part-time after school for wages. As another woman put it, "[i]t was mostly boys that worked after school." In her early to mid-teens, Katie-Jean Kurtz was restricted from working outside the home after school by her parents, particularly her father. Katie-Jean was quite vigorous as she described the general context: "When I was young, boys had a great number more opportunities than girls—there's no doubt about it. My brother left home at sixteen and earned a man's salary ... When I was a child, my parents wanted—felt—that I should be a secretary—that would be an excellent job for a woman. That would mean I wouldn't have to scrub floors." Her experience illuminates the simple but important point that "family life" is actually experienced differently by each individual member of the family. It also illustrates that parental fear of what might befall an unaccompanied female is one critical underpinning of the sexual division of labour within a patriarchal system.

*Source:* Arruda (1998, pp. 225–233)

---

What's the pattern in this next example?

# Sample 3

### Mark Kirby, "Feminist, Populist, Humanitarian?: Progressive Thinking and Images of Princess Diana"

The claim that Diana was an inspiration to women, whose life contained some commentary on gender politics seems to be the strongest argument. It was aired quite widely in the media. Beatrix Campbell, for example, argued that Princess Diana had survived victimhood to realise her true self identity (Channel 4's "After Dark" special, 14/9/97). Similarly, Suzanne Moore noted: "Had she been born 20 years earlier she would have been expected to put up with her husband's infidelity, to grin and bear it. In refusing to do so, she laid open the cynical workings of monarchy, patriarchy and hereditary privilege that had used her as little more than a brood mare. When the fairy tale fractured we saw another story altogether, one that many, particularly women, could relate to" (*Independent*, 1/9/97). Writing from this same perspective, Joan Smith claimed: "Diana's unhappy marriage charted a familiar course for millions of women and made them feel that, however disastrous their lives, they were not alone" (*Guardian*, 2/9/97). Although Smith was also willing to point to the tendency to overlook the faults of Princess Diana in all of this (*Independent on Sunday*, 14/9/97), *Cosmopolitan* editor, Mandi Norwood, writing in the *Express on Sunday* (14/9/97), even went so far as to argue that: "Diana personified feminism, new feminism—a force of nature rather than a mere brand of politics," and went on to argue that she, along with Mother Teresa, showed that "feminine" values of kindness, compassion, radiance and good humour were "worth a lot." This was rejected by Nicci Gerard (*Observer*, 21/9/97) who also noted that she felt like "the personal had washed the political away." Gerard presents a more hard-headed view of feminism than allowed for by the adulation of Diana, and highlights the criticisms of Joan Smith made by Beatrix Campbell who, she says, argued that there was a problem with "Smith's insufficiently reverential attitude to Diana."

*Source:* Kirby (1998, pp. 29–30)

## Sample 4

### Donna Cox, "*Diana: Her True Story*: Post-Modern Transgressions in Identity"

In the classic scenario of romance fiction, there is an evacuation of identity in the *jouissant* encounter of one and other so that two subjectivities merge in a fantasized situation of perfect blissful union. Lacan refers to "*jouissance*" as an intense and excessive pleasure/pain associated with sexual coming and religious mysticism (Lacan, 1982). In *A Touch of Love*, the heroine experiences "an ecstasy and a rapture that was indescribable sweep through her body. It was so vivid, so intense that it was partly a sharp pain" (p. 158). [Barbara] Cartland [one of Diana's favourite novelists] goes on to associate this with the "very essence of love" which results in an ultimate out-of-body experience for the united couple (p. 158). The undoing/dissolution of "I" is here so intense that it evacuates identity and translates into the bodily location by which we orientate ourselves in time and space. In his study of the structure of romance, Northrop Frye identifies its "structural core [as] the individual loss or confusion or break in the continuity of identity" (Frye, 1976, p. 104). Here is a romantic diaspora of dispossessed identity which Diana had textual recourse to, writing herself into the heroine's place so that textuality might be said to have had its effects in her lived bodily experience.

*Source:* Cox (1999, pp. 331–332)

## Sample 5

### Annette Hill, "Fearful and Safe: Audience Response to British Reality Programming"

The connection with American commercial television and popular factual entertainment led to accusations that European reality programming was populist and an example of the lowest common denominator television. Bondebjerg (1996, p. 28) noted how programs such as *SOS-liveller död* (Sweden), *Sagan ukopklaret* (Denmark), and *999* (United Kingdom) exported and adapted the format of American reality programs to fit "European ... [and] formerly very traditional public service cultures." Similarly, Dauncey (1996) commented on how French reality programs such as *La Nuit des héros* (France 2, 1991), *Urgences* (La Cinq, 1991), or *Témoin No. 1* (TF1, 1993) also developed out of the American tradition of reality TV (Dauncey, 1996, p. 95). In France, concern about reality programming led to debate about the negative impact of reality TV, specifically its tendency to encourage tabloidization and voyeurism (Dauncey, 1996, pp. 97, 99, 101). Dauncey (1996) criticizes the American and British approaches to popular factual entertainment that, according to him, sacrifice quality in favour of commercial interests: "France should realise that by producing its own, inexpensive, popular and populist television in the form of reality shows, it is undermining its higher order ambitions to be the foremost purveyor of quality culture" (p. 101).

*Source:* Hill (2000, p. 195)

As mentioned, other topographical patterns are certainly possible. For example, it's not uncommon to encounter a benchland landscape in which high-level guiding sentences are supported by mid-level generalizations that precede narrower canyons of reported speech. A photograph version of such a landscape looks like this:

Benchland topography

Now here's a sample paragraph. Watch for a guiding sentence followed by a first main point that the author presents as a subordinate generalization, then supporting details, a second main point, supporting details, a third main point, supporting details, and a concluding sentence. The subordinate main points are underlined.

# Sample 6

### Pamela den Ouden, "The Madwoman in the Arctic: Fear of the Feminine—A Circumpolar Perspective"

Throughout his life, Danish author Hans Christian Andersen never rose above his self-perception as an Ugly Duckling and experienced rejection on all sides. <u>He was often harshly criticized by the Danes.</u> In 1843, while travelling in France, Andersen received word that a Danish newspaper had reported that the opening of the stage version of "Agnete and the Merman" "had been hissed at" (*Diaries* 137). On hearing this, he complained bitterly in a letter to a friend that "[f]rom Denmark are always coming the chill draughts that turn me to stone" (137). Feeling unappreciated by the Danes, Andersen stated: "I don't believe in love in the North, but in evil treachery. I can feel it in my own blood, and it's only in that way I know I am Danish" (138). <u>Furthermore, he felt rejected by his friends, who could not accept his fame. This rejection led to morbid and suicidal thoughts.</u> In January 1841, he wrote: "How lonely I am! Every now and then I even think it might be a good thing if I were killed ... I have nothing to live for any more....My need to be noticed is so great that the idea of sudden death intrigues me" (103). <u>Finally, he was rebuffed by women. He was unsuccessful in love several times and remained a bachelor all his life.</u> His first love, Riborg Voight, married another, but the only letter she ever wrote to Andersen was found in a leather pouch on Andersen's chest when he died (Lederer 140). His second love, Louise Collin, was already in love with someone else and made sure that she and Andersen were never alone together once she realized he had feelings for her. His third attempt at love was also unsuccessful. When he was 35, he fell in love with Swedish singer Jenny Lind, who regarded their relationship as that of a brother and sister, referring to him both as a "child" (*Diaries* 154) and a brother. In 1847, Lind wrote to Andersen while he was in London: "My dear Brother! Welcome to England! I am looking forward to having a chat with you, dear Brother. Your sisterly friend, Jenny Lind" (206). Lederer suggests that Andersen's lack of aggressiveness in courting these women and his reticence in declaring his intentions constitute a "failure of nerve" that may have caused them to reject him (102).

*Source:* den Ouden (1998)

Whereas samples 1–5 present solid blocks of reported speech along the valley floor or middle portion of paragraphs, Sample 6 breaks up the reported speech into smaller sections. In the topographical analogy, remember, the subordinate generalizations create that mid-level benchland for the author's own voice while reported speech is found in a narrower bottom-land of supporting details. This pattern may resemble composition models that you've encountered in high school, where "topic sentences" are followed by main points. The pattern can also serve academic writers provided paragraphs contain appropriately sophisticated abstractions and sources.

Remember, too, that these samples merely present common patterns. An analysis of published academic writing reveals other patterns. Sometimes, for example, a core paragraph may consist only of brief, high-level comments that forecast the direction of a particular section in the core; or perhaps low-level details will comprise first-hand observations of the writer and not involve a lot of reported speech. On still other occasions, readers may even encounter paragraphs that seem to begin low, with reported speech, and stay on a relatively flat prairie. Alternatively, a paragraph might begin with low-level details and conclude with a high-level generalization. Consider the following photographs and samples.

Prairie topography

Here's a sample core paragraph from a paper on grizzly bear attacks on humans:

# Sample 7

**Stephen Herrero and Andrew Higgins, "Human Injuries Inflicted by Bears in British Columbia: 1960–97"**

In 3 of 44 incidents involving grizzly bears, poor physical condition of the bear was identified by inspecting B.C. Conservation Officers. Body weights of 2 bears were judged to be low. These bears were reported to have had little fat and generally poor body condition. The inferred motivation in 1 of the attacks was a female acting in defense of her cubs. The second incident involved a male bear, and the inferred motivation was a bear attempting to claim a hunter's kill. The third case involved an adult male bear who, when autopsied, had apparently normal fat reserves but infected teeth. The bear was not in hibernation in January at the time of the attack. The inferred motivation of this incident was possible predation.

*Source:* Herrero & Higgins (1999, pp. 214–215)

Low-high topography

This sample is from the same paper:

## Sample 8

Grizzly bears inflicted most (68%, 49 of 72) serious or fatal injuries (Table 1). Grizzly and black bears were responsible for equal numbers of fatal injuries. The number of serious and fatal injuries inflicted by bears increased each decade from the 1960s to the 1990s (Fig. 1). While the number of serious injuries and fatalities varied from year to year, the overall trend for 1960-97 was up, as shown by a 3-year running average (Fig. 2). The injury rate from both species of bears combined (the mean number of residents of B.C./bear inflicted injury) increased during the 1980s and 1990s (Table 2). The rate of increase in injuries significantly exceeded the rate of human population increase during the 1990s (Fig. 2). All differences are significant because we are describing population of events, not samples.

*Source:* Herrero & Higgins (1999, p. 211)

We suggest that prairie and low-high topographies are more common in scientific writing, where high-level generalizations are harder to come by. Conversely, in the territory of the humanities and social sciences, where generalizations and supporting details appear along a more rugged horizon, the high-low, high-low-high, and benchland topographies are usually the most effective. Know the country you're in.

**Core paragraphs** in the humanities and social sciences are generally typified by different levels: in the high places (at the outset and perhaps at the end), we hear the voice of the primary writer; in the lower middle-ground, we hear the voices of others.

The basic patterns we are emphasizing raise some questions about proportion. First, it is evident that variations in elevation produce core paragraphs that are quite bulky. The low-level details, in particular, take up a lot of room, so that paragraphs as a whole may extend to half a page or more. Further, given the amount of space devoted to the presentation of low-level details, a large percentage of the core of a research paper may consist of reported speech. Hyland's work showed that reported speech tends to be particularly heavy in the humanities and social sciences (1999, p. 341), where knowledge emerges through a managed conversation among sources. In the hard sciences, there is a greater tendency for knowledge to be produced through original laboratory procedures. Even in the sciences, however, reporting structures play an important role.

These assumptions are supported by the preceding sample passages from the humanities and social sciences. Sample 1 (Theberge) consists of 11 sentences. Four present the observations of Theberge, the primary writer; seven entail reported speech that presents the observations of someone else. Thus, about 63 percent of the paragraph involves another voice—that of sports columnist James Lawton. The percentages for Sample 2 (Arruda) are similar. Depending on how one accounts for ellipses, this paragraph also consists of 11 sentences. Once again, four present the observations of Arruda, the primary writer; seven present the observations of Williams Lake residents. If this pattern were to hold true in other papers in other disciplines, more than half of the core in research papers would involve reported speech.

In actuality, a wider sampling of core paragraphs, even within Theberge's and Arruda's respective papers, would probably reveal a lower ratio of reported speech, but the overall percentage would remain quite high—probably within 35 to 55 percent. Thus, real examples of academic writing, involving discipline-based articles published by professional scholars, indicate that other voices play a *major role* in the language of research. The emphasis on reported speech reveals a genre-based concern for evidence that supports generalizations.

Given the precedents established by published research, the temptation for students to simply give in to other voices may be strong. This impulse can become even stronger when writers are pressed for time or when they feel intimidated by other voices in the knowledge domain. Surrounded by experts, student writers may begin to doubt the value of their own ideas and become reluctant to claim even the high-level room for themselves. Remember, however, that the high-level observations are rarely pulled out of thin air; they are born, instead, from the assimilation and synthesis that accompany careful research and reading. In this sense, even the high-level points are founded on other voices—on accumulated evidence that will be presented in due course. Academic writers neither surrender to other voices nor ignore them: the concept of academic argumentation hinges on an interplay between generalization and evidence, a process whereby academic writers strategically situate their own voice in relation to others.

## Guiding Sentence Outlines

Given our understanding of methods of development and paragraph topography, we are now in a position to think about outlining the core of a paper. Techniques for outlining vary, and may range from rough notes or diagrams to highly detailed plans that identify the highs and lows of individual core paragraphs.

Whichever outlining technique you choose, outlines can help the development of a paper. Outlines provide an embellished sense of direction, and some writers prefer to draft with a blueprint in front of them. However, other writers find it difficult to compose an outline before they begin drafting and prefer to discover their sense of direction by working in the environment of rough paragraphs. Thus, as we consider outlining, we are again faced with the variability of the writing process. Different writers work differently.

This text simply asks you to consider a certain kind of outline, one that strikes a compromise between the very rough and the very detailed. Such an outline provides a bird's-eye view of a paper's peaks or hilltops, the places that are so crucial to management and direction. Such outlines consist of the guiding sentences for prospective individual paragraphs. As noted above, these guiding sentences are generated from the research process, and more specifically, from the ongoing work on your research notebook. By this point in the semester, you've gone through your sources carefully, taking lots of notes. By now, you've also sorted your notes into major categories that correspond to major sections in the core of the paper. You should also now be able to make finer subdivisions, creating smaller clusters of details that will comprise the bulk of individual paragraphs. As you study these clusters, you should be able to make connections among the details, connections that will lead to the paragraph's overarching claim (guiding sentence). This practice shows that guiding sentences are "umbrella" statements under which all paragraph details must fall. Guiding sentences make a claim that explicitly connects the details. In this sense, there is an aspect of originality in the creation of a guiding sentence, which foregrounds your own voice, yet, at the same time, guiding sentences do not mysteriously appear out of thin air. They are derived from the research process. Here's an example of how a guiding sentence can emerge from clustered details in your research notebook. The topic under consideration deals with the psychological effects of playing *Dungeons and Dragons*.

---

# Brandy Little, "Rolling a Critical Failure: Psychological Well-Being among *Dungeons and Dragons* Players"

## Clustered Low-Level Details:

- A number of teenage suicides and runaways have been attributed to *Dungeons and Dragons* under the rationale that players lose touch with reality because of the macabre aspects of the adventures themselves (Adler & Doherty, 1985; Brooke, 1985; Shuster, 1985; as cited in Simon, 1997).
- Some psychiatrists have flatly stated that "the game causes young men to kill themselves and others" (Adler & Doherty, 1985; as cited in Simon, 1997).
- However, some people are concerned that role-playing games reduce the ability of players to distinguish between fantasy and reality (Abeyta and Forrest, 1991).
- The National Coalition on Television has linked the games to 29 suicides and murders since 1979 (Schuster, 1985). One woman blamed her son's suicide on his involvement with *Dungeons and Dragons*. Because of this she formed the organization "Bothered About *Dungeons and Dragons*" (B.A.D.D.) to call attention to its perceived ill effects (Schuster, 1985).
- The Christian Information Council has stated that, "Playing these games can desensitize players to murder, suicide, rape, torture, robbery, the occult, or any other immoral or illegal act..." (Brook, 1985, B-1)
- There are significant differences between the variances of role players and non-role players in relation to Psychoticism. Eysenck and Eysenck (1975) describe the characteristics of a person scoring very high on the Psychoticism Scale as an individual who may be solitary, troublesome, not caring for people, and lacking in sympathy and feeling. The Psychoticism Scale has been shown by Eysenck and Eysenck to be significantly higher in both male and female prisoners. In the present study it was the non-role players who reported more criminal activity and obtained the higher Psychoticism score although their Psychoticism scores were not in the

range of those for male prisoners ... or even above their age norms
(16 to 19) for male university students (as cited by Abeyta & Forrest, 1991).

*Source:* Little (2009)

**Guiding Sentence Derived from Clustered Low-Level Details Above**

Popular media has condemned *Dungeons and Dragons* for purportedly having
detrimental effects on players.

**Another Cluster of Low-Level Details:**

- Hicks, Larson, and Pulling indicate that the media has reported that
  many of the personality profiles of role players are indistinguishable from
  those who practice Satanism (as cited in Leeds, 1995).
- Richardson, Best, & Bromley state that occultists "assume that there is
  power inherent in black or white magic, witchcraft, or Satanism" and have
  classified Satanists as "those who may be obsessed with fantasy role-playing
  games" (p. 178).
- Hicks states that educational workshops for police and social workers
  recognize four levels of satanic involvement, with those who play *Dungeons
  and Dragons* on the first tier of belief (Richardson, Best, & Bromley).
- Evans notes that multiple media reports have claimed that D & D players
  are vulnerable to belief in the occult and Satanism, while Larson and
  Hicks claim that the game may be a "soft induction technique" into
  Satanism (as cited in Leeds, 1995).
- The game allegedly uses authentic "spells, incantations, and demons"
  and, Pulling states, has raised questions concerning the "power of magic,
  mythical beasts and the abundance of demons and devils as character
  opponents" (as cited in Leeds, 1995; Richardson, Best, & Bromley).
- The media states that Sean Sellers had claimed he was motivated to
  murder his mother, stepfather, and a cashier, because of reading satanic
  literature and playing D & D (Richardson, Best, & Bromley).

**Guiding Sentence Derived from Cluster of Low-Level Details Above**

The game has also received negative publicity for allegedly promoting Satanism.

There are key moments in the research and writing process. Discovering
your topic and developing the thesis are two of these moments. Another key
moment involves the practice of creating guiding sentences from the low-level

details in your research notebook. Strung together, such guiding sentences direct the flow of your argument, creating *thesis-driven narrative coherence.* The merit of a guiding-sentence outline is that it enables you to examine the overall *coherence, proportion,* and *relevance* of the core of your paper.

**Coherence:** Guiding sentences should logically follow one another (in effect, they should tell an intelligible story).

**Proportion:** Guiding sentences should reflect an appropriate distribution of emphasis on aspects of the argument.

**Relevance:** Guiding sentences should stay in touch with topic and contribute to thesis development.

The guiding sentence outline presented below charts peaks in the core of James Keller's "Masculinity and Marginality in *Rob Roy* and *Braveheart*," a paper we referred to earlier. For the purposes of this demonstration, the outline begins by confirming topic and thesis. Subsections in the core are designated by Roman numerals, and core paragraphs are marked by Arabic numerals. In preparing this outline, we studied every paragraph individually. While we assumed that the first or second sentence in each paragraph would be high-level guiding sentences, we consistently checked this. We are impressed by how the high points in this author's paragraphs keep the topic in view and by how these high points tell a coherent narrative or story as they engage in thesis development.

---

# Sample Guiding Sentence Outline of James Keller's "Masculinity and Marginality in *Rob Roy* and *Braveheart*"

Topic: Masculinity and marginality in *Rob Roy* and *Braveheart*
Thesis: Films such as *Rob Roy* and *Braveheart* are structured on a dichotomy that codes homosexuality as the negation of traditional masculinity.

## I. *Rob Roy*

1. Michael Caton-Jones's *Rob Roy* (MGM, 1995) is one of the two recent films that depict the struggle of the Scottish for self-determination.
2. Archibald Cunningham's behavior sets him up as the antithesis of the MacGregor clan and its values of honor, fidelity, and fraternity; but

mostly, Cunningham is contrasted with the brutish masculinity of Rob.

3. Archie's mannerisms do not at all correspond with the gender codes of twentieth-century America.

4. The audience's anxiety over Archie's sexuality is permitted to linger through one intervening scene in which Rob and his wife make love.

5. Archie's sexual marauding extends beyond the seduction and discarding of servant maids.

6. In contrast to Archie Cunningham, Rob Roy is constructed as the quintessential family man, who looks after not only his wife and children but also his clan.

7. Rob's position as the symbolic repudiation of subversive desire is reinforced by dialogue.

8. Rob's honor is set against the deceit of the Englishmen, particularly Archie.

9. There are stronger visual images that reinforce the opposition between the two masculinities.

10. The contest between brawn and effeminacy is settled in favor of brawn, but what does this mean in terms of gender politics?

## II. *Braveheart*

11. Mel Gibson's *Braveheart* (Paramount, 1995) deals with some similar themes, particularly the juxtaposition of competing masculinities.

12. Seldom in recent films has there been a more stereotypical and negative portrayal of a gay man than that offered in *Braveheart.*

13. Gibson's William Wallace, like Rob Roy, is represented as the ideal of raw manhood.

14. Wallace's marriage is an important point of divergence between the two representations of masculinity.

15. The director constructs Edward as the symbolic antithesis of manhood, incapable and unworthy of a place within the affairs of war and government.

## III. Conclusion

16. I contend that the values embraced by William Wallace and Rob MacGregor are clearly intended to refer to contemporary American politics; thus the implicit message of the films reinforces the conservative agendas of the past decade and perpetuates the current trend to scapegoat homosexuals.

The above outline enables us to evaluate Keller's paper in terms of *coherence*, *proportion*, and *relevance*, and for this reason it is a valuable tool. After considering the outline, we notice that Keller devotes more space in his argument to *Rob Roy* than to *Braveheart*, but this is not necessarily a problem. Clearly, the thesis-driven narrative coherence of Keller's paper is strong, and this is something to aspire to in your own paper.

Here is another example of a guiding sentence outline. This one is for Jennifer Mitchell's "Indian Princess #134: Cultural Assimilation at St. Joseph's Mission."

---

## Sample Guiding Sentence Outline of Jennifer Mitchell's "Indian Princess #134: Cultural Assimilation at St. Joseph's Mission"

Topic: Cultural assimilation at St. Joseph's Mission
Thesis: My paper will demonstrate that attendance at St. Joseph's Mission negatively affected the cultural identity of the Native children who were schooled there, including my mother.

### I. An Historical Overview of the Residential School System

1. The Canadian government and the Roman Catholic Church worked together to assimilate the Native population into a supposedly more civilized and superior European style of living.
2. The policy of assimilation was formally adopted in the *Indian Act* of 1880.
3. The government of Canada provided the Catholic Church with funds for the operation of residential schools.
4. The priests, nuns, and teachers who ran the missionary schools were devout in the Christian belief that the second coming of Christ would occur only when the gospel had been spread throughout the world.

### II. Life at St. Joseph's

5. Mission schools were intentionally situated away from Native communities and families, and St. Joseph's Mission was no exception.
6. Given their distance from Native communities, residential schools limited the contact between children and families.
7. Upon their arrival at the mission, Native children were immediately submerged in a lifestyle alarmingly different from their own.

8.  As Native children lost the way of life they had known, they also lost all sense of personal identity.
9.  In addition to isolating Native children, missionaries also sought to transform them through discipline.
10. Since teaching Catholicism to the Natives was an important part of the missionary objectives, prayer was a large part of the students' day-to-day lives.
11. An integral part of the mission schools' focus on cultural suppression and assimilation involved the ultimate extinction of the Native languages.
12. Furthermore, missionaries gained the obedience of Native students through punishment that incorporated public humiliation.
13. Poor food, food shortages, and constant hunger were as common at St. Joseph's as punishment and humiliation.
14. Another painful aspect of the residential school system was the eventual return home.

### III. The Long-Term Effects of Residential Schools

15. For former students, the long-term effects of residential schools are potentially devastating.
16. The contrast between Catholic beliefs and traditional spirituality in Aboriginal communities is also a cause of much present-day confusion among those who attended residential schools.
17. Summarizing her life at St. Joseph's, Beverley does not recall ever feeling loved or cared for by the nuns.

### IV. Conclusion

18. In British Columbia, the last residential school closed in the 1980s.
19. Through corporal punishment, humiliation, destruction of language, segregation, prayer, and other tactics, the missionaries of residential schools, including St. Joseph's, tried to destroy Native culture.
20. Beverley, however, has been lucky in several ways.

## The Jenna Files

Notes to self:

- I feel like things are starting to come together. I'm now quite confident about my topic and thesis.
- Also, it looks as though the core of my paper will have two sections—the first section will be on the distinguishing characteristics of cyberbullying; the second section is on negative effects that may lead to suicide, especially among teenage girls. My method of development in Section One is exemplification. My method of development in Section Two seems to be more exemplification, but I'm also using cause and effect.

In Jenna's outline below, numbered instructor comments appear at the end of the outline.

## The Jenna Files

### Guiding Sentence Outline for Jenna's "'That Dead Girl': Cyberbullying and Suicide among Teenage Girls"

Thesis: I argue that cyberbullying is a unique social phenomenon whose "virtualness" further isolates victims and often leads to suicide among teenage girls.

### I. The Unique Characteristics of Cyberbullying

1. Nowadays, technology is very important to our lives and almost nothing can be done without technological processes.[1]
2. Cyberbullying and traditional bullying both involve victims and offenders; however, the similarities end at this.[2]
3. In the context of cyberbullying, offenders do not have to expose their information and this gives them freedom to express themselves without weighing the costs.[3]
4. Further, from a victim's perspective, there can be a perception of wider humiliation in an online environment because the "onlooking" community is not limited to those who are physically nearby.[4]

5. Because cyberbullying occurs online, it may seem as though victims can more easily escape their tormentors simply by going offline; yet such an escape may not be as simple as it appears.
6. Cyberbullying is also unique because its virtual nature may raise questions about whether bullying has actually occurred.
7. Additionally, teen victims of cyberbullying may lack the kinds of adult support available to victims of traditional bullying.
8. It follows that in cases of online bullying, teens may be more inclined to attempt to resolve their situation without adult support.
9. Cyberbullying may be unique in other respects, and is more likely to take the form of sexual harassment.

## II. The Negative Effects of Cyberbullying

10. The characteristics of cyberbullying have led to a variety of negative effects.
11. Because men and women are different both physically and psychologically, they have different reactions toward cyberbullying.
12. Anger, sadness, and frustration are common responses among girls who are cyberbullied.
13. Ongoing cyberbullying can lead to depression.
14. Ultimately, girls are at higher risk of suicidal thoughts and of attempting suicide.

## III. Conclusion

15. This paper focuses on the relationship between cyberbullying and suicide among teenage girls.
16. Because cyberbullying can cause suicidal thoughts and behaviors, researchers and social organizations have been trying to solve these problems.
17. There remains a need for more research and new practical solutions to deal with the silence of victims, the unawareness of parents, and the lack of empowerment among educators.

**Instructor comments:**

1. "Nowadays" is too general. Be more specific. Technology may be "very important" to our lives, but you could perhaps be more precise by saying technology "is integrated into every aspect of our lives."

2. I would disagree! Motives and psychopathology are surely related!
3. "Information" is too general. Do you mean "personal information"? "Without weighing the costs" is very colloquial; "without accountability" is more precise.
4. Jenna, the rest of the guiding sentences look good and display strong thesis-driven narrative coherence! I see you've made the shift to two sections. Good idea. There just seems to be an imbalance in the lengths of Section 1 and Section 2. As you proceed with drafting, you may be able to address this by building on Section 2. Onward!

# Documentation

Different disciplines have different ways of acknowledging information borrowed from sources. Thus, once you are ready to begin drafting, it is a good idea to know what style of documentation your paper calls for. In academic writing, there are four major styles of documentation: the American Psychological Association style (APA); the Chicago (or Turabian) style; the Council of Science Editors style (CSE), and the Modern Language Association style (MLA). APA is used in the social sciences, in disciplines like psychology and sociology. The Chicago style, which involves bibliographic footnotes or endnotes, is commonly used in history. CSE is standard in the sciences, and for disciplines such as engineering. MLA is used in English studies and philosophy. There are also other styles of documentation that tend to be quite discipline specific, for example, the Harvard System of Referencing, a name-date style used in law, medicine, and natural, social, and behavioural sciences; or the SBL (Society of Biblical Literature) style, used in ancient near eastern, biblical, and early Christian studies. While all of this may seem daunting to someone approaching styles of documentation for the first time, documentation is actually a fairly straightforward process, one that is governed by genre expectations that reflect social needs.

The various styles of documentation may look different, but they share an underlying structure in that all involve a *two-step process*. Regardless of style, documentation at the first step involves an *in-text acknowledgement* of the source. "Citations" are an important component of Step 1 acknowledgement.

APA, CSE, and MLA all use parenthetical citations that provide bits of information in round brackets or parentheses; Chicago, on the other hand, uses raised or superscript numerals. At the second step, entries in *a list of sources* at the end of the paper correspond to the in-text citations. Step 1 indicates that the primary writer is drawing on a source. Step 2 provides complete publication information about the source.

Since Step 1 citations and Step 2 lists complement each other, they can be envisioned as partners in a dance. The information associated with the in-text citation is joined arm-in-arm to an entry in the list. These two partners perform together, creating a harmonious whole.

The samples below show the two-step process of documentation in a variety of passages:

| | |
|---|---|
| **MLA** | |
| **Step 1: From Pamela den Ouden's "My Uttermost Valleys"** | In their well-known 1979 study of the patriarchal literary tradition, entitled *Madwoman in the Attic: The Woman Writer and the Nineteenth Century Literary Imagination*, Sandra Gilbert and Susan Gubar, two American feminist critics, argue that many male writers, including such luminaries as Dante, |

Milton, Swift, and Dickens, have presented their female characters as angels (21–27) or as monsters (27–35).

Works Cited

Gilbert, Sandra, and Susan Gubar. *The Madwoman in the Attic: The Woman Writer and the Nineteenth Century Literary Imagination.* New Haven: Yale UP, 1979. Print.

**Step 2: From the Works Cited at the end of the paper**

# APA

**Step 1: From Shari Harrison's "Empowering Life Long Learners: Using Authentic Assessment to Enhance Learning in Post-Secondary Writing Courses"**

According to Fischer and King (1995), "authentic assessment is a positive and dynamic form of evaluation. It is a system that documents what students can do; promotes the collaboration of teacher [and] student ... in the learning process; and places ownership of learning on the student" (p. 33).

References

Fischer, C., & King, R. (1995). Authentic assessment: A guide to implementation. Thousand Oaks, CA: Corwin Press.

**Step 2: From the list of references at the end of the paper**

# Another Example of APA

**Step 1: From Alice Carlick's "The Girl and the Grizzly"**

Anthropologists suggest that narratives provide windows on the way people think about and live in the world (Ridington, 1988, p. 70; Cruikshank, 1983, p. 5).

References

Cruikshank, J. (1983). *The stolen woman: Female journeys in Tagish and Tutchone narrative.* National Museum of Man Mercury Series, paper No. 87. Ottawa: National Museums of Canada.

Ridington, R. (1988). *Trail to heaven: Knowledge and narrative in a northern Native community*. Vancouver: Douglas and McIntyre. Print.

**Step 2: From the list of references at the end of the paper**

# CSE

**Step 1: From Chapter 3 in the *CSE Manual***

A detailed source on phonetic symbols is *Phonetic Symbol Guide* (Pullum and Ladusaw 1986).

### References

Pullum GK, Ladusaw WA. 1986. *Phonetic symbol guide*. Chicago: Univ. Chicago Pr.

**Step 2: From the list of references at the end of the manual**

# Another Example of CSE

**Step 1: From David Hamer's paper on Grizzly Bears in Banff**

In years of high fruit production, roots are dug infrequently by grizzly bears during autumn, but if the buffaloberry crop fails, roots can dominate the diet from August until hibernation in later October or November (Pearson 1975, Russell at al. 1979, Hamer and Herrero 1987a).

### References

Hamer D, Herrero S. 1987a. Grizzly bear food and habitat in the Front Ranges of Banff National Park, Alberta. Int. Conf. Bear Res. Manage. 7:199–213.

Pearson AM. 1975. The northern interior grizzly bear Ursus arctos L. Canadian Wildlife Service Report Series No. 34. 84 p.

**Step 2: From the list of references at the end of the paper**

Russell RH, Nolan JW, Woody NG, Anderson, GW. 1979. A study of the grizzly bear in Jasper National Park, 1975–1978. Final report. Canadian Wildlife Service, Edmonton, Alberta. 136 p.

## Chicago

**Step 1: From I. S. MacLaren's "Retaining Captaincy of the Soul"**

Conventional modes of perceiving nature comprised no less a part of the Arctic explorer's baggage than they did the Grand Tourist's because, as Stephen Fender has stated recently in his study of the response to landscape in the early American West, "People confronted by unfamiliar landscapes have often needed the reassurance of frames or focusing devices, whether physical or conceptual, brought along from their own cultural base."[1]

Notes

**Step 2: From the list of notes at the end of the paper**

1. Stephen Fender, *Plotting the Golden West: American Literature and the Rhetoric of the California Trail* (Cambridge: Cambridge University Press, 1981), p. 16.

The precise mechanics for each style of documentation vary according to the kind of source (journal article, book, website). For example, Step 2 entries for books look a little different from Step 2 entries for journals. It is also worth remembering that some publishers use their own versions (in-house versions) of a given style, so that APA and CSE formatting, in particular, may differ from journal to journal. In the case of papers prepared for college and university classes, students should follow the style manual for their discipline, unless instructors state otherwise. The official style manuals are listed below:

**APA:** *Publication Manual of the American Psychological Association*
**Chicago:** *The Chicago Manual of Style*
**CSE:** *Scientific Style and Format: The CSE Manual for Authors, Editors, and Publishers*
**MLA:** *MLA Handbook for Writers of Research Papers*
**Turabian:** *A Manual for Writers of Term Papers, Theses, and Dissertations*

Normally, these style manuals can be found in the reference section of your library, and they are often supplemented by a host of abridged style manuals. Be sure to follow the most up-to-date edition. Many composition handbooks also provide abridged information on the different styles, as do innumerable websites devoted to documentation. The problem with websites, however, is that they can be "here today, gone tomorrow." The following sites may be accessible:

**The Official APA Site**
www.apa.org

**The Official MLA Site**
www.mla.org

**The Chicago Manual of Style Online**
www.chicagomanualofstyle.org

**Scientific Style and Format (CSE) Online**
www.scientificstyleandformat.org

If your instructor requires a particular style, it would be a good idea to ask him or her to approve abridged style manuals, whether they are in print or online.

Documentation can be a time-consuming process. Nevertheless, it deserves your careful attention, for meticulous documentation enables readers to check and verify information for themselves. In relation to genre theory, thoroughness serves a scholarly need for precision, accuracy, and reliability. It will impress your instructors, just as it impresses journal editors.

An overview of the documentation process as a whole shows that Step 1 involves choices and Step 2 is highly prescribed. At Step 1, scholars have sentence-level flexibility in how they acknowledge their sources. Step 2, by comparison, is mechanical—following patterns stated in style manuals. In the next section, we will delve more deeply into Step 1 and the sentence-level considerations associated with reported speech.

## Sentence-Level Considerations and Reported Speech

Once you know what style of documentation you will be using, there are some further sentence-level considerations that warrant attention as you acknowledge sources in core paragraphs. The practice of acknowledging sources throughout a paper is a crucial skill for academic writers. Hyland (1999) has observed that Step 1 citation involves "choices that carry rhetorical and social meanings [through] a wide range of signaling structures and reporting forms" (p. 344). Let's begin with the basics. Each time you employ a source, you need to decide whether you will

- quote,
- paraphrase, or
- paraphrase and quote

and whether you will acknowledge the source

- by naming it in an attributive expression (integrated reference), or
- by naming the source in the citation only (non-integrated reference).[1]

It is possible to mix and match these choices in a variety of ways:

- integrated reference with quotation
- integrated reference with paraphrase
- integrated reference with paraphrase and quotation
- non-integrated reference with quotation
- non-integrated reference with paraphrase
- non-integrated reference with paraphrase and quotation

The chart below illustrates these choices.

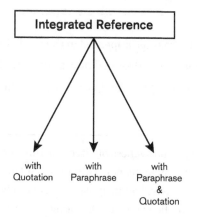 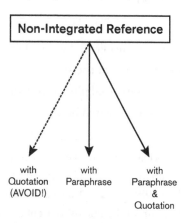

Making choices when presenting reported speech

**Caution:** Among the potential patterns for presenting reported speech, beware of non-integrated reference with quotation. This pattern results in what Hacker and Sommers (2012) refer to as a "dropped quotation" (p. 171). A dropped quotation is a sentence consisting of *only* a quotation and possibly a citation. Dropped quotations have no contextual material provided by the primary writer, whether in the form of an attributive expression, transitional phrase, paraphrase, or other bridging device. Dropped quotes are like guests who suddenly appear at a wedding without any introduction or invitation. No one has made way for them. These wedding crashers are strangers who disrupt the flow of the conversation. Their appearance comes as a jolt to guests at the party, that is, to readers. In the sample below, we imposed a dropped quote on a published article. The dropped quote is in bold.

---

Rhetorical criticism is concerned with the persuasiveness of discourse through the "creation of social forms in human symbolic behavior" (Klumpp and Hollihan, 1989, p. 88). That is, the salience of rhetorical propositions is largely based upon the correspondence of the symbolic value of a discourse with the established meaning of the existing social order. **"The concept of visual argument is an extension of rhetoric's paradigm into a new domain ... rhetoric in a broader sense is the use of symbols to communicate ... [A]ny form of persuasion, including visual persuasion, belongs within rhetoric's province" (Blair, 1996, p. 37).**

*Source:* Adapted from Todd (2002, p. 67)

---

Did you feel the jolt? Below we show how the passage appeared in the published article. Notice that the sentence shown above as a dropped quotation actually carries a contextual phrase and an attributive expression in the original. These features are shown in bold.

---

Rhetorical criticism is concerned with the persuasiveness of discourse through the "creation of social forms in human symbolic behavior" (Klumpp and Hollihan, 1989, p. 88). That is, the salience of rhetorical propositions is largely based upon the correspondence of the symbolic value of a discourse with the established meaning of the existing social order. **Stating the case for visual**

> **communication, Blair (1996) argues that** "the concept of visual argument is an extension of rhetoric's paradigm into a new domain ... [R]hetoric in a broader sense is the use of symbols to communicate... [A]ny form of persuasion, including visual persuasion, belongs within rhetoric's province" (p. 37).
>
> *Source:* Todd (2002, p. 67)

## More on Quotation or Paraphrase

As mentioned in the discussion of summary writing, the general rule is to quote only when the precise words of the source are important. Otherwise, paraphrase is preferable. Note, however, that it is possible to strike a compromise between quotation and paraphrase: quoted phrases can appear embedded inside a paraphrase.

## More on Integrated and Non-Integrated Reference

Remember that integrated reference means the researcher integrates the name of his or her source into a sentence through an *attributive expression* that comes before a citation. When integrated reference occurs, attribution is incorporated into the grammatical structure of a sentence so that sources (authors' names, titles, and/or personal pronouns) appear as one of the following:

- the subject of a verb: Smith notes that ...
- a possessive adjective: Smith's observation indicates ... His work shows ...
- the object of a preposition: In the work of Smith, ...
- the object of a prepositional phrase: According to Smith, ...

Non-integrated reference, on the other hand, marginalizes attribution, pushing it exclusively into citations, the form of which (parenthetical citations or superscript numerals) depends on the style of documentation. In non-integrated reference, attribution is an aside in which citations supply publication details about the information just mentioned. Grammatically, such citations function like a non-restrictive appositive element.

Some Step 1 examples of integrated and non-integrated reference follow:

## Integrated Reference with Paraphrase

(An Attributive Expression [Phrase or Clause] Plus a Citation)
**Chicago:** According to Christy, Bedaux's ability to create a favourable impression of himself led to the multimillionaire's success.[1]
**APA:** According to Christy (1980), Bedaux's ability to create a favourable impression of himself led to the multimillionaire's success (p. 23).
**MLA:** Christy argues that Bedaux's ability to create a favourable impression of himself led to his success (23).

## Non-Integrated Reference with Paraphrase

(Citation Only)
**Chicago:** Bedaux's ability to create a favourable impression of himself led to his success.[1]
**APA:** Bedaux's ability to create a favourable impression of himself led to his success (Christy, 1980, p. 23).
**MLA:** Bedaux's ability to create a favourable impression of himself led to his success (Christy 23).

When you employ integrated reference, you are shining a spotlight on your source, as though it were at centre stage. When you employ non-integrated reference, sources are more shadowy figures that inhabit peripheral regions. The use of integrated and non-integrated reference involves discretion, but student writers should also be aware of different disciplinary patterns. In the humanities and social sciences, for example, integrated reference is much more common than in the natural sciences. Hyland suggests this is because the softer disciplines have a greater acceptance of individual agency in the knowledge-making process; in the sciences, on the other hand, "citation behavior" creates the impression that facts speak for themselves (Hyland, 1999, pp. 342, 344–348; note Hyland's interesting use of nominalization: "citation behavior"!).

So, be aware of your stylistic choices, and make informed, sensitive decisions. Here are some guidelines:

## *Use Integrated Reference*

✓ When referring to an important source for the first time
✓ When referring to an important source at the beginning of a paragraph
✓ When returning to an important source after employing other sources
✓ On an intermittent basis because integrated signalling structures are a well-established pattern in scholarly discourse

## *Use Non-Integrated Reference*

✓ When providing a brief description of a tradition of inquiry
✓ Whenever a source does not need to be highlighted
✓ When ongoing statements of attribution amid low-level paragraph detail may begin to clutter your writing

## More on Grammatical Constructions in Integrated Reference

We've noted that integrated reference is associated with certain grammatical structures. The following examples elaborate on these patterns, showing how attributive expressions may be situated at different points in a sentence.

---

**Source passage:** "The decision whether or not to marry belongs properly to individuals, not to the government" (Thomas Stoddard, "Marriage is a Fundamental Right," p. 45).

The samples below employ MLA documentation.

- Attributive expressions may be written as prepositional phrases before, between, or sometimes after a quotation or paraphrase.

   According to Thomas Stoddard, "[t]he decision whether or not to marry belongs properly to individuals, not to the government" (45).

   "The decision whether or not to marry," according to Thomas Stoddard, "belongs properly to individuals, not to the government" (45).

   "The decision whether or not to marry belongs properly to individuals, not to the government," according to Thomas Stoddard (45).

---

- Attributive expressions may be written as subordinate clauses preceding a quotation or paraphrase. In these cases, the quotation or paraphrase must comprise a main clause.

    As Thomas Stoddard notes, "[t]he decision whether or not to marry belongs properly to individuals, not to the government" (45).

    As Thomas Stoddard notes, choices about marriage are matters of individual discretion, rather than governmental decree (45).

- Attributive expressions may be written as part of a main clause, consisting of a subject and a transitive verb. The quotation or paraphrase (often the object of the transitive verb) may complete the main clause.

    In "Marriage is a Fundamental Right," Thomas Stoddard argues that "[t]he decision whether or not to marry belongs properly to individuals, not to the government" (45).

    In "Marriage is a Fundamental Right," Thomas Stoddard notes that choices about marriage are matters of individual discretion, rather than governmental decree (45).

- Attributive expressions may also be written as complete main clauses that precede a quotation.

    Thomas Stoddard argues that personal freedom is a paramount concern: "The decision whether or not to marry belongs properly to individuals, not to the government" (45).

## Choosing Attributive Verbs for Integrated Reference

When integrated reference involves subject/predicate constructions, you have a host of attributive verbs to choose from. Writers can indicate their attitude toward a source by exploiting the connotative meaning of such verbs. "Claims," for example, can carry a pejorative implication, hinting that the researcher is standing at a critical distance from what the source says (cf. Giltrow, 2002, p. 251). "Illustrates," on the other hand, has a more objective, authoritative ring, possibly because it implies the existence of empirical evidence, and can be used to validate information. Sample attributive verbs are listed below:

| argues | emphasizes | relates |
|--------|-----------|---------|
| asserts | explains | reports |
| believes | illustrates | reveals |
| claims | implies | says |
| comments | insists | sees |
| concludes | maintains | shows |
| condemns | notes | speculates |
| considers | observes | suggests |
| declares | points out | writes |

On occasion, the colouring force of attributive verbs can be emphasized through the use of adverbs. Consider the effect of the adverb/verb constructions in an essay by Kerry Abel, entitled "Of Two Minds: Dene Response to the Mackenzie Missions, 1858–1902":

> Even those who would agree with revisionist historians that the fur trade did not cause as great a disruption as once believed, still would argue that the case of the missionary was quite different. As one author confidently asserts,
>
> > Things started to change permanently and fundamentally when the missionaries started to take over the souls of native people ... There is no question that the practical result has been the destruction of one of the cornerstones of native culture.[5]
>
> *Source:* Abel (1989, p. 78)

In this case, Abel proceeds to disagree with this "confident" assertion. The confidence that Abel attributes to the source signals what *she* regards as an overly confident approach to knowledge-making. Reading between the lines, one may even detect a hint of sarcasm in Abel's citation behaviour (how's *your* citation behaviour?!). Such interrelationships suggest that the production of knowledge is a complicated and potentially adversarial business in which writers occasionally pit themselves against their sources. However, ethics of politeness are part of academic culture, so debate is carried on in more restrained tones than encountered, say, in blog comments.

## Maintaining Contact with Sources

It is important to maintain ongoing contact with your sources. You should not, for example, introduce a source once, through integrated or non-integrated reference, then continue to draw on it without further attribution, leaving your reader to guess where information is coming from. This means that integrated and non-integrated reference, two basic patterns involved in reported speech, should make ongoing appearances throughout the core of your paper. What's at stake here is building clear *attributive frames* for the presentation of low-level detail in core paragraphs. All information drawn from a source should be clearly tied to that source. In the passages that follow, the information after the guiding sentence (the first sentence) has been drawn from John Berger. Passages 1 and 2 provide weak examples of attributive framing; Passages 3 and 4 provide better examples.

---

### Passage 1

[inadequate reporting: the beginning of the frame is vague]
When we look at art, whether portraits, photographs, or advertisements, we should note where people in the picture are looking. In advertisements in women's magazines, for example, there is a tendency for "*men* [to] *act* and *women* [to] *appear.* Men look at women and women watch themselves being looked at." In such cases, women are depicted as conscious recipients of a male gaze. Similarly, in Renaissance paintings of female nudes, the woman's expression reflected her subordination to the male owner of the painting. Accordingly, the ideal viewer is typically male and the female model appeals to his ego (Berger, 1972, pp. 52–64).

---

### Passage 2

[inadequate reporting: the frame dissolves too soon]
When we look at art, whether portraits, photographs, or advertisements, we should note where people in the picture are looking. According to Berger (1972), in advertisements in women's magazines, for example, there is a tendency for

*"men* [to] *act* and *women* [to] *appear.* Men look at women and women watch themselves being looked at" (p. 52). In such cases, women are depicted as conscious recipients of a male gaze. Similarly, in Renaissance paintings of female nudes, the woman's expression reflected her subordination to the male owner of the painting. Accordingly, the ideal viewer is typically male and the female model appeals to his ego.

## Passage 3

**[adequate but cumbersome documentation: consecutive citations]**
When we look at art, whether portraits, photographs, or advertisements, we should note where people in the picture are looking. In advertisements in women's magazines, for example, there is a tendency for *"men* [to] *act* and *women* [to] *appear.* Men look at women and women watch themselves being looked at" (Berger, 1972, p. 52). In such cases, women are depicted as conscious recipients of a male gaze (p. 54). Similarly, in Renaissance paintings of female nudes, the woman's expression reflected her subordination to the male owner of the painting (p. 55). Accordingly, the ideal viewer is typically male and the female model appeals to his ego (pp. 52–64).

Passage 4, below, presents an alternative to the consecutive non-integrated references in Passage 3. The citation that accompanies integrated reference is delayed so that the attributive frame encompasses more information. This "envelope technique" can be clear and economical, but if the frame becomes too large, readers may lose track of its edges. An envelope should not expand beyond the scope of one paragraph.

## Passage 4

**[adequate and unobtrusive documentation: the envelope technique]**
When we look at art, whether portraits, photographs, or advertisements, we should note where people in the picture are looking. According to Berger (1972), in advertisements in women's magazines, for example, there is a tendency for *"men* [to] *act* and *women* [to] *appear.* Men look at women and women watch themselves being looked at." In such cases, women are depicted as conscious

recipients of a male gaze. Similarly, in Renaissance paintings of female nudes, the woman's expression reflected her subordination to the male owner of the painting. Accordingly, the ideal viewer is typically male and the female model appeals to his ego (pp. 52–64).

## More on Attributive Frames

In the sample paragraph that follows, we have underlined the researcher's guiding sentence and concluding sentence. *Within* the valley of reported details, we have annotated reporting structures for each attributive frame.

---

Until the late 1950's, when government policy towards residential schools changed, the Canadian government supported the Roman Catholic Church in its quest to assimilate the Native population into a supposedly more civilized and superior European style of living. Furniss (1992) notes that the state saw the Natives' way of life as something to be destroyed and absorbed into mainstream culture, calling this the "Indian problem" (p. 13).[1] Furniss adds that it was the Federal government's ideal to transform all Native peoples physically and culturally into an image that was more pleasing to the European sensibilities (p. 16).[2] The common ideal of the Catholic Church and Canadian officials was to assimilate the Native culture as quickly as possible.

**Notes:**
1. Integrated reference with paraphrase and quotation
2. Integrated reference with paraphrase

*Source:* Mitchell (2001)

---

Another annotated example follows:

---

The priests, nuns, and teachers who ran the missionary schools were devout in the Christian belief that the second coming of Christ would only occur when the gospel had been spread throughout the world. In fact, missionaries believed the native culture had to be forcefully destroyed if there was any chance of saving the Natives' souls (Furniss, 1992, p. 16).[1] Such salvation clearly depended on the

Natives' acceptance of the Christian faith and on their renunciation of pagan beliefs (p. 18).[2] In particular, Furniss (1992) notes that the missionaries felt it was crucial to remove the Native children from homes and families, influences that were viewed as deleterious to cultural adjustment (p. 27).[3] According to Haig-Brown (1988), the resulting segregation of children and families reveals the invasive nature of the missionary's work (p. 35).[4] Indeed, Native children were taught the European way of life on a live-in, full time basis.

**Notes:**
1 and 2. Non-integrated reference with paraphrase
3 and 4. Integrated reference with paraphrase

*Source:* Mitchell (2001)

Try blocking, labelling, and annotating the following paragraphs on your own.

Mission schools were intentionally situated outside and away from the native communities and families. St. Joseph's Mission was no exception. Indeed, a bus would routinely come to pick up children attending the school. According to Haig-Brown (1988), this bus was originally called the "school truck" and then later the "cattle truck." The arrival of this bus involved most Native peoples' first introduction into a way of life that was in startling contrast to the one they had always known. Native children began to recognize and fear the mission school bus, and its arrival in their community (pp. 47, 48). Indeed, Beverley remembers the bus in a negative light: "a bus came and got us and took us to the mission. I never left for four years. No one came to get me, no one came to visit me." Beverley says that this memory, of the bus taking her away from home, is especially vivid (personal communication, Oct. 19th, 20th, 2001). Others who attended residential schools have similar memories of a first bus (Haig-Brown, 1998, p. 48). Perhaps such memories, for Beverley and others, are especially vivid because the experience marked the loss of home and family.

*Source:* Mitchell (2001)

Given their distance from Native communities, residential schools limited the contact that children had with their parents and families. Furniss (1992) claims that the Oblates saw "the physical removal of children from their families and communities [as] a central ingredient of the residential school system" (p. 51). Beverley remembers that there were older students at St. Joseph's who told her that they had been her age when they first arrived there. The school went up to grade eight and they wouldn't be allowed to leave until they had completed grade eight. Beverley also could not recall a time in the four years that she spent at St. Joseph's that her mother was allowed to visit her. She recalls receiving a gift from her mother only once during her stay at the mission: one Christmas she received a plastic candy cane filled with chocolates. She had no other contact with her family in her four year stay (personal communication, Oct. 19th, 20th, 2001). This form of segregation was the norm within residential schools in British Columbia. Distancing Native children from their families, including siblings in attendance at the same school, was seen as beneficial to the missionary goal of bringing the Natives into popular European society.

*Source:* Mitchell (2001)

## The Jenna Files

Notes to self:

- I'm at a low point, and I don't mean low-level detail. It's mid-terms, and I'm swamped. I'm also really tired. This is all so much work. Next week, I have four tests, and I'm supposed to be making progress on my research paper. Maybe five courses wasn't a good idea.
- I'm trying to build on my guiding sentence outline by developing whole paragraphs. I'm going to try to set aside an hour each day this week to go through my research notebook and continue to cluster the details into paragraph groupings. I've started on that process and it does make writing the core paragraphs easier, but it's still slow going. Some of my paragraphs seem a little disconnected.
- Also, I have to watch for all those little mistakes that my instructor has already commented on, like parallel structure, syntax, even the logic of some of my statements. And proofread—he even found a spelling mistake.

## Several Core Paragraphs from Jenna's Paper with Instructor Feedback

In the twenty-first century,✓ technology is integrated into every aspect of our lives.✓ Over 1.8 billion people used the Internet in 2009: 42.4% were Asian users, 23.6% European users, and 14.4% North American users, and numerous[1] of them were teenagers (Bhat, Chang & Linscott, 2010, p. 35). ~~However, as technology has been rapidly growing, problems have occurred one after another. One of the newest and most serious problems is cyberbullying.~~[2] Unlike traditional bullying that happens in person and involves continuous physical assaults, cyberbullying is more likely to harm people mentally.[3] A lot of[4] research has been conducted on traditional bullying, but only little research on cyberbullying. As a result, there is no exact definition even though it has become an important social issue. However, in general, cyberbullying is defined as a harmful and aggressive action through the Internet or any electronic devices (Dooley, Pyzalski & Cross, 2009, p. 182).

Cyberbullying and traditional bullying both involve victims and offenders, and they have similar processes.[5] Offenders choose a target and humiliate him or her in front of people, or they ruin his or her social life. However, the most identifiable difference is that cyberbullying only occurs through telecommunication devices. Offenders do not have to expose their personal information,✓ and this gives them freedom to express themselves anonymously and without accountability.✓[6] This can be very humiliating for victims, as it is not only a private dispute between victims and the bullies, but involves the whole community [7] (Schneider, O'Donnell, Stueve, & Coulter, 2010, p. 171). Dooley, Pyzalski, and Cross (2009) exemplified that [8] an offender can upload shameful pictures of a victim to the Internet which anyone can see, and this one action can cause the victim more humiliation than what the offender thought because of the pervasiveness of the Internet (p. 183). Moreover, because the incidents happen through the Internet, cyberbullied victims still have to deal with them out of school. As long as they are connected to the Internet, they are exposed to the possibility of victimization; therefore, it is very hard for the victims to evade their victimization, whereas victims of traditional bullying can avoid the situations after school (Dooley, Pyzalski, & Cross, 2009, p. 184).

According to Hinduja and Patchin (2011), "two-thirds of youth go online every day for school work, to keep in touch with their friends, to learn about celebrities, to share their digital creations, or for many other reasons" (p. 23).[9] Because teen-agers spend more time on the Internet than any other age groups, cyberbully-ing mostly occurs among adolescents (p. 21). Schneider, O'Donnell, and Stueve (2012) noted that 93% of teenagers use the Internet everyday, and 75% of teen-agers have their own cell phones (p. 171). Therefore, they have a high chance of being cyberbullied; Hinduja and Patchin indicated that 20% of 11-to-18 year-old students have been victims of cyberbullying (p. 21). Add to this that, in America, youth suicide is the third leading cause of death among teenagers, 13.8% of whom reported seriously considering suicide; another 6.3% reported that within the 12 months before the survey they had attempted suicide (Bauman, Toomey, & Walker, 2013, p. 341). Cyberbullying affects the increasing numbers of attempted and completed suicides among teenagers (p. 342). However, despite the studies examining the connection between cyberbullying and suicide being relatively small (Bauman, Toomey, & Walker, 2013, p. 342), these researchers do point out that victims of cyberbullying are at high risk of suicide (p. 342). [10]

**Instructor comments:**

1. "Numerous" + noun; "numerous" can't be used with a preposition.
2. Wordy. Compress into one sentence.
3. Logic? Are you disregarding the possibility of mental harm occurring through physical assaults?
4. Tone?
5. Nice improvement over your guiding sentence outline.
6. Good work. Looking back at your guiding sentence outline, I can see you've rethought paragraph structure.
7. How so? I'm not following your argument. You start out by referring to the anonymity of offenders, but suddenly move to the scope of the victim's humiliation. These are different points. The argument needs to be "unpacked."
8. Exemplify + noun (don't use "that" with "exemplify")
9. Are you sure you want to start a paragraph with reported speech? Here, maybe try to adhere more closely to your guiding sentence outline. Overall, these sample paragraphs are a bit rough at the moment, but there's time to work on them.
10. Check the syntax of this sentence. Your meaning is not clear.

# Case Study: Staying in Touch with Sources

The following case study shows how attribution can be improved in successive drafts. Here, we witness a student paper progressing from a first draft to a second draft, with improved attribution along the way. For emphasis, attributive expressions have been placed in **bold**; arrows point to superscript citations.

---

## First Draft: Weak Attribution

### Champagne and Caviar: Geographical Exploration and the Bedaux Expedition

In the summer of 1934, the Bedaux expedition rolled into the Peace country on its way to find a gateway to the Pacific. Charles E. Bedaux, the leader of the expedition, was born in the small French village of Charenton-le-Pont. Bedaux's father, a railroad engineer, and his mother, a dressmaker, both hoped that their son would proceed through school and become a lawyer; however, a year and a half before he was to have graduated, Bedaux was expelled. For the next couple of years, Bedaux worked at several part-time jobs but was consistently drawn towards the "red-light" districts of urban France. After working as a hawker for night clubs, he met a pimp who offered to teach him the tricks of his trade. One aspect of this education was a keystone to Bedaux's success: "the necessity of keeping up a front no matter how down on his luck he might be."[1] This, along with his ability to convince men of their need for his services and his alluring personality, led to his success in selling his efficiency system which eventually made him a multimillionaire. It also led to his two marriages and numerous affairs. After setting a record for crossing the Sahara Desert for the first time in rubber-tired vehicles, touring the South American rain forest region, and sailing throughout the South Seas, Bedaux turned towards what he considered the last unconquered corner of the world, the northern section of British Columbia.

Note:
1.   Jim Christy, *The Price of Power* (New York: Knopf, 1981), p. 21.

## Second Draft: Adequate Attribution

### Champagne and Caviar: Geographical Exploration and the Bedaux Expedition

In the summer of 1934, the Bedaux expedition rolled into the Peace country on its way to find a gateway to the Pacific. **In *The Price of Power*, Jim Christy chronicles Bedaux's early life:** the leader of the expedition was born in the small French village of Charenton-le-Pont; Bedaux's father, a railroad engineer, and his mother, a dressmaker, both hoped that their son would proceed through school and become a lawyer; however, a year and a half before he was to have graduated, Bedaux was expelled; for the next couple of years, Bedaux worked at several part-time jobs but was consistently drawn towards the "redlight" districts of urban France; after working as a hawker for night clubs, he met a pimp who offered to teach him the tricks of his trade.[1] **According to Christy**, one aspect of this education was a keystone to Bedaux's success: "the necessity of keeping up a front no matter how down on his luck he might be."[2] This, **Christy asserts**, along with Bedaux's alluring personality and his ability to convince men of their need for his services, led to his success in selling his efficiency system which eventually made him a multimillionaire. **Christy adds that** Bedaux's ability to create a favourable impression of himself also led to the multimillionaire's two marriages and numerous affairs.[3] After setting a record for crossing the Sahara Desert for the first time in rubber-tired vehicles,[4] touring the South American rain forest region, and sailing throughout the South Seas, Bedaux turned towards what he considered the last unconquered corner of the world, the northern section of British Columbia.

**Notes:**

1. Jim Christy, *The Price of Power* (New York: Knopf, 1981), 21.

2. Ibid.

3. Ibid., p. 22.

4. Ibid., p. 23.

# Plagiarism

Plagiarism is the act of presenting someone else's work as your own. The most extensive forms of plagiarism may involve purchasing or simply copying all or large parts of a paper, whether from another student or from the Internet. Paying someone else to write your paper for you would be another example of extensive plagiarism. More limited forms of plagiarism occur when a writer copies select passages from another work without adequate attribution. Both the extensive and the more limited types of plagiarism are regarded as serious forms of misconduct in academic communities. Nevertheless, there is a widespread perception among teaching faculty at universities and colleges that plagiarism is on the rise. What we can be sure of is that it's easier to plagiarize than ever before. A quick Google search reveals thousands of "paper mills" that promise A+ papers in exchange for credit card information. Further, search engines also offer immediate access to millions of documents that can easily be copied.

The way to avoid plagiarism is to follow the Step 1 and Step 2 attribution practices and patterns described earlier in this chapter: adequate scholarly documentation at Step 1 involves the creation of attributive frames through integrated and non-integrated attribution to acknowledge the quotation, paraphrase, and summary of someone else's ideas; at Step 2, a corresponding list of references is needed at the end of a paper. It's important to follow such attribution practices at *both* Step 1 and Step 2. Some students arrive in university and college classrooms believing that it's acceptable to simply copy, without attribution, large chunks of information into the text of a paper, if a list of references is presented at the end. This belief is misguided. Proper scholarly documentation involves practices that must be followed *throughout* a paper.

But if the avoidance of plagiarism is really such a straightforward matter, why are instructors and professors spending countless hours addressing plagiarism? There is no simple answer to this question although it is apparent that frequently students are working from a different set of understandings and priorities from their instructors. Students may be pressured by lack of time, lack of sleep, heavy course load, and also may have entered the post-secondary community without a full appreciation of how seriously that community regards plagiarism. Indeed, less stringent approaches to the acknowledgement of intellectual property are common in other contexts, for example, website images and YouTube videos. Further, research papers themselves inherently involve a complex interplay between borrowing and creating, between presenting the voices of others and finding a legitimate space for one's own voice. We've covered this territory in our discussion of paragraph topography. Writers who become familiar with this topography can competently deal with genre expectations, but for novice student writers, such patterns may at first be difficult to manage. Instructors, on the other hand, have spent years working in their disciplines and have a deep intellectual, emotional, and financial investment in attribution practices. In academic culture, the chain (tradition) of inquiry matters; being first counts. For these reasons, perhaps, we have seen instructors respond with a mix of intense disbelief and even anger when they encounter student plagiarism.

The goal, then, is to have students and instructors on the same page, working from the same set of genre expectations. This involves a process of acculturation in which students become members of a community of discourse. Students whose writing practices fall outside the community norms proceed at their own risk. The consequences for plagiarism can be severe, including failure in an assignment, failure in a course, and even expulsion from an institution. The best way to avoid plagiarism is to pay strict attention to the nuances of attribution.

Below, we present history instructor Dr. Eva St. Jean's overview of plagiarism. Eva describes the kinds of plagiarism that she's encountered.

---

Plagiarism takes many forms in student essays. Here are some common types and examples:

### 1. Copying an entire essay, or "cutting-and-pasting" other writers' words without providing sources.

Example:

> The Veterans' Land Act, passed 20 July 1942, followed a Canadian tradition dating from the 17th century of settling ex-soldiers on the land. In 1919 a Soldier Settlement Act had provided returned WWI veterans who wished to farm with loans to purchase land, stock and equipment. According to Sarah Carter, these soldier settlements "constitut[ed] a significant erosion" of First Nations land.[1]

The underlined section has been cut and pasted from the online *Canadian Encyclopedia*, which the student didn't cite, nor did the student enclose the copied portion in quotation marks. Faulty framing causes the reader to assume that the first two sentences are the student's interpretation of Carter's article, but a quick Internet check shows that they were copied from the online *Canadian Encyclopedia*.

**2. Providing wrong sources. The student cites a source, but the source does not contain the material quoted or paraphrased.**

Example:

The underlined portion shows words borrowed from Erin Hanson's "Reserves," *Indigenous Foundations*, UBC.ca (http://indigenousfoundations.arts.ubc.ca/home/government-policy/the-indian-act.html).

> Today it is evident that the Canadian government's attempt to segregate First Nations on reserves isolated from non-native communities has failed. This policy was based on <u>the widely held colonial belief that in time Aboriginals would either die out or enfranchise and assimilate into mainstream Euro-Canadian society</u> (The Indian Act, 2009).

Possible correction:

> Today it is evident that the Canadian government's attempt to segregate First Nations on reserves isolated from non-native communities has failed. This policy was based on "the widely held colonial belief that in time Aboriginals would either die out or enfranchise and assimilate into mainstream Euro-Canadian society" (Hanson, 2009).

**3. Quoting without using quotation marks.**

Example 1:

The underlined section in the following sentence indicates "borrowed" words, which should be enclosed in quotation marks. A citation has been supplied, but the sentence structure suggests the information was paraphrased, when most of the words are quoted.

> Furthermore, <u>neither the armed forces, nor the RCMP knew much, if anything, about any Japanese Canadians</u> who were loyalists to the Japanese Empire.[1]

Possible correction:

> Canadian authorities had no information about any Japanese Canadians who remained loyal to Japan.[1]

Example 2:

> In addition, the Tsilhqot'in established a reputation for ferocity which kept the road out of their territory as well as most travellers.[1]

Possible correction:

> In addition, the Tsilhqot'in established a "reputation for ferocity" which kept the road out of their territory as well as most travellers.[1]

Another possible correction:

> In addition, the Tsilhqot'in became famous for quickly resorting to violence, which kept the road out of their territory as well as most travellers.[1]

### 4. Providing the correct source but the wrong page number or unnecessarily listing a wide range of pages in a text.

Example:

> According to Sarah Carter, soldier settlements "constitut[ed] a significant erosion" of First Nations land. Carter suggests that the federal government's protection of the interests of white war veterans and railway companies was done at the cost of the people living on Indian reserves. Quoting historian Brian Titley, who states that many government officials saw reserve land as "idle," she agrees that the government wanted to increase the agricultural output on Aboriginal land by making it available to white farmers and land speculators.[4]

**Note:**

4.  Sarah Carter, "'An Infamous Proposal:' Prairie Indian Reserve Land and Soldier Settlement After World War I." *Manitoba History* 37 (1999): 9-21.

If we used the online version of this article, pagination wouldn't be available, but we would have to provide the link so that the reader could use search options to find the correct page; if, on the other hand, we used a paper or pdf version, we must provide the exact page number(s).

### 5. Giving detailed disciplinary information without showing the source, perhaps mistakenly believing the information is "common knowledge" that doesn't need a citation.

Example:

Frederick Law Olmsted was so adept at concealing the artificial quality of his landscape paintings that his reconstruction of the natural world has been largely overlooked by the public.

Possible correction:

Anne Whiston Spirn and other scholars have shown that Frederick Law Olmsted was so adept at concealing the artificial quality of his landscape paintings that his reconstruction of the natural world has been largely overlooked by the public.[1]

### 6. Not creating accurate attributive frames.

Below, the single footnote at the end of the passage suggests that both the point about Reserve lands near Fort St. John and the larger point about "a significant erosion" of Aboriginal land come from the same source. However, the source does not mention the specific case of the Fort St. John Reserve lands.

Example:

Reserve lands near Fort St John, B.C. that were appropriated through the War Veterans' Land Act have been the object of a specific claims process since the initial agreement failed to take mineral rights into effect. This is just one example of "a significant erosion of the lands remaining to Aboriginal people."[1]

Possible correction:

Reserve lands near Fort St John that were appropriated through the Veterans' Land Act have been the object of a specific claims process since the initial agreement failed to take mineral rights into effect.[1] Apparently this is not an isolated incident. Sara Carter notes that the earlier Soldier Settlement Act also led to "a significant erosion of the lands remaining to Aboriginal people."[2]

In summary, to avoid plagiarism, remember the following:

- Use quotation marks and citations when you are quoting;
- Even paraphrased material requires attribution; and finally,
- Stay in touch with your sources—consistently provide your reader with attributive frames.

## Related Unacceptable Academic Practices

There is some debate about whether resubmitting one's own work for another course should be regarded as a form of plagiarism (self-plagiarism). Strictly speaking, we would consider this practice to be "multiple submission," rather than plagiarism. Like plagiarism, however, multiple submission will be viewed as a form of academic misconduct unless your institution allows multiple submission when permissions have first been secured. Check your institution calendar and course syllabi for applicable guidelines.

Similarly, there is some question about whether extensive "cut-and-paste" copying with attribution should be regarded as plagiarism. Imagine, for example, a 14-page paper that opens with a quotation mark, then provides a closing quotation mark and parenthetical citation at the end of the conclusion! Given the presence of attribution, such practice may not be regarded as plagiarism, per se, but it is plagiarism in spirit. The writer, despite quotation marks and a citation, has, for all intents and purposes, submitted someone else's work as his or her own. Do not expect your instructor to look favourably on a 14-page block quote. Even less extreme use of block quotes—even block quotes from multiple sources—will not be well received.

## Common Knowledge

You need to be able to distinguish between knowledge that arises from someone's particular research and knowledge widely available in tertiary sources (encyclopedias, Wikipedia, etc.).

Most handbooks inform students that "common knowledge" does not require attribution or documentation. Thus, common knowledge is presented as an exception to the rule that all borrowed information must be documented. However, this exception is neither as simple nor as reliable as it may sound. In this book, we would like to make a distinction between common non-disciplinary knowledge that does not require attribution and common disciplinary knowledge that does require attribution.

Common non-disciplinary knowledge is not generated under the carefully monitored conditions of academic research. For example, easily accessible biographical or historical information can be regarded as common non-disciplinary knowledge:

- Ernest Hemingway was born in 1899 in Oak Park, Illinois.
- American Independence occurred in 1776.
- Nelson Mandela served as president of South Africa from 1994 to 1999.

This kind of common knowledge does not require documentation. Even though it may not technically constitute *common* knowledge in the sense that people walk around with such information in their heads, such facts may be found in popular sources such as encyclopedias and other reference books. Generally speaking, this kind of knowledge is not produced through any original thinking or empirical investigation.

On the other hand, common disciplinary knowledge embodies generally accepted understandings that have been developed through academic research and original thinking in particular fields. For example:

- Although he adopted an anti-intellectual persona in his public life, Hemingway, the writer, employed many of the literary techniques associated with the high modernism of writers such as T. S. Eliot.
- The influences that led to American independence were fundamentally different from the processes that led to Canadian confederation.

This kind of common knowledge should be documented. In fact, such assertions have emerged from a tradition of inquiry, and we already know that scholars are under an obligation to acknowledge the work of their disciplinary predecessors, even when the previous studies present what have become agreed-on principles in the field.

In the student paper below, the attributive frame begins a little too soon—Black's birthdate doesn't require attribution, although the curriculum at the "proper ladies' school" probably does:

## From Gold Rush Pioneer to the
## Second Female Member of Parliament:
## Martha Black's Trek to Success

According to William Morrison, Martha Black was born in Chicago in February 1866. She was a child of privilege with a taste for pranks, and she attended proper ladies' schools, where she learned the skills meant to assure wealthy girls of her day a successful marriage: deportment, needlework, elocution, tennis, riding, and botany.[1]

**Note:**
1.   Martha Louise Black, *My Ninety Years* (Anchorage Alaska: Alaska Northwest Publishing, 1976), p. 138.

In the sample below, attribution has been appropriately delayed.

Martha Black was born in Chicago in February 1866 to wealthy parents and attended upper-class schools. According to William Morrison, she had "a taste for pranks," and she attended proper ladies' schools, where she learned the skills meant to assure wealthy girls of her day a successful marriage: deportment, needlework, elocution, tennis, riding, and botany.[1]

At the end of the day, writers may still experience some uncertainty about the type of common knowledge they are dealing with, and whether, in fact, it does require attribution. When in doubt, cite. Use and acknowledge sources extensively, but make sure that your own voice retains a managing role at the higher levels.

## English Language Learners

Students who have not been schooled in an English-speaking environment (a country with English language school systems/institutions) may be especially at risk of plagiarizing. They may struggle to express themselves in English; summary and paraphrase may be difficult. In addition, there is a popular belief, expressed by some international students themselves, that strict standards of attribution are not applied in their home countries. For many international students, then, it's both particularly important and challenging to internalize disciplinary norms regarding attribution. In such cases, there is a lot to learn and understand in the process of academic acculturation. If your first language is not English, be sure to check with your professor, sign up for help at your institution's writing or tutorial centre, and get the support you need.

## Ideas for Further Study

1. After studying your research notebook, identify a main method of development for the paper you are working on.
2. Prepare a guiding sentence outline for your own paper. Does your outline demonstrate the kind of narrative coherence that was evident in the outline of James Keller's paper?
3. Using concepts discussed under "Sentence-Level Considerations and Reported Speech," analyze the management of other voices in several core paragraphs in one of your sources.

## Note

1. Our terms "integrated" and "non-integrated" represent a modification of terminology used by Swales and Hyland.

## References

Abel, K. (1989). Of two minds: Dene response to the Mackenzie missions, 1858–1902. In K. S. Coates & W. R. Morrison (Eds.), *Interpreting Canada's North: Selected readings* (pp. 77–93). Toronto: Copp Clark.

Arruda, T. F. (1998). "You would have had your pick": Youth, gender, and jobs in Williams Lake, British Columbia, 1945–75. In R. Sandwell (Ed.), *Beyond the city limits: Rural history in British Columbia* (pp. 225–234). Vancouver: UBC Press.

Berger, J. (1972). *Ways of seeing.* London: BBC and Penguin Books.

Clouse, B. F. (1995). *Patterns for a purpose.* New York: McGraw Hill.

Cox, D. (1999). *Diana: Her true story:* Post-modern transgressions in identity. *Journal of Gender Studies, 8*(3), 323–337.

Davis, R. (1989). Thrice-told tales: The exploration writing of John Franklin. In J. Carlsen & B. Streijffert (Eds.), *The Canadian North: Essays in culture and literature* (pp. 15–26). Lund: Lund University Press.

den Ouden, P. (1998). *The madwoman in the Arctic: Fear of the feminine—a circumpolar perspective.* Unpublished manuscript, Northern Lights College, Fort St. John, Canada.

Giltrow, J. (2002). *Academic writing: Writing and reading in the disciplines* (3rd ed.). Peterborough, ON: Broadview Press.

Hacker, D. & Sommers, N. (2012). *A pocket style manual* (6th ed.). Boston: Bedford/St. Martin's.

Herrero, S., & Higgins, A. (1999). Human injuries inflicted by bears in British Columbia: 1960–97. *Ursus, 11,* 209–218.

Hill, A. (2000, May). Fearful and safe: Audience response to British reality programming. *Television and New Media, 1*(2), 193–213.

Hyland, K. (1999). Academic attribution: Citation and the construction of disciplinary knowledge. *Applied Linguistics, 20*(3), 341–367. doi:10.1093/applin/20.3.341

Keller, J. (1997). Masculinity and marginality in *Rob Roy* and *Braveheart. The Journal of Popular Film and Television, 24*(4), 146–151.

Kirby, M. (1998). Feminist, populist, humanitarian?: Progressive thinking and images of Princess Diana. *Class and Capital, 22*(1), 29–41.

Levine, S. J. (2005). Portraits of criminals on Bruce Springsteen's *Nebraska*: The enigmatic criminal, the sympathetic criminal, and the criminal as brother. *Widener Law Journal, 14*(3), 767–785.

Little, B. (2009). *Rolling a critical failure: Psychological well-being among Dungeons and Dragons players.* Unpublished manuscript, Northern Lights College, Fort St. John, Canada.

Mitchell, J. (2001). *Indian princess #134: Cultural assimilation at St. Joseph's Mission.* Unpublished manuscript, Northern Lights College, Fort St. John, Canada.

Norris, F. (1992). Popular images of the North in literature and film. *Northern Review 8–9,* 53–72.

Stoddard, T., & Fein, B. (1990). Gay marriage. *ABA Journal, 76*(1), 42.

Swales, J. (1990). *Genre analysis: English in academic and research settings.* Cambridge: Cambridge University Press.

Theberge, N. (1989). A feminist analysis of responses to sports violence: Media coverage of the 1987 World Junior Hockey Championship. *Sociology of Sport Journal, 6*(3), 247–256.

Todd, A. M. (2002). Prime-time subversion: The environmental rhetoric of *The Simpsons.* In M. Meister & P. M. Japp (Eds.), *Enviropop: Studies in environmental rhetoric and popular culture* (pp. 63–80). Westport, CT: Praeger Publishers.

Waldman, N., & Norton, S. (Eds.). (2012). *Canadian content* (7th ed.). Toronto: Nelson Educational.

# CHAPTER 7

# Crossing the Finish Line:
## Rhetorical Moves in Scholarly Conclusions

The end crowns the work.

—Anonymous

The major function of conclusions in the humanities and social sciences is to confirm what has already been said. For this reason, many conclusions in fields such as English or sociology do not labour under the intense knowledge-making burdens that introductions are prone to. Putting the finishing touches on an argument is not as difficult as getting the argument under way. If we were to describe the situation in more academic language, we could say that scholarly conclusions are not under as much *epistemological pressure* as scholarly introductions.

Nevertheless, conclusions perform an important rhetorical function. As the writer's last chance to clarify his or her contribution to knowledge, conclusions represent what a reader is left with. Moreover, conclusions can do more than simply repeat or confirm knowledge. Sometimes, for example, writers in the humanities and social sciences choose not to present their overarching knowledge claim or thesis until the end of the paper, so that conclusions provide a *delayed thesis*. This strategy can contribute to the appearance of objectivity: evidence is considered before a position is sharply drawn. Other things happen in scholarly conclusions. Readers may encounter *solutions to a problem*, a *call to action*, a *statement of relevance*, and *questions for further research*. Once again, academic writers can choose from a set of rhetorical features—in this case, rhetorical features that typically appear in the discourse of scholarly last words. Thus, just like introductions, conclusions merit close attention.

# Rhetorical Features in Scholarly Conclusions

The remainder of this discussion describes more precisely the particular rhetorical features commonly present in scholarly conclusions. Any given conclusion may incorporate one or more of these gestures in a variety of sequences.

### Repeating or Initiating Knowledge Claims

We already know that conclusions may repeat or initiate a thesis. In either case, the presentation of a thesis may also be accompanied by a review of main points in the core of the paper. Thus, conclusions can offer a brief summary of the knowledge that a writer has to offer. Such knowledge summaries are often accompanied by metadiscourse in the present perfect tense or simple past tense: for example, "This paper has shown ...," "We have illustrated ...," "My research has suggested ...," "We identified...." Further, knowledge summaries can occupy merely a sentence if scholars are only recapping a thesis. In other cases, though, when academic writers recap both a thesis and main points, knowledge summaries can expand to a paragraph or more. We think the pattern of thesis followed by main points is the most common, but it's possible that a knowledge summary could move from main points to thesis. Conclusions that repeat what's been said earlier are likely the most familiar and exemplify another piece of high school composition advice: "tell them what you're going to say; tell them; tell them what you've told them."

When this summary function occurs in scholarly conclusions, however, you may witness writers paying particular attention to marking out the limits of their knowledge, especially in sciences. In *Keeping Our Cool: Canada in a Warming World* (2008), Andrew Weaver notes that "Getting a yes or no from scientists is almost impossible. They may offer a yes, but will immediately follow it with a list of circumstances under which the yes is valid and invalid. Their answer will be framed in caveats, a discussion of uncertainty and what it means ..." (p. 29). Thus, we might expect to encounter a range of hedging or qualifying words, constructions that Janet Giltrow has identified as *limiting expressions*. Note the tables below, which have been adapted from Giltrow's book *Academic Writing* (2002, pp. 290–291):

# Limiting Expressions

### Limiting Adverbs and Auxiliaries

| | |
|---|---|
| allegedly | particularly |
| apparently | partly |
| appears | perhaps |
| approximately | possibly |
| could | presumably |
| evidently | probably |
| generally | rarely |
| hardly | roughly |
| may | seems |
| might | some |
| most | sometimes |
| often | somewhat |
| ostensibly | typically |
| ought to | usually |

### Limiting Metadiscursive Verbs

| | |
|---|---|
| I attempt | I sense |
| I believe | I speculate |
| I claim | I suppose |
| I feel | I think |
| I infer | |

### Limiting Prepositional Phrases

| | |
|---|---|
| at least | in part |
| for me | in the sense that |
| in one case / in this case / in some cases | to a lesser extent |
| in one sense | to me |

Using limiting expressions in academic writing defies the standard advice that is often given to students in basic composition courses: make bold and forceful claims. Conventional wisdom says that to waffle is bad! However, here are some real examples of scholars "hedging their bets" in academic conclusions. Limiting expressions are italicized.

The first sample is taken from biology:

# David Hamer, "Forest Fire's Influence on Yellow Hedysarum Habitat and Its Use by Grizzly Bears in Banff National Park, Alberta"

The high density of hedysarum shoots in the 2 burns *may* have no biological significance given that *typically* only a small fraction of available plants are dug by grizzly bears. Mattson (1997) found that biscuitroot density contributed little to distinguishing dug from undug biscuitroot sites in the Yellowstone ecosystem. However, *it is possible that* greater hedysarum density increases the *likelihood* of hedysarum growing or being abundant in specific microhabitat preferentially dug by bears, owing to a greater ease of digging or other factors. In addition, high hedysarum density *could* result in bears exposing more than one taproot per excavation. This *could be* important in late autumn when bears *appear to have* difficulty digging frozen ground. At this time bears *sometimes* enlarge a single excavation rather than break into the frozen topsoil of a new digging site, and can be observed enlarging the same excavation for > 1 h (Hamer and Herrero 1983, p. 138). [italics added]

*Source:* Hamer (1999, p. 1519)

The next sample comes from cultural studies in the humanities. Note the examples of nominalization: "indexicality," "transmutation," and "digitalization."

## Arild Fetveit, "Reality TV in the Digital Era: A Paradox in Visual Culture?"

I have *suggested* that reality TV, itself, *might be* read partly as a symptom of unsettled issues in this transmutation. More precisely, it *might* express a longing for a lost touch with reality, prompted by the undermining and problematizing of indexicality. Not only does reality TV powerfully reclaim the evidential quality of photography said to be lost after digitalization, it also *seems to be* obsessed with conveying a sense of connectedness, of contact with the world—a trait that also, albeit on a less tangible psychological level, *might seem to be* lost in an era where silicon has replaced the silver of Daguerre and Talbot. [italics added]

*Source:* Fetveit (1999, p. 800)

Alternatively, scholars may be equally concerned about expressing their sense of certainty. Andrew Weaver (2008) has something to say about this as well, noting the language used by the International Panel on Climate Change (IPCC) in its Fourth Assessment Report:

> Warming of the climate system is unequivocal, as is now evident from observations of increases in global average air and ocean temperatures, widespread melting of snow and ice, and rising global average sea level.
>
> Most of the observed increase in global average temperatures since the mid-20th century is *very likely* ... due to the observed increase in anthropogenic greenhouse gas concentrations. (pp. 34–35)

Weaver (2008) observes that "scientists rarely use words such as *unequivocal,* but when they do, they are absolutely certain" (p. 35). In presenting the passage above, he also notes that in the context of the IPCC report *"very likely"* has a statistical meaning, indicating a greater than 90 percent probability (p. 35). The IPCC report actually quantifies many markers of obviousness and limiting expressions, providing a percentage of assurance associated with particular words. Note the table below, adapted from Giltrow (2002), which emphasizes markers of obviousness (pp. 292–294):

---

## Markers of Obviousness

| | |
|---|---|
| certainly | of course |
| clearly | overwhelmingly |
| decidedly | surely |
| it is evident that | undoubtedly |
| obviously | without question |

---

The following example is taken from a conclusion in a paper from art studies. The emphasis here is on certainty, but do you see any examples of hedging?

---

## Ann Davis, "A Study in Modernism: The Group of Seven as an Unexpectedly Typical Case"

The Group of Seven were *clearly* conservative modernists, skeptical of the artistic modes of the past, dedicated to creating a new, autonomous Canadian aesthetic. While trumpeting stylistic autonomy in their painting, the group usually retained enough forms and colours to allow the viewer a representational reading. At the same time their ideology was *thoroughly* objective and intuitive, based on mystical principles. These traits *firmly* link the Group of Seven to European modernism. [italics added]

*Source:* Davis (1998, n.p.)

---

In the next example, from history, we see a more evenly distributed mix of hedging and certainty.

## David Peterson del Mar, "Pimping and Courtship: A 1940 Court Case from Northern British Columbia"

If one does not expect to find prostitutes and pimps in love, one does not expect to find them in small towns. British Columbians have *usually* associated rural areas with innocence and virtue, not vice and immorality. The court case explored here *suggests* that prostitution, pimping, and courtship violence has a history in urban and rural North America alike, although locale has *certainly* shaped the nature of that history. [italics added]

*Source:* del Mar (1998, p. 223)

## Exploring Solutions to a Problem

Looking beyond knowledge summaries, conclusions may also explore solutions to a problem that has been identified and demonstrated in the core of the paper.

## Elizabeth C. Pomeroy, "The Bully at Work: What Social Workers Can Do"

Workplace bullying is a silent disease within organizations that can reach epidemic proportions during tough economic times. When unemployment rates are high and jobs are at a premium, workers feel compelled to hold onto their livelihoods regardless of the stressful work conditions they may be experiencing. Employee-employer training and workshops on workplace bullying need to be provided to increase awareness of this problem. Professionals in employee assistance programs and human resources departments need to take complaints of bullying as seriously as allegations of harassment if substantial changes are to be made. Finally, social workers are in a pivotal position to provide assistance to employees who experience workplace bullying and, by doing so, can make a significant difference in the lives and careers of people who are working hard to make a living for themselves and their families.

*Source:* Pomeroy (2013, p. 7)

Here's another conclusion that presents solutions to a problem. The following is from an article on bobcat kill sites of white-tailed deer. Now that we're into the sciences, notice how heavy the nominalization becomes (see Chapter 8).

## N. J. Svoboda, J. L. Belant, D. E. Beyer, J. F. Duquette, and J. A. Martin, "Identifying Bobcat *Lynx rufus* Kill Sites Using a Global Positioning System"

We identified factors that can improve researchers' ability to detect bobcat kill sites before field investigation, and thereby reduce the overall field effort. When using cluster data to identify bobcat kill sites of white-tailed deer, we recommend investigating clusters when predator presence exceeds 50 locations. Further, we suggest that researchers should investigate clusters as soon as practical after cluster formation, if possible within seven days following cluster initiation. When applying this approach to other study areas, we recommend that researchers select a random sample of identified kill sites and evaluate the ability of the model to identify these kill sites. We further recommend refitting our top model using this data and reevaluating the ability of the model to correctly distinguish between kill sites and non-kill sites.

*Source:* Svoboda et al. (2013, p. 84)

## Call to Action

Conclusions may also present a call to action, encouraging readers to address a problem. At times, a call to action may be closely related to exploring solutions to a problem, but we suggest that the former tends to make a direct appeal to the reader. The following example is from mechanical engineering studies.

## S. Brown, "Rebranding Engineering"

Our message to the public, and most importantly to youth, is ours to craft. We need to ensure we are training the next generation to be risk takers, dynamic decision makers, and creative designers whose unique talents are appreciated—not taken as a commodity. As a profession we also need to show that we regularly partner with other professions; that our role is to complement and collaborate with artists, designers, lawyers, etc. to make the best products possible. Such connections drive business and innovation, and pull us from the sideline to the mainstream.

Consider the following actions to join as a united profession to rebrand ourselves and reverse the commoditizing of the profession.

- Be the face of engineering: Visit schools and after-school clubs and tell your stories of why you choose your profession and who you are—"I love soccer," "I read all the Harry Potter books," "I was a Girl Scout."
- Pay attention to your language: Just as the engineering societies are doing, recognize your need to tie engineering to life's problems that you solve and people you help. "I work for an automotive supplier. Our antilock brakes save over 100 lives a day by avoiding collisions."
- Tell friends why you vote as you do: Know who supports public education, supports infrastructure projects, etc.
- Tell adult friends what you do, too: Your neighbor may be contracting other engineers as commodities—you'll make a difference in places you didn't expect.
- Treat the youth that you know as adults and teach them rational debate, inquiry, and a love for exploration: From a young age, my grandfather would engage me in debate, believing in me enough to challenge my thoughts and expect me to challenge his. He showed me how creative and innovative mechanical engineering is. Do the same for a potential next generation mechanical engineer you know.

*Source:* Brown (2011, p. 45)

Here's another call to action, this time from a music educators' journal:

# Britain Scott and Christiane Harrassowitz, "Beyond Beethoven and the Boyz: Women's Music in Relation to History and Culture"

We enthusiastically encourage our colleagues to consider how they might include more women's music in their classes. We do not believe that instructors must be experts in gender analysis to address topics like those we included in our class. The resources we list in the Resources sidebar, although by no means a comprehensive bibliography of relevant materials, provide a wealth of information and ideas for class topics and activities.

*Source:* Scott & Harrassowitz (2004, p. 55)

The next example is from counselling psychology:

## June Slakov and Mary Leslie, "A Creative Model for a Post-Treatment Group for Women with Cancer"

We cannot take away the uncertainty or fear that characterizes this time after treatment [of women with cancer], but we can support the process of confronting the fear and facing one's mortality. We can introduce skills and a perspective to help anchor the participants in present reality and to hold uncertainty in a transformed way. While the experience of cancer is different for each woman, "borderland" will be part of the rest of their lives, as the possibility of recurrence is always with them.

*Source:* Slakov & Leslie (2003, p. 14)

## Providing a Statement of Relevance

As previously noted, statements of relevance may occur in introductions, but they are perhaps most at home in conclusions. If introductions often lead *into* a topic by providing contextual information that functions as background, conclusions frequently lead *out* by providing contextual information that tells us why we should care about the author's research.

Thus, we could say that statements of relevance recontextualize topic and thesis by pointing toward a bigger, *moral* picture that lies beyond the immediate research domain (Giltrow, 2002, pp. 15, 314). In this sense, statements of relevance tend to reveal a concern for the collective welfare. Such gestures bridge the gap between highly focused or specialized scholarly activity and the lives of people beyond the academy.

The following example is from political science. It begins with a summary of the knowledge claim, and then moves to a statement of relevance:

## Michael Orsini, "The Politics of Naming, Blaming, and Claiming: HIV, Hepatitis C, and the Emergence of Blood Activism in Canada"

This article views the emergence of blood-tainted blood activism in Canada, especially among victims of Hepatitis C, through the lens of social movement theory. While blood-tainted victims were a difficult constituency to mobilize, they did so successfully and in a short time, securing not only compensation victories for victims but influencing the decision to overhaul Canada's blood system. This article sought to expand our understanding of public inquiries as sites for contestation over meaning. Inquiries not only provide a forum for groups to express their interest, but as Jane Jensen has explained, they also contribute to the ways in which these interests are re-articulated.... While victims were "successful" in securing compensation—a "textbook" outcome—they also succeeded in creating a collective identity for tainted-blood victims and altering public notions of the proper role of "sick" people in society.

*Source:* Orsini (2002, p. 497–498)

The next example is from composition studies:

## Wendy Bishop, "Suddenly Sexy: Creative Non-Fiction Rear-ends Composition"

I believe the recent and continuing discussions taking place between composition and creative writing at, on, and about [the issue of creative non-fiction] have the possibility of infusing our classrooms with needed energy and offer a chance for teachers and students, together, to sideshadow the future in a manner that will allow them to discover what they don't yet know, to clarify what they don't yet understand, to preserve what they value, and to share their discoveries with others while writing essays that matter.

*Source:* Bishop (2003, p. 273)

## Presenting Opportunities for Further Research

The emphasis in some conclusions is on suggestions for further research. In this sense, papers may end as they begin, by identifying a *knowledge deficit.* For example, in "The Paradox of Probation: Community Supervision in the Age of Mass Incarceration," M. S. Phelps identifies a number of areas that researchers could tackle. This sample comes from legal and policy studies:

---

### M. S. Phelps, "The Paradox of Probation: Community Supervision in the Age of Mass Incarceration"

Second, this work suggests that scholars of punishment still have much to learn about probation and its role in the criminal justice system. Focusing on the paradox of probation model, research might examine in more detail the varied state structures that affect central institutional practices. For example, scholars might further investigate how the sentencing process is affected by larger structural factors and how these state characteristics in turn influence what kinds of cases are sentenced to probation versus incarceration. Scholars might also research how the bureaucratic structure of probation shapes institutional decision making around supervision practices and revocation policies. Scholars interested in the emergence of the discourse around "evidence-based practices" might examine how such practices are popularized in the context of probation supervision and when and why such practices are adopted by probation departments.

*Source:* Phelps (2013, p. 73)

---

The following example comes from counselling psychology:

---

### Shann R. Ferch and Marleen I. Ramsey, "Sacred Conversation: A Spiritual Response to Unavoidable Suffering"

Although clients have consistently reported experiencing a greater sense of personal development and relief from their suffering, we re-emphasize that empirical studies are needed to investigate the effectiveness of empathy, intentional forgiveness, and Sacred Conversation in relieving unavoidable suffering. Systematic quantitative and qualitative studies investigating the role of Sacred Conversation will bring greater understanding to how the approach enhances an individual's ability to create transcendent meaning from suffering and bring relief to physical and psychological pain. Survey research delineating the nature of this approach, along with experimental research measuring outcomes of the approach with regard to curative effects in anxiety, depression, stress, anger, and immunodeficiency levels are warranted. Phenomenological studies revealing the meaning of the approach for individuals and families are also warranted. Such studies will provide an important bridge toward clinical discernment with regard to suffering, emotion, and transcendent meaning.

*Source:* Ferch & Ramsey (2003, p. 25)

## Additional Features in Conclusions

The preceding list of concluding features is not exhaustive. We encourage you to watch for additional rhetorical elements in scholarly conclusions. For example, depending on journal style, conclusions may carry their own subheading: "Conclusion" or "Summary." Further, it is interesting to note that questions may have a role in conclusions, underscoring the open-ended nature of academic inquiry. You may even see conclusions that begin with their own epigraph. As we move from core paragraphs to conclusions, we generally leave the valley floors of heavy reported speech. Indeed, because conclusions invite high-level generalization, they open sustained space for the author's own voice. Nevertheless, we may still encounter passages of reported speech with documentation.

# The Sequence of Rhetorical Moves in Academic Conclusions

As is the case with introductions, the rhetorical features in scholarly conclusions reveal a familiar sequence of "moves." For example, while you will commonly see that conclusions begin with knowledge summaries, it is also common to encounter opportunities for further research as a final concluding gesture. Yet there is room for flexibility. The flow of concluding rhetorical features can be determined through your own judgment calls based on topic and disciplinary norms. Here are two potential patterns:

Restatement of Thesis → Recap of Main Points → Statement of Relevance → Call to Action → Opportunities for Further Research

Or

Restatement of Thesis → Solutions to a Problem → Call to Action → Statement
of Relevance

## Seeing Conclusions in Their Entirety

The following passages present full conclusions to papers. Block and label the
flow of rhetorical features in each.

---

### Barbara Zecchi, "All About Mothers: Pronatalist Discourses in Contemporary Spanish Cinema"

This brief survey of maternal paradigms in contemporary Spanish cinema [has
illustrated] that women are still subjected to traditional values without any
real alternative to the patriarchal archetype, and that motherhood is still generally conceived in Spanish society as the ultimate fulfillment for a woman.
All the films I have analyzed (with the sole exception of *El milagro de P. Tinto*)
coincide in representing the birth of a child as the only meaningful event in
a woman's life. Moreover, all the movies ... present motherhood and work as
antithetical realities, since all the mothers we have seen belong to the domestic
sphere and do not show any professional aspiration.

In a social context of pronatalism, such a vindication of maternity not only contributes to the return of a traditional model of womanhood, but also transforms
all the "yermas"—non-mothers—into otherness: negative (or absent) models. As
happened during the Franco regime, the overriding concern about depopula-
tion "mark[s] women off as a separate species and identif[ies] them exclusively as
mothers whose offspring would check the tendency towards declining birth rates
and thus prevent the decadence of Spain" (Nash, 1991, p. 160).

However, in democratic Spain there is also room for "minority reports" and
the hegemonic pronatalist and pro-domestic discourse that attributes a low
birth rate exclusively to women's insertion in the workplace, and that invokes a
return of women to the domestic sphere, is challenged by a variety of different
perspectives....

To conclude, Iciar Bollain's film *Flores de otro mundo* (1998) is worth mentioning as an exceptional case in the landscape of contemporary Spanish cinema, since it departs from traditional discourses on maternity and presents a
perfect synthesis of and reflection upon the alternative to domesticity that I
have illustrated above. Bollain's "female gaze" offers a future full of hope and
optimism; a future in which "women's choices are dictated by personal dig-
nity" and are not bound to patriarchal conventions or social opportunism, a
future in which women's solidarity has the power to overcome cultural differences and defeat racism.

*Source:* Zecchi (2005, pp. 158–159)

This next conclusion is from a paper in a nursing journal. Which rhetorical
features do you see?

## M. Gawthrop, "Travelling with Babies and Toddlers"

Package holidays can be a safe and positive experience for the whole family
and health professionals have an important role in preparing and advising
families prior to travel.[9]

However, parents may underestimate the hazards associated with more
exotic package holiday destinations and can be unaware of specific health
risks. For example, they may not realise young children with malaria are likely
to become more severely ill than adults and older children.

Without being alarmist, practice nurses need to provide realistic, consistent advice, encompassing nationally recognised recommendations. The ability
to clarify information, often diplomatically, is also required. Undertaking a
collaborative risk assessment is an integral part of enabling parents to make
informed choices about their family's health.

*Source:* Gawthrop (2012)

The following example is again from the field of nursing.

# D. Dews and B. Bostock-Cox,
# "Nurses in Commissioning Groups:
# Exciting Challenge or Poison Chalice?"

Since the late 1980s practice nurses have been an integral part of the primary healthcare team and practice nursing has become a recognised career choice. Practice nurses are experienced clinicians, capable of critical thinking and innovation, who strive to deliver good quality, evidence based, cost effective care in an ever changing healthcare landscape. Practice nurses often hear first-hand from patients their experiences of the current healthcare systems, both positive and negative, and this information could provide a valuable contribution to discussions around service development. For many years practice nurses have adapted to change with integrity and dedication for the benefit of patients. It is important that the nursing voice is heard, our input valued and that we remain an integral part of future developments.

CCGs [Clinical Commissioning Groups] are a fact of life. Criticising decisions once they are made will be pointless. Nurses need to get ready to meet the challenge of the brave new world of the NHS [National Health Service] by making sure they are part of the decision-making processes. The NHS has a history of hierarchical structures, but we should not allow subtle bullying, the doctor-nurse game or sexual politics to reduce the potential we have to make a real impact on the NHS of the future.

We should celebrate the opportunities that are now presenting to us and prepare to face them, head on. We should look to our leaders to help us develop the necessary negotiating, leadership and business skills that will allow to us to be fully functioning and contributing members of the CCG. We should show our colleagues on the CCGs that we can and do effectively contribute to their decisions and we should use our influence as CCG board members to show exactly why there should be no question as to the relevance of our position on it.

*Source:* Dews & Bostock-Cox (2012)

Next up is a conclusion from the field of education.

## T. Loveland, "Professional Development Plans for Technology Education: Accountability-Based Applications at the Secondary and Post-Secondary Level"

Why would continuous improvement and learning be applicable to technology educators? As a field that teaches about technological changes, it is important for educators to keep up with those technological changes. One method to keep up with change is through professional development training, whether offered locally, statewide, or through national associations like ITEEA. By writing professional development plans that link performance-based goals to standards and specific training, technology teachers and postsecondary faculty will go a long way toward ensuring that their students are taught through standards-based methods and content, thereby leading to effective student learning and increased technological literacy.

*Source:* Loveland (2012, p. 31)

The next example is also from the discipline of education. This summary is short but strong.

## P. J. Katsioloudis and M. V. Jones, "Green Transportation for a Green Earth"

A quote found in a Greenpeace advertisement states: "It wasn't the Exxon Valdez captain's driving that caused the Alaskan oil spill. It was yours" (ADEC, 1993). It is vital that we promote the protection of the environment and strengthen the laws that prohibit waste dumping so the surroundings stay clean and healthy; otherwise, the direct output of this concept—the existence of humanity in the years to come—will be questionable.

*Source:* Katsioloudis & Jones (2012, p. 24)

Here is one from acoustical physics.

## N. N. Kanev, A. A. Livshits, and H. H. Möller, "Acoustics of the Great Hall of the Moscow State Conservatory after Reconstruction in 2010–2011"

The reconstruction of the Grand Hall of the Moscow Conservatory in 2010–2011 did not have a significant impact on its acoustics. The acoustic quality of the hall remained at the same high level, which has been confirmed by acoustic parameter measurements before and after renovation. Small differences in some parameters at low and high frequencies can be interpreted as positive, since they made it possible to balance the frequency response of these parameters. Performers and listeners appreciated the acoustics of the Great Hall after renovation. No one noted a deterioration in the acoustic characteristics.

It should be noted that over time, there may be some changes in the acoustic parameters of the hall, primarily because of stabilization of the temperature and humidity in the hall; elapse of the first rapid aging phase of individual building materials (paints, fillers, adhesives, and primers); release of excess moisture from wooden structures, cement-sand screeds, and concrete; and final nail fixation and lapping of nail and self-drilling compounds in wooden structures. The problem of acoustic evolution of halls after construction or reconstruction has not been sufficiently covered in the current literature and is of independent interest. In connection with this, a series of measurements of acoustic parameters of the Great Hall at six month intervals is planned. These measurements should also record the presence or absence of differences in acoustic parameters of audience halls in summer and in winter, when the temperature and humidity characteristics of fresh air differ greatly.

*Source:* Kanev, Livshits, & Möller (2013, pp. 367–368)

The following conclusion is from an early medieval history journal.

## S. Ashley, "What Did Louis the Pious See in the Night Sky? A New Interpretation of the Astronomer's Account of Halley's Comet, 837"

Does it matter exactly what two men saw in the night sky almost 1200 years ago? I think it does, not least because it shows that new knowledge can be won from even the most well-mined texts, especially when they strike up conversations in places outside those they normally socialize in, like historical astronomy or T'ang Chinese records. But it also shows that the most transparent empirical claims of texts that have been edited, studied and used for generations can never be taken for granted. But neither can those claims be rejected out of hand. Perhaps this should be obvious. And yet generations have simply assumed that the Astronomer knew what he was talking about when he said he saw what we now call Halley's Comet that spring evening. It appears that he did not. Yet he also managed to describe accurately what he thought he witnessed over Aachen, and he succeeded to such an extent that twelve centuries later his work continues to inspire historians and astronomers to look upwards into the night sky.

*Source:* Ashley (2013, p. 49)

The conclusion below is drawn from a journal dealing with the history of science and medicine.

## H. Higton, "Instruments and Illustration: The Use of Images in Edmund Gunter's *De Sectore et Radio*"

As we have seen, instruments are illustrated in many different ways in Gunter's *De Sectore et Radio*. They appear as schematic diagrams, reduced to their most basic form, in order to demonstrate the mathematical principles according to which they work. They feature in simplified form in illustrations designed to demonstrate their use out in the field, whether for measuring the height of tall objects, for observing the angles subtended by the stars or for calculating the angle of an inclined plane. They grace the elaborately decorated title page, assisting in a commentary on the role of different instruments in the mathematical culture of early modern England. They are reproduced as fine copies of the real thing, engraved by the foremost instrument maker of the day. And they can be made in paper from separate parts provided for their construction. It is rare to discover so many different ways in which a book can be illustrated. Perhaps the close interaction of Gunter with the instrument makers, and his preoccupation with making the understanding of how mathematical instruments work accessible to a wider range of users than had been the case, led him to pay close attention to the methods by which diagrams of instruments could be used in varied ways to meet the needs of the text at a particular point. What is certainly true is that such a project could not have been undertaken without the symbiotic relationship between mathematician and maker that had begun to flourish in the seventeenth century, and which shows itself in the enhancement of books on instruments to such a fine level, beginning with Gunter but continuing throughout the seventeenth and eighteenth centuries.

*Source:* Higton (2013, pp. 199–200)

The field of occupational therapy provides the next example.

## C. Andersson, M. Eklund, V. Sundh, K. Thundal, and F. Spak, "Women's Patterns of Everyday Occupations and Alcohol Consumption"

To summarize, we found a strong correlation between problematic alcohol consumption and patterns of everyday occupations characterized by low engagement in leisure activities and a large amount of spare time. When planning for preventive and treatment actions, the findings provide new options and ideas. On a societal level, one example would be providing alcohol-free activity areas. On the individual level, another example would be finding suitable and engaging activities in several everyday domains, as opposed to focusing on specific risk factors. When supporting women in not developing additional negative alcohol consumption habits, discussing the role of alcohol consumption in the performance of different everyday activities could prove to be of great importance. Occupational therapists, with a specific knowledge of engagement in occupations, on both individual and population levels, could contribute in this endeavour.

*Source:* Andersson et al. (2012, p. 236)

In this next conclusion, watch for nominalization and reported speech amid the larger concluding rhetorical features.

# A. J. McGowan and K. M. Strang, "Ammonoids and Mash-ups: The Potential of Geobrowsers to Enhance Public Awareness of Geodiversity Sites and Objects in Their Spatial Context"

The most interesting questions aren't around individual nuggets of data, but rather how we can corral it to create an information architecture which serves up the whole picture.

—Ben Goldacre Bad Science Blog (2011)

The quotation above sums up the power of data integration and the need to make tools available that make the integration of heterogeneous data types possible to a wider user group. Geobrowsers offer a powerful, low-cost means of introducing geodiversity sites to a wide audience through a familiar medium, where these data are spatially-explicit. Geobrowsers are more limited in their capabilities than semantic web-based solutions but their usability and functionality for displaying spatial data makes them ideal for data with a strong spatial context. As well as making access to specialist data sets easier, geobrowsers can allow researchers to validate spatially attributed data without the use of expensive GIS programs. Without such tools, the release of spatially attributed data lays data-providing organizations open to the charge of suffering from data-rich information-poor syndrome (Ward et al. 1986).

By offering motivated, but non-specialist, users the tools and information to tackle geodiversity projects related to particular areas geobrowsers could help a wider group of people experience geodiversity as a high-level, absorbing "flow" activity on an equal footing with other areas of natural history that benefit from well-organized, skilled and determined voluntary efforts (Butterfield & Long 2001).

*Source:* McGowan & Strang (2012, p. 309)

## The Jenna Files

Notes to self:

- I'm so glad mid-terms are over. That was a brutal three weeks. There's light at the end of the tunnel!
- My core paragraphs are holding together better now.
- For my conclusion, I understand that I can do more than just recap the thesis and main points. I can have solutions to a problem, a call to action, and a statement of relevance. I'm working on this, but I know my conclusion isn't there yet, but at least I can work with my instructor's comments and make improvements.

### Jenna's Draft Conclusion

In conclusion, this paper is focused[1] on the relationship between cyberbullying and suicide among teenage girls. While technology has rapidly developed, the negative sides, such as cyberbullying, have not been researched very much despite the fact that cyberbullying is now known as a social issue. Moreover, the occurrence of cyberbullying is on the rise since more adolescents have their own telecommunication devices (Hinduja and Patchin, 2011, p. 23). The negative effects of cyberbullying have been spotlighted by researchers because cyberbullying can cause suicidal thoughts and behaviors.[2] As a result, researchers and social organizations have been trying to solve these problems.[3] Some of the solutions Hinduja and Patchin (2011) suggested that students, parents, and educators could try in order to reduce the occurrence of cyberbullying were: students should let their parents know which websites they use and trust parents and teachers; parents should put more effort into communicating with their children; and educators should keep "a safe and respectful school climate" (p. 24-26). However, because victims of cyberbullying often feel reluctant to report incidents of bullying to their guardians, and because most parents are not aware if their children are being bullied, and because preventing cyberbullying is hard for educators when students are out of school, the amount of cyberbullying is increasing. In the face of this increase, there is a need for more research and new practical solutions to deal with the reluctance of victims, the unawareness of parents, and the lack of empowerment of educators.[4]

**Instructor comments:**

1. Reconsider tense. You're wrapping up. This paper "has focused on."
2. It sounds like you're trying to recap the argument here, but you could do that more clearly. Try to more explicitly recap your thesis and main points from the core.
3. You're moving on to solutions to a problem. It might be good to have a paragraph break here.
4. Ending with a call for further research (that is, a knowledge deficit). Good move, but you seem to be missing an opportunity for a statement of relevance.

# Ideas for Further Study

1. Think about the precise way in which you might wish to recap the argument in your paper, especially with regard to limiting expressions and markers of obviousness. Also think about employing other rhetorical features typically found in academic conclusions, such as exploring solutions to a problem, statements of relevance, and questions for further research.
2. Identify the rhetorical features in the conclusion to one of the articles in your research notebook.

# References

Andersson, C., Eklund, M., Sundh, V., Thundal, K., & Spak, F. (2012). Women's patterns of everyday occupations and alcohol consumption. *Scandinavian Journal of Occupational Therapy, 19*(3), 225–238. doi:10.3109/11038128.2010.527013

Ashley, S. (2013). What did Louis the Pious see in the night sky? A new interpretation of the Astronomer's account of Halley's Comet, 837. *Early Medieval Europe, 21*(1), 27–49. doi:10.1111/emed.12008

Bishop, W. (2003). Suddenly sexy: Creative non-fiction rear-ends composition. *College English, 65*(3), 257–275.

Brown, S. (2011). Rebranding engineering. *Mechanical Engineering, 133*(12), 42–45.

Davis, A. (1998). A study in modernism: The Group of Seven as an unexpectedly typical case. *Journal of Canadian Studies, 33*(1), 108–121.

del Mar, D. P. (1998). Pimping and courtship: A 1940 court case from northern British Columbia. In R. W. Sandwell (Ed.), *Beyond the city limits: Rural history in British Columbia* (pp. 212–224). Vancouver: UBC Press.

Dews, D., & Bostock-Cox, B. (2012). Nurses in commissioning groups: Exciting challenge or poison chalice? *Practice Nurse, 42*(4), 34–39.

Ferch, S. R., & Ramsey, M. I. (2003). Sacred conversation: A spiritual response to unavoidable suffering. *Canadian Journal of Counselling, 37*(1), 16–27.

Fetveit, A. (1999). Reality TV in the digital era: A paradox in visual culture? *Media, Culture & Society, 21*, 787–804.

Gawthrop, M. (2012). Travelling with babies and toddlers. *Practice Nurse, 42*(2), 26–30.

Giltrow, J. (2002). *Academic writing: Writing and reading in the disciplines* (3rd ed.). Peterborough: Broadview Press.

Hamer, D. (1999). Forest fire's influence on yellow hedysarum habitat and its use by grizzly bears in Banff National Park, Alberta. *Canadian Journal of Zoology, 77*(10), 1513–1520.

Higton, H. (2013). Instruments and illustration: The use of images in Edmund Gunter's *De Sectore et Radio. Early Science & Medicine, 18*(1/2), 180–200. doi:10.1163/15733823-0007A0007

Kanev, N. N., Livshits, A. A., & Möller, H. H. (2013). Acoustics of the Great Hall of the Moscow State Conservatory after reconstruction in 2010–2011. *Acoustical Physics, 59*(3), 361–368. doi:10.1134/S1063771013030068

Katsioloudis, P. J., & Jones, M. V. (2012). Green transportation for a green Earth. *Technology & Engineering Teacher, 71*(7), 19–25.

Loveland, T. (2012). Professional development plans for technology education: Accountability-based applications at the secondary and post-secondary level. *Technology & Engineering Teacher, 71*(7), 26–31.

McGowan, A. J., & Strang, K. M. (2012). Ammonoids and mash-ups: The potential of geobrowsers to enhance public awareness of geodiversity sites and objects in their spatial context. *Scottish Geographical Journal, 128*(3/4), 304–311. doi:10.1080/14702541.2012.725857

Orsini, M. (2002). The politics of naming, blaming, and claiming: HIV, Hepatitis C, and the emergence of blood activism in Canada. *Canadian Journal of Political Science, 35*(3), 475–498.

Phelps, M. S. (2013). The paradox of probation: Community supervision in the age of mass incarceration. *Law & Policy, 35*(1/2), 51–80. doi:10.1111/lapo.12002

Pomeroy, E. C. (2013, January). The bully at work: What social workers can do. *Social Work, 58*(1), 5–8. doi:10.1093/sw/sws055

Scott, B., & Harrassowitz, C. (2004). Beyond Beethoven and the Boyz: Women's music in relation to history and culture. *Music Educators Journal, 90*(4), 50–56.

Slakov, J., & Leslie, M. (2003). A creative model for a post-treatment group for women with cancer. *Canadian Journal of Counselling and Psychotherapy / Revue Canadienne de Counseling et de Psychothérapie, 37*(1), 6–15. Retrieved from http://cjc-rcc.ucalgary.ca/cjc/index.php/rcc/article/view/225

Svoboda, N. J., Belant, J. L., Beyer, D. E., Duquette, J. F., & Martin, J. A. (2013). Identifying bobcat *Lynx rufus* kill sites using a global positioning system. *Wildlife Biology, 19*(1), 78–86. doi:10.2981/12-031

Weaver, A. (2008). *Keeping our cool: Canada in a warming world.* Toronto: Penguin Canada.

Zecchi, B. (2005). All about mothers: Pronatalist discourses in contemporary Spanish cinema. *College Literature, 32*(1), 146–164.

# CHAPTER 8

# Freight-Train Nouns:
## The Density of Scientific Writing

> Every great advance in science has issued from
> a new audacity of imagination.
>
> —John Dewey

Scientific discourse has a reputation for being one of the more challenging forms of academic writing. It often involves highly technical language, numbers, graphs, equations, and tables that are unintelligible to the layperson. Some of us may feel as though scientists speak another language. Nevertheless, on the whole, we tend to tolerate and even respect such difficulty because we sense that something important is at stake. The goal of much science writing, after all, is to reveal patterns in nature, and that activity can have real and immediate significance in our lives. Further, scientific reports present data and interpretation in an effort to persuade others to accept or reject the hypotheses under consideration. Thus, while the humanities often struggle to justify their existence, science and technology research tends to be more firmly entrenched as a funding priority in universities.

> Whereas the goal of writing in the humanities may be to speculate philosophically on the human condition, the goal of much science writing is to reveal patterns in nature. Scientists want to let nature speak for itself.

Given their search for an "unmediated" version of reality, scientists place a particularly high value on objectivity or empiricism (the pursuit of knowledge by observation and experimentation), and try to place careful controls on how knowledge is generated. Scientists want to say, with reasonable certainty, that something—some pattern, or relationship, or fact—exists "out there," on its own, and their language reveals this desire. More than any other form of academic discourse, science writing tries to eliminate subjectivity. Thus, while self-disclosure may be an increasingly popular rhetorical gesture in the humanities and social sciences, it is not a part of the rhetoric of the natural sciences. In research articles, biologists, for example, will not write about their personal background; instead, they will explain their methods—methods that others may, hypothetically at least, test and repeat.

The rhetoric of science has received considerable attention. Groundbreaking books such as *Laboratory Life: The Construction of Scientific Facts* (Latour & Woolgar, 1986) and *Opening Pandora's Box: A Sociological Analysis of Scientists' Discourse* (Gilbert & Mulkay, 1984) demonstrate that academic knowledge-making, even in the core sciences, is a form of storytelling. Gilbert and Mulkay, for example, contend that the cultural values of the sciences result in an "empiricist's repertoire" that involves an array of textual or *stylistic* practices. Superficially, perhaps, these practices downplay the role of the researching self, yet, at a deeper level, they also suggest that knowledge-making is a social phenomenon, a rhetorical activity that hinges, in part, on language use. Such studies show that the researcher is a highly socialized being who constructs knowledge claims according to disciplinary customs and expectations.

Most of the articles that we have looked at so far belong to the humanities and social sciences. These articles have consisted of introductions, cores, and conclusions, but despite these broad similarities, the authors have exercised a lot of narrative freedom. They have told their stories in different ways, using different methods of development, varying degrees of self-disclosure, and so on. In the natural sciences, however, where academic writers often want to describe a controlled investigation or empirical study, a more rigidly structured kind of storytelling is evident. Scientists who want to explain the results of an experiment adhere to what is called the "report format," which has a predetermined narrative structure.

The *Publication Manual of the American Psychological Association* (6th ed.) (American Psychological Association, 2010) recognizes the report of empirical studies as a distinct *type* of scholarly article, one that "typically consist[s] of distinct sections that reflect the stages in the research process" (p. 10). Scientific reports give unprecedented attention to a detailed, step-by-step account of how knowledge was generated. Perhaps the most noticeable sign of the report genre is a series of subheadings in a sequence something like this:

1. Abstract
2. Introduction
3. Methods (may be called Materials and Methods)
4. Results
5. Discussion
6. References

In the remaining portions of this discussion, we will touch on a few of the rhetorical structures that are evident in scientific reports.

# Front Matter

## Title and Title Page

Unlike many titles in the humanities and social sciences, which often contain an allusive phrase as part of a two-part title, titles in scientific reports tend to simply reflect the factual content of the report in a straightforward manner, often in fewer than a dozen words. Such titles contain keywords that other researchers and Internet search engines recognize. Note the directness of the following examples:

- Climate change in the North Pacific region over the past three centuries
- Green tea inhibits vascular endothelial growth factor (VEGF) induction in human breast cancer cells
- Lead in grain size fractions of road deposited sediment
- Mercury, zinc, and copper accumulation in mangrove sediments surrounding a large landfill in southeast Brazil
- Properties of a fetal multipotent neural stem cell (NEP cell)
- Changes in soil physical characteristics during transition from intensive tillage to direct seeding
- Residential segregation of visible minorities in Canada's gateway cities

- Songbird community composition versus forest rotation age in Saskatchewan boreal mixed-wood forest
- Bioavailability of heavy metals in soils amended with sewage sludge
- Reviving central Brandon in the early twenty-first century

Compared to titles in the humanities and social sciences, these titles are "missing" more than just an allusive phrase. They are also missing an explicit abstraction, providing only the research site. In the sciences, where disciplinary problems are often agreed-on, prestige abstractions or Big Issues may be implicit. Note some possible abstractions that hover around a few of the research sites listed above.

- Mercury, zinc, and copper accumulation in mangrove sediments surrounding a large landfill in southeast Brazil [*environmental pollution*]
- Changes in soil physical characteristics during transition from intensive tillage to direct seeding [*agricultural ecology*]
- Reviving central Brandon in the early twenty-first century [*urban renewal*]

See the *CSE Manual* or other style guide for detailed instructions on title pages. Students should check with their instructor for further guidelines.

## Running Head

The running head is a shortened form of the complete title. It is identified as such on the title page and reappears at the top right of each page of the paper. The following examples show the reduction of the complete title to a running head.

---

**Title:** Winter severity, survival, and cause-specific mortality of female white-tailed deer in north-central Minnesota

**Running head:** Survival of white-tailed deer

**Title:** Effect of fall-applied manure practices on runoff, sediment, and nutrient surface transport from silage corn in south coastal British Columbia

**Running head:** Manure effects on runoff, sediment, and nutrient transport

**Title:** Breeding bird response to midstory hardwood reduction in Florida sandhill longleaf pine forests

**Running head:** Bird response to midstory hardwood reduction

## Abstract

The abstract, placed after the title page and before the first page of text, provides readers and other researchers with a summary of the purpose of the report, the data presented, and the major conclusions. In presenting the abstract clearly and concisely (about 200 words), researchers generally use the past tense to describe actions related to the carrying out of the experiment or research (for example, "we developed," "I investigated," "we compared," "we estimated," "I included," "we recorded," "I identified," "we gathered," "we classified," "I documented," and so on) and the present tense to describe results, conclusions, or the activity of the paper itself (for example, "we detail," "we review," "we propose," "we support," and so on). Although published scholarship contains abstracts using the personal pronouns *I* or *we* to refer to the researchers themselves (but not in the more general editorial sense), and abstracts that adopt a less personal approach (for example, "the data suggest," "these results indicate," "this study shows," and so on), individual instructors may prefer abstracts without the use of *I* or *we* (see "Passive Voice," below).

Note the various features in the following abstract for an article by Ross et al. (2002) entitled "Abundance and Distribution of Breeding Waterfowl in the Great Clay Belt of Northern Ontario." Although key words are not part of the abstract, in journal articles they are usually listed right after the abstract and before the start of the introduction.

# R. J. Ross et al., "Abundance and Distribution of Breeding Waterfowl in the Great Clay Belt of Northern Ontario"

## Abstract

The abundance and distribution of breeding waterfowl in the Great Clay Belt of northern Ontario was determined through helicopter surveys of 177 fixed plots (2 x 2 km each) during the nest initiation periods from 1988 to 1990. This area has higher fertility, flat topography, high water table and better access than the surrounding Boreal Forest, and therefore has greater potential for increased waterfowl production through habitat management. Overall breeding density averaged 112.5 indicated breeding pairs per 100 km$^2$, 68% being of the four most common species [Mallard (*Anas platyrhynchos*), Ring-necked Duck (*Aythya collaris*), American Black Duck (*Anas rubripes*), and common Goldeneye (*Bucephala clangula*)]; 13 other species were encountered. The average total of breeding waterfowl for the region was estimated at 59,330 pairs. Distributions of the species were related to ecodistrict and to surficial geology. The more northerly of the two main ecodistricts had higher densities of American Black Ducks, Ring-necked Ducks, Common Goldeneyes, and Canada Geese (*Branta canadensis*). Mallard and Hooded Merganser (*Lophodytes cucullatus*) distributions correlated with presence of surficial clay and moraines, respectively. Less common species including Green-winged Teal (*Anas crecca*) and American Wigeon (*Anas Americana*) appeared to be concentrated in smaller-scaled habitat features (beaver pond sequences and estuarine marshes, respectively). Results generally agreed with those of earlier Clay Belt surveys. Total breeding density of waterfowl is slightly higher than that of surrounding regions.

*Key Words:* ducks, populations, habitat, boreal, forest, Ontario.

*Source:* Ross et al. (2002, p. 42)

# Introduction

Introductions in scientific reports serve similar purposes to introductions in reports in the humanities and social sciences: they set the stage for what follows, define the subject of the report, and answer the question: Why was this study performed?

## Setting the Stage

The opening sentences of Stephen Herrero and Andrew Higgins's "Human Injuries Inflicted by Bears in British Columbia: 1960–97" (1999) sound very much like an opening we might encounter in the humanities or social sciences, which sets the stage for what follows: "In 1967, 2 young women were killed during a 24-hour period by different grizzly bears in Glacier National Park, Montana. These were the first fatal grizzly bear–inflicted attacks in the park" (p. 209). In fact, these first two sentences could easily launch an essay about the psychology of fear, the sociology of outdoor recreation, or even a personal essay about surviving a bear attack.

In science writing, however, the introduction quickly focuses on the problem under investigation, often by providing a condensed history of pertinent research in the same or similar area of study through a *tradition of inquiry* (see Chapter 5 and below). As in the humanities and social sciences, researchers may go on to identify a *knowledge deficit* or gap (see Chapter 5) that will signal the importance of their own study.

## Traditions of Inquiry

As we have already seen in the discussion on traditions of inquiry in Chapter 5, researchers are under an obligation to acknowledge what has previously been published relating to their study. The tradition of inquiry is, in a sense, a very brief literature review that contextualizes the study undertaken by acknowledging foundational work on which the present study is built. This part of the introduction may be densely packed with citations, as in the following example. In science writing, there is a convention, perhaps for purposes of economy, to present a tradition of inquiry through paraphrase and non-integrated reference. Note that the results of research, and not the researchers themselves, are foregrounded through the use of non-integrated reference:

## A. Wall and J. Heiskanen, "Effect of Air-Filled Porosity and Organic Matter Concentration of Soil on Growth of *Picea abies* Seedlings after Transplanting"

Soil aeration is positively related to air-filled porosity (AFP) and negatively to water content (Glinski & Stepniewski 1985). For mineral soils, an AFP of 10% is usually presented as the minimum limit for gaseous diffusion and 10-15% for root respiration and growth, although these values may actually vary in situ from 5 to 30% (Wesseling & Wijk 1957, Vomocil & Flocker 1961, Magnusson 1992, Xu et al. 1992, Zou et al. 2001). In organic soils, such as peat, optimum AFP for tree seedlings may even be over 40% (Puustjärvi 1977, Lähde & Savonen 1983, Heiskanen 1995). Seedlings may tolerate waterlogging for several days (Zaerr 1983). Owing to rain or irrigation and evapotranspiration, the actual in situ AFP in the growth medium varies over time.

*Source:* Wall & Heiskanen (2003, p. 344)

On the other hand, when presenting a tradition of inquiry in an article on human injuries inflicted by black bears, Stephen Herrero and Andrew Higgins (1999) use integrated reference to draw attention to their own previous studies. In this case, integrated reference highlights the importance of their earlier work. In the first paragraph of the methods section, integrated reference further emphasizes the importance of Herrero's foundational work in the knowledge domain. Thus, given the extent of his research and the length of time he has been publishing on bear–human interactions, it is not surprising that Herrero makes repeated appearances through both integrated and non-integrated reference in his own work.

Digressing for a moment, we might reconceive traditions of inquiry as a way of showing the "pedigree" of the knowledge about a certain area of study. Susan Peck MacDonald (1994) argues that scientific knowledge, in particular, tends to build on established points of consensus, foundational laws, or agreed-on problems to be solved (pp. 21–24). In this sense, scientific knowledge is more linear than knowledge in the humanities, which may demonstrate little, if any, progression, but instead, seems to be "recursive and reiterative" (Becher, as cited in MacDonald, 1994, p. 24), or "diffuse" (p. 22). In English studies, for example, there will never, in all probability, be an agreed-on meaning for Milton's *Paradise Lost*. Hence, literary scholars are destined to discuss forever, without any foundational consensus on which to build. Scientific knowledge, on the other hand, hinges on established laws and agreed-on problems that provide starting points for new studies. For this reason, the introductions that one encounters in scientific report format often place special emphasis on a tradition of inquiry. Scientists, in particular, place a high value on citing their predecessors and showing how knowledge in the current study is descended from previous work. In addition to the "pedigree" of the knowledge a researcher is using, other things may be at stake. Especially in cases where there are immediate practical applications for scientific research, such as patentable processes or products, the order of published research becomes even more important.

MacDonald's concept of a "diffuse" knowledge-making model in the humanities may be one reason why humanities students sometimes advance to the upper levels of an undergraduate degree without developing a sense that previous studies on their topic are important to their own work. If we return to English studies, first- and second-year students are not always required to use the library for research, but may be encouraged instead to rely on their own close reading of a text, without referring to previous studies. In essence, meaning is generated and presented in a vacuum. And while "the library" is supposed to become more important at the senior-undergraduate levels, in third and fourth year, the initial disregard for traditions of inquiry may be hard to reverse. Looking for analogies, one might point to the different emphases placed on prerequisites in the humanities and sciences. In the humanities, where MacDonald says diffusion prevails, prerequisites may not always be as vital as they are in the sciences.

## Knowledge Deficit

As in the humanities and social sciences, a tradition of inquiry is sometimes followed by a knowledge gap. Here are some examples of how scientists express a knowledge deficit:

- We are not aware of any other publication where such a comparison has been made.
- No other study of ... has been conducted.
- This study is one of the first attempts to demonstrate ...
- Limited information exists on ...
- Hence, the objective of this study was ...

## Topic

We have already touched on some of the rhetorical configurations of topic in the sciences. It is also worth noting that in the sciences, topic is often flagged as a statement of purpose or as an announcement of an objective somewhere toward the end of the introduction. Here are some examples:

- The objectives of this study were ...
- The primary objectives of this study were to ...
- The objective of this research was ...
- Hence, the objective of this study was to examine ...
- Therefore, we focus our research on ... but we also present some evidence about ...
- ... is the focus of this study
- This paper reports on ...
- In this paper, we summarize ...

In the examples above, topic again sounds like general forecasting (see Chapter 5).

## Hypothesis

At the simplest level, a hypothesis is a premise or an assumption that will be tested; it is a statement that is deemed plausible and that will be tested in the course of an experiment. In effect, a hypothesis in the sciences takes the place of a thesis in the humanities. A hypothesis represents a kind of sophisticated guess. The *hypo-* prefix in *hypothesis* means *under* or *below*. So a hypothesis is "below the surface," serving as a foundation or basis for investigation. Sometimes, the hypothesis is implied in the objective or statement of purpose (topic). A hypothesis can never be "proven," but the results of the investigation can either support or negate the hypothesis.

The presence of a hypothesis in scientific writing implies a cautious approach to the generation of knowledge. Rather than beginning with a claim, scientific writing begins with a plausibility or a tentative assumption, which is then tested. When the same results are obtained with many repeated testings, a hypothesis may become accepted knowledge. Like thesis claims in the humanities and social sciences, hypotheses are usually stated in the final paragraph or sentence of the introduction.

Here is an example in which George et al. (2002) present an objective followed by two hypotheses:

> The objective of this study was to determine changes in stream channel morphology in response to 2 seasons (wet and dry) and 3 intensities (no grazing, moderate, and concentrated) of grazing. Our first hypothesis was that grazing induced bank erosion along the bedrock limited intermittent streams at the San Joaquin Experimental Range would increase stream channel width at bank full compared to that measured in the baseline year or in the ungrazed channel reaches. Our second hypothesis was that bedload deposition was dynamic and would result in yearly fluctuations in stream channel depth.

Alternatively, science writers might express something called a null hypothesis. Whereas a hypothesis anticipates a particular result, a null hypothesis rejects that anticipated result. It may be useful, in thinking about the purpose of an experiment, to suggest a hypothesis and the countering null hypothesis as exploratory steps in arriving at a statement of purpose. In the example below, at the outset of the experiment, the results are unknown: it is possible that the application of herbicide might not damage seed production and viability. Alternatively, analysis of the experimental data may very well show that there was an effect. The hypothesis and null hypothesis represent the "on the one hand" and "on the other hand" possibilities for the outcome of the experiment.

As a **Statement of Purpose:** The objective of this study was to determine if herbicide treatments damage seed production or seed viability.

As a **Hypothesis:** The hypothesis was that herbicide treatments would damage seed production and seed viability.

As a **Null Hypothesis:** The null hypothesis was that herbicide treatments would not damage seed production and seed viability.

Another way of thinking about all this is to say that in a null hypothesis, scientists state that what they *really* think is going to happen isn't going to happen. In this sense, a null hypothesis is a fictitious prediction, a form of make-believe. Rhetorically, at least, the null hypothesis is a way of pre-empting assumptions. In effect, scientists play the devil's advocate with themselves. Nowhere, perhaps, is the production of scientific knowledge more openly "constructed" than in the articulation of a null hypothesis. The null hypothesis is a rhetorical artifice.

# Methods

While we have encountered methods sections in our reading so far, such sections become even more important as we deal with report format in the sciences. In fact, methods sections sometimes comprise a large part of scientific reports, taking several pages. Perhaps more than any other discursive feature in the sciences, methods sections reveal a concern for objectivity. The function of a methods section is to demonstrate properly controlled observation through the use of instruments, measurements, and so on. Thus, methods sections describe scientific procedure in an effort to ensure reliability (see Chapter 5 for methods in the social sciences).

The methods section lists materials used, describes any special pieces of equipment needed, tells how they were used, and explains where and when the work was done. This last point is especially important in field studies, where the particular locale or season in which the experiment or investigation was carried out can be a crucial factor in the results. This section is often divided further by subheadings such as site description, experimental design, data collection, sampling procedure, and data analysis. Inclusion of various subheadings will, of course, depend on the specifics of the experiment undertaken or the phenomenon being studied.

In Chapter 5, we noted that methods sections often defy standard notions of good writing, presenting choppy sentences and agentless or passive-voice constructions. Moreover, Swales (1990) notes that in some methods sections, particularly in the natural sciences, "an enormous amount is taken for granted ... [and] this belies the common belief that the purpose of methods sections is to permit replication" (pp. 120–121). In fact, some would "deny that replication is really possible" (p. 121). The peculiarities and complications that Swales notes should remind us that methods sections, like every other feature of academic writing, are highly mediated forms of expression.

# Results

The results section answers the question: What did the researcher find? It presents data, measured values (quantitative results), and observations, but no interpretation, implications, or conclusions. In the text, researchers usually summarize the data from the experiments as opposed to discussing every individual result. Tables, graphs, and other illustrative material ( for example, photographs, maps, drawings), which should always be referred to in the text of the report, can be used to illuminate or supplement the text. Data in a table should not be duplicated in a graph or figure, and readers should be alerted as to what information to look for in a table or figure. For example, "Bats responded most to light intensity and colour treatments used during experimental tours (Table 1). In general, all responses were highest during full-white light level and lowest during the no-light level (Fig. 1)." Figures and tables are referred to in the text by their number, for example, "Figure 1 shows that the activity ..." or "The activity decreases after five minutes (Figure 9.1)."

# Discussion

Discussion and conclusion sections in scientific reports present many of the rhetorical gestures that we have already discussed in relation to conclusions in the humanities and social sciences (see Chapter 7). In the discussion section, researchers interpret the data that they gathered during the experiment or the field research. They may relate the results to existing theory and knowledge, and explain the logic that allows them to accept or reject the original hypothesis.

The discussion may also include suggestions to improve experimental technique, explain some influence that may have unexpectedly affected results, or clarify areas for additional research, thus identifying a further *knowledge deficit.* Alternatively, in the following example, the research team draws attention to the limitations of the study:

---

## D. L. Shek, "Predictors of Perceived Satisfaction with Parental Control in Chinese Adolescents: A 3-Year Longitudinal Study"

There are several intrinsic limitations to studies of predictors of satisfaction with parental behavioral control in the literature. First, as mentioned, few studies have examined the predictors of perceived satisfaction with parental control (Shek, 2006c, in press). In addition, few studies have examined predictors of perceived parental control with reference to both fathers and mothers (Shek, 2005).

Second, most of the studies in this area were conducted predominately in Western contexts with few studies conducted in different Chinese communities (Shek, 2006a). A computer search using the key words of "trust," "parental control," and "Chinese" in May 2007 revealed only 6 relevant citations and all of them were written by the author. An examination of popular Chinese beliefs shows that the parent-adolescent relationship was governed by duties and obligations rather than trust in the traditional Chinese culture, as exemplified by the sayings "fu yao zi si, zi bu neng bu si" ("if a father wants the child to die, the child cannot have the option of not dying"), and strong emphasis on filial piety, as shown in the saying "bai xing xiao wei xian" ("among all acts of a person, filial piety is the most important"). In addition, as parent-adolescent communication was unilateral in the traditional Chinese culture, with parents (particularly the fathers) playing a dominant role, a child's readiness to communicate with the parent might not be great in the Chinese culture.

The third limitation is that there are few longitudinal studies in this field (Shek, 2007, in press). While multiple regression analyses based on cross-sectional data can give some clues to the predictors of perceived parental control, the findings are not definitive. It is argued that a longitudinal design can provide a better understanding of the predictors of perceived parental control and their changes over time.

*Source:* Shek (2008, p. 155)

Similarly, in the following example, researchers van Lommel, van Wees, Meyers, and Elfferich point out possible limitations to their study on near-death experiences (NDE):

---

## P. van Lommel, R. van Wees, V. Meyers, and I. Elfferich, "Near-Death Experience in Survivors of Cardiac Arrest: A Prospective Study in the Netherlands"

One limitation of our study is that our study group were all Dutch cardiac patients, who were generally older than groups in other studies. Therefore, our frequency of NDE might not be representative of all cases—e.g., a higher frequency could be expected with younger samples, or rates might vary in other populations. Also, the rates for NDE could differ in people who survive near-death episodes that come about by different causes, such as near drowning, near fatal car crashes with cerebral trauma, and electrocution. However, rigorous prospective studies would be almost impossible in many such cases.

*Source:* van Lommel et al. (2001, pp. 2043–2044)

---

In the next example, the first part of the discussion section of a study of the survival of white-tailed deer centres around assumptions outlined in a previously published study. Note how the researchers contextualize their study by relating their findings to that earlier work. Here, then, a *tradition of inquiry* emerges relatively late in the paper.

---

## G. DelGiudice, M. Riggs, P. Joly, and W. Pan, "Winter Severity, Survival, and Cause-Specific Mortality of Female White-Tailed Deer in North-Central Minnesota"

**Discussion**

**Survival Analysis**

*Assumptions:* Tsai et al. (1999) discuss 7 assumptions for statistical inference based on survival data from radiotagged animals. They include (1) animals in the study cohort constitute a representative sample of the target population, (2) survival times of individuals are uncorrelated, (3) radiocollars do not affect survival, (4) animals recruited at different calendar times and ages have the same underlying survival function, (5) death times are exact, (6) censoring is random (noninformative), and (7) the underlying hazard is constant or at least piece wise exponential. We consider each of these as they relate to our study.

*Assumption 1.* We standardized all aspects of Clover trapping (e.g., trap size, door height, trap locations) in this study to preclude a trapping bias for any age class of does....

*Assumption 2.* The deer in our study were competing for the same progressively declining winter resources; thus, the clustering of >80% of the death times in winter strongly suggests correlation....

*Assumption 3.* We excluded from our analysis 12 deer that died within 7 days of capture because their deaths may have been capture-related. The remaining deer gave no evidence of any adverse effects.

*Source:* DelGiudice et al. (2013, pp. 707–708)

In the discussion section, researchers may also address connections to other phenomena or the significance of their experimental results, gestures that are akin to a *statement of relevance*. In the article on near-death experience, for example, the authors say that "NDE pushes at the limits of medical ideas about the range of human consciousness and the mind–brain relation" (p. 2044).

Furthermore, scientific writers may also speculate about the meaning of the experimental results. In a passage in the previously mentioned NDE article (see pg. 282), the researchers speculate about why people have near-death experiences—they consider neurophysiology and changing states of consciousness, but clearly state that their experiments did not show that psychological, neurophysiological, or physiological factors caused the experiences. If speculation is part of the discussion, it should be clearly identified as such.

# Conclusion

The conclusion section gives the researchers the chance to summarize the particular data and discussion, and draw conclusions about the experiment or research they have conducted. Often, metadiscursive "flags" explicitly signal the summary function of conclusions. In the examples below, the metadiscursive verbs point to the emergence of a *thesis* or *knowledge claim* at the end of the study:

- The results of this study showed ...
- This study showed that ...
- Our data from four experiments ... indicate that ...
- This study provides evidence of ...

As in the humanities and social sciences, we should not be surprised to encounter *limiting expressions* in the articulation of knowledge claims (see Chapter 7).

In the following examples, note how the conclusion contains a rejection of the hypothesis.

---

## M. R. George et al., "Influence of Grazing on Channel Morphology of Intermittent Streams"

In conclusion, we detected no significant streambank erosion, thus we must reject our hypothesis that grazing increases width in these bedrock limited stream channels. We detected a significant increase in depth in the control treatments. Additionally, we found significant year effect on morphological parameters that included depth in their measurement or calculation, supporting our hypothesis that annual stream flow dynamics have a large effect on depth of the stream channels we studied. The large year effect and weaker year x grazing effect on stream morphology confirms the need for long-term studies to separate natural variation in stream morphological parameters from those caused by land management activities.

*Source:* George et al. (2002, p. 556)

---

In conclusions, researchers can also give direction about further studies that need to be carried out. We've seen this in other disciplines, where at the end of a paper, scholars present *opportunities for further research*. See the following example:

---

### M. Fend, J. Muras, J. Steffen, R. Battista, and A. Elfessi, "Physiological Effects of Bouldering Activities in Upper Elementary School Students"

Therefore, further research is needed on the physiological exertion put forth by students when playing different bouldering games, as well as on the physiological effects of bouldering for different age groups. It may also be beneficial to investigate the motivational influence of bouldering games in the physical education classroom to determine what games are most well-liked and provide the most excitement for the students.

*Source:* Fend et al. (2011, p. 208)

---

A brief review of journal articles in various disciplines, however, shows that not all published articles have a conclusion section. Sometimes, conclusions are incorporated into the discussion section. Depending on the discipline and the topic, a variety of other subheadings may be used in place of conclusions:

- Intended Applications
- Implications
- Management Implications
- Modification and Future Development
- Recommendations

## Acknowledgements

Scientists often receive help from various sources. In a short paragraph at the end of the written report of their studies, often just before the literature cited, researchers acknowledge the help they receive from assistants, funding agencies, university libraries and facilities, and other agencies or individuals:

We thank observers ... for assisting in field trials. We gratefully acknowledge the University of Washington's Friday Harbor Laboratories for providing boat dockage and office support. We appreciate the helpful reviews by ... of earlier drafts of this manuscript. This work was funded by ...

# References

This section presents an alphabetized list of references cited in the paper, and not a general bibliography of works consulted on the topic. Individual instructors may request a particular style of documentation, for example, APA or CSE, and student researchers should diligently observe formatting requirements. Our suggestion is that unless otherwise advised by their instructor, students should follow the official style manual for the documentation style that they choose for their papers, and not one of the many variations that individual journals adopt as their "house" style. Following is a sample references page, showing some of the most often used kinds of references, formatted first according to APA style, and then according to CSE style. Students should check the most recent editions of the *Publication Manual of the American Psychological Association* and *Scientific Style and Format: The CSE Manual for Authors, Editors, and Publishers* for complete details on formatting citations and references.

## APA Style

### References

Evans, R. A., & Love, R. M. (1957). The step-point method of sampling: A practical tool of range research. *Journal of Range Management, 10*, 208–212.

Hosmer, D. W., & Lemeshow, S. (2000). *Applied logistic regression* (2nd ed.). New York: John Wiley & Sons.

Morgan, K. A., & Gates, J. E. (1983). Use of forest edge and strip vegetation by eastern cottontails. *Journal of Wildlife Management, 47*, 259–264.

National Oceanic and Atmospheric Administration. (2001). National Climatic Data Center Climate Data Online. Retrieved January 21, 2001 from http://cdo.ncdc.noaa.gov/plclimprod/plsql/poemain.poe

Worton, B. J. (1989). Kernel methods for estimating the utilization distribution in home-range studies. *Ecology, 70*, 164–168.

## CSE Style

### References

Evans RA, Love RM. 1957. The step-point method of sampling: A practical tool of range research. Journal of Range Management 10:208–12.

Hosmer DW, Lemeshow S. 2000. Applied logistic regression. 2nd ed. New York: J Wiley. 373 p.

Morgan KA, Gates JE. 1983. Use of forest edge and strip vegetation by eastern cottontails. Journal of Wildlife Management 47:259–264.

Worton BJ. 1989. Kernel methods for estimating the utilization distribution in home-range studies. Ecology 70:164–168.

### The Jenna Files

Notes to self:

– They have to write papers in *science* courses??

# Sentence-Level Considerations

There is much that could be said about how sentence patterns in the natural sciences differ from sentence patterns in other disciplines. In this chapter, we will limit the scope of our discussion to the passive voice and nominalization, stylistic features also observable in the humanities and social sciences. In the natural sciences, however, these tendencies are even more apparent. Among scientists, the passive voice may sometimes be preferred over the active voice, and bulky noun phrases are especially common.

## Active Voice and Passive Voice

In English grammar, "voice" shows the relationship between the subject and the verb of the sentence. We can construct sentences in the active voice or the passive voice. In the active voice, the doer of the action is the subject of the sentence; for example, "Mary ate the apple." The active voice shines a spotlight on the subject of the sentence as the doer of the action. On the other hand, the passive voice presents the subject of the sentence as the receiver of the action, often leaving the doer of the action unstated and implied. The passive voice uses a grammatical construction that consists of a form of the verb "to be" (*is, are, was, were, has been*) plus the past participle of another verb. Basic composition instructors usually frown on the passive voice because it often sounds wordy and can be a form of agentless expression that disguises or downplays the doer of an activity. For instance, we could simply say, "The apple was eaten." In this case, the doer of the action has not been named.

Yet in certain sections of scientific reports, the passive voice is useful. Note how the doers of the action—that is, the researchers—are relatively unimportant in the following examples:

- The study was established in 1993 at Lacombe, Alberta, Canada ...
- Seeding was followed by harrowing.
- All paddocks were hand weeded during the summer.
- Baseline data were collected in 1994.
- The preliminary study was followed by four years of treatment application and data collection.

The above examples are from materials and methods sections, parts of scientific reports often written in the passive voice. Note, however, the following sentences that use the active voice, which were also found in materials and methods sections:

- We identified three vegetation associations within the study area based on field reconnaissance and following Hernandez (1998).

- We followed Lehr (1978) for plant nomenclature.
- We determined diets of desert bighorn sheep based on fecal pellets collected two times each season.
- We systematically travelled the area on foot across washes, ridgetops, and cliffs and observed sheep with a pair of 10 x 50 binoculars and a 30 x 16 spotting scope.
- We avoided disturbing the animals.

We advise students to check with their instructors for preferences concerning active and passive voice, as well as for use of the personal pronouns *I* and *we* to refer to the researchers themselves. Beyond materials and methods, other sections of research papers may also employ the passive voice. Note, for instance, how often it is used in the introduction to John Theberge's "Ecological Classification, Status, and Management of the Gray Wolf, *Canis lupus*, in Canada" (1991, p. 460):

> The Gray Wolf *is listed* as a furbearer in all jurisdictions. None provide quotas for trappers. It *is listed* as a game species in all jurisdictions except Alberta and Labrador. Only in British Columbia *is* it actually *managed*, with area-specific bag limits. Wolves *are killed* to protect livestock in most jurisdictions (Table 1). [italics added]

## Nominalization

The word "nominalization" comes from the Latin *nomen*, meaning name. Thus, in the most basic sense, *nominalization* simply refers to the act of naming. We can see this Latin root in terms such as *nominate*, *nomenclature*, and *nom de plume*. In studies of academic writing, however, nominalization has acquired a more specialized meaning. It refers to instances in which noun phrases replace subject-predicate constructions, thereby turning actions into "things." This kind of nominalization is often what's at stake when readers complain that academic writing is hard to read, or that it is jargon-ridden.

"O.K.! Time to investigate calcium-induced conformational switching."

The words that tend to trouble people the most are the nouns or noun phrases that "absorb" subjects, verbs, and prepositions. Like the passive voice, nominalization is not limited to scientific writing, but it has a familiar home there. The following examples of nominalization are drawn from published scientific articles:

- Rent-appropriation opportunities
- Accessibility research
- State energy program outputs
- Methodology of energy demand forecasting
- Corporate competence building
- Energy-efficient procurement practices
- Economic optimal stocking rates
- Cricket paralysis virus internal ribosomal entry site
- Calcium-induced conformational switching
- First-principles molecular dynamics investigation
- Anaerobic ammonium-oxidizing micro-organisms
- Microbial secondary metabolite formation
- Penicillin-susceptible target proteins

- Microbial cellulose utilization
- Osmotic stress signalling
- Quantization
- Plant-associated symbiotic growth states

Nominalization can be a good thing. It can be used to accomplish the following:

- Stabilize phenomena, permitting cause/effect analysis
- Economically reinstate high-level concepts
- Precisely identify specific concepts
- Replicate the kind of language that academics are used to

On the other hand, as previously noted, nominalization can also make prose difficult to read. When readers complain that writing is wordy, nominalization is frequently the grammatical culprit causing the problem. Too much nominalization can obscure meaning with excessively long noun phrases, making some sentences nearly unintelligible. Academic writers should make informed judgments about the use of such "freight-train phrases" (*Scientific Style and Format*, 1999, p. 119), weighing the advantages with the disadvantages. Remember that your reader seeks meaning and clarity.

# Ideas for Further Study

1. Find your own examples of the passive voice and nominalization in scientific sources. A good method is simply to browse the titles of articles in databases such as the General Science Index. Nominalization will appear under virtually any subject.
2. Using the sample titles given earlier in this chapter, write appropriate running heads.
3. Still working with these titles, see if you can supply abstractions for a few more of the research sites.
4. Look back at the examples of nominalization earlier in this chapter. Rewrite each as a simpler phrase that restores subjects, verbs, and/or prepositions.
5. In a video entitled *Science, Culture, and the Modern World* (Ideas Channel, 1993), two scientists, Michael Rose and Gregory Benford, claim that the humanities and sciences are "piling up against each other in some gigantic

academic football game." Do you see any signs of competition between the humanities and sciences at your college or university? On a related point, do you think that different stereotypes accompany popular conceptions of people in the humanities and people in the sciences?

# References

American Psychological Association. (2010). *Publication manual of the American Psychological Association* (6th ed.). Washington, DC: American Psychological Association.

DelGiudice, G., Riggs, M., Joly, P., & Pan, W. (2002). Winter severity, survival, and cause-specific mortality of female white-tailed deer in north-central Minnesota. *Journal of Wildlife Management 66*(3), 698–717.

Fend, M., Muras, J., Steffen, J., Battista, R., & Elfessi, A. (2011). Physiological effects of bouldering activities in upper elementary school students. *Physical Educator, 68*(4), 199–209.

George, M. R., et al. (2002). Influence of grazing on channel morphology of intermittent streams. *Journal of Range Management, 55*(6), 551–557.

Gilbert, G. N., & Mulkay, M. (1984). *Opening Pandora's box: A sociological analysis of scientists' discourse.* Cambridge: Cambridge University Press.

Herrero, S., & Higgins, A. (1999). Human injuries inflicted by bears in British Columbia: 1960–97. *Ursus, 11*, 209–218.

Ideas Channel. (1993). *Science, culture, and the modern world.* Videotape. Discussion between Michael Rose & Gregory Benford.

Latour, B., & Woolgar, S. (1986). *Laboratory life: The construction of scientific facts.* Princeton: Princeton University Press.

MacDonald, S. P. (1994). *Professional academic writing in the humanities and social sciences.* Carbondale: Southern Illinois University Press.

Ross, R. J., Abraham, K. F., Gadawski, T. R., Rempel, R. S., Gabor, T. S., & Maher, R. (2002). Abundance and distribution of breeding waterfowl in the great clay belt of northern Ontario. *Canadian Field-Naturalist, 116*(1), 42–50.

*Scientific style and format: The CSE manual for authors, editors, and publishers.* (1999). Cambridge: University of Cambridge.

Shek, D. L. (2008). Predictors of perceived satisfaction with parental control in Chinese adolescents: A 3-year longitudinal study. *Adolescence, 43*(169), 153–164.

Swales, J. (1990). *Genre analysis: English in academic and research settings.* Cambridge: Cambridge University Press.

Theberge, J. B. (1991). Ecological classification, status, and management of the gray wolf, *Canis lupis,* in Canada. *The Canadian Field-Naturalist, 105*(4), 459–463.

van Lommel, P., van Wees, R., Meyers, V., & Elfferich, I. (2001, December 15). Near-death experience in survivors of cardiac arrest: a prospective study in the Netherlands. *The Lancet, 358*(9298), 2039–2045. doi:10.1016/S0140-6736(01)07100-8

Wall, A., & Heiskanen, J. (2003). Effect of air-filled porosity and organic matter concentration of soil on growth of Picea abies seedlings after transplanting. *Scandinavian Journal of Forest Research, 18*(4), 344–350.

# CHAPTER 9

# A Last Review:
## Revising and Proofreading

I see but one rule: to be clear.
If I am not clear, all my world crumbles to nothing.

—Stendhal

One of the clichés in the field of composition is that good papers are not written, they are rewritten. Like a number of other clichés, this one is reliable. However carefully you may have worked throughout the term to develop a first-rate paper, your work will benefit from revision and correction. This means that it is advantageous to complete a draft well before the paper is due. With a completed draft in hand, you can begin to reconsider your work and look for ways in which it might be improved. In actuality, of course, completing a draft ahead of time is not easy: it is a feat that calls for organization and commitment throughout the term. In order to foster a situation in which revising and proofreading are possible, we advise instructors and students to plan ahead and set aside time from the beginning of term. One way for instructors to do this is to incorporate revising and proofreading into their course syllabus, devoting entire classes to these activities near the end of a semester.

In the discussion that follows, we frame revising and proofreading as peer activities, but students should also consider these practices on their own and enlist the help of instructors or tutors where permissible. Indeed, the peer approach is simply one facet of a larger process of rewriting. Granted, peer evaluation sometimes makes students feel uncomfortable. You may not like the idea of commenting on another student's work and be even less comfortable about having another student comment on yours. Nevertheless, the peer approach can turn revising and proofreading into mutually rewarding exercises, presenting opportunities to improve both your paper and someone else's. If your class adopts the peer model, be prepared to offer and receive *constructive* criticism, and remember that this kind of exchange exemplifies the critical thinking skills that colleges and universities are supposed to promote. Moreover, comments can take the form of questions rather than brusque or forceful demands. In such cases, readers and writers can learn together.

The guidelines presented here involve a minimum of two sessions, each consisting of approximately one-and-a-half hours. Thus, if your class meets for a three-hour block once a week, the entire block could be devoted to peer evaluation. If your class meets for two one-and-a-half–hour blocks per week, the two sessions could be held on separate days. The entire process should be initiated by an exchange of papers, so that all students have someone else's paper in front of them. Try to ensure that you are handing over a *complete* draft, including the references or works cited; otherwise, you will compromise the help that your partner will be able to provide.

# Session One: Revising

People who are unfamiliar with rewriting tend to focus on small, local details—on spelling, sentence structure, the fine points of documentation, and so on. All of these considerations are important, but we're not there yet. Genuine *revision* involves a reconsideration of even more important elements that relate to the overall structure of a paper. This macrostructure involves such things as the ongoing use of a particular prestige abstraction, the wording of topic and thesis, the order of sections within the core of a paper, and paragraph structure. *The Allyn & Bacon Handbook* (Rosen & Behrens, 1994) has this to say about revision:

> Accomplished writers expect to revise. They know that good revision reaches deep; that it is not, for the most part, about cosmetic changes (a word scratched out here, another added there) but about fundamental changes and redirections that help you discover meaning. Above all, readers expect *clarity* of ideas in your writing. When you revise, you rethink and you clarify; you will serve your own interests and your reader's by committing yourself to meaningful revision. (p. 99)

In the first session, try to avoid tinkering. Think big. The steps we've outlined correspond to the introduction–core–conclusion pattern often found in the humanities and social sciences. If you are reading a scientific report, you will need to reconceptualize the steps.

## Step 1: Review the Introduction

- ❑ Highlight the border between the introduction and the core.
- ❑ Identify the rhetorical gestures in the introduction and comment on their placement and effectiveness. Pay special attention to the placement and clarity of the thesis claim. (Use the margins to make your comments.)

## Step 2: Review the Core

- ❑ As you proceed through the core of the essay, start with an overview: try to highlight borders between main sections. Are these section borders clear? Are there effective methods of development throughout the paper?

❑ In light of the thesis, comment on the relevance of each main section.

❑ Now dig in: consider paragraph structure within each of the main sections. Do paragraphs have adequate guiding sentences and low-level detail? Is there effective thesis-driven narrative coherence? (Once again, use the margins to make your comments.)

## Step 3: Review the Conclusion

❑ Does the conclusion clearly recap the argument? If not, should it? What other typical concluding features does the conclusion contain? Are there opportunities to present more concluding features?

## Step 4: Discussion

❑ Gathering in groups of two or three, allow about 10 minutes to discuss each paper. Where there is uncertainty about the merit of some suggestions, instructors might offer their opinion.

# Session Two: Proofreading

In this second session, pairings can remain the same or be changed. Whether or not you have the same paper in front of you, now is the time to dwell on details. If revising involves significant structural adjustments, proofreading descends more to the level of microstructure. The recommended procedure is relatively simple: once again, we will read papers from beginning to end, but this time watch for the following:

❑ Are sentences clear and grammatically correct? Are there spelling errors?

❑ Is the level of discourse appropriate for a college- or university-level research paper? (Is the language too colloquial? Do you see effective or ineffective examples of nominalization?)

❑ Does the paper provide adequate documentation? (Is it using an effective mix of integrated reference, non-integrated reference, paraphrase, and quotation?)

❑ Do you see effective examples of the envelope technique? Do the citations in the essay clearly correspond to a list of references at the end of the paper?

❏ Does the paper consistently and correctly employ a particular style of documentation?

❏ Gathering in groups of two or three, again allow about 10 minutes to discuss each paper. Remember that instructors might be willing to offer suggestions.

We've been following Jenna's progress on her paper throughout this text. Here, in the final chapter, we present a version of Jenna's paper that is ready for peer revision and proofreading. As you prepare your own paper for peer review, analyze Jenna's paper and offer constructive comments that could be shared in the context of your class. You'll notice that we have also included several instructor comments on Jenna's complete draft, but there is still room for you to say more.

## The Jenna Files

"That Dead Girl":
Cyberbullying and Suicide among Teenage Girls[1]
Jenna Sin
Northern Lights College

On September 13, 2013, Rebecca, a 12-year-old girl, completed suicide after 15 middle-school students repeatedly bullied her in person and online. Rebecca was bullied for over a year, and the bullies urged her though online websites and smart phone applications to kill herself. In response, Rebecca changed her online identity to "That Dead Girl" (Speere, 2013, para. 2). When Rebecca's mother, Tricia Norman, found out that Rebecca was being bullied, Norman withdrew her daughter from school and closed down her Facebook account (Alvarez, 2013, pp. 1-2). However, according to Hinduja and Patchin (2011), adolescents value the Internet community websites very highly, and they cannot "live" without the Internet: "two-thirds of youth go online every day for school work, to keep in touch with their friends, to learn about celebrities, to share their digital creations, or for many other reasons" (p. 23). Therefore, Rebecca felt she could not stop using social media and opened a new community website account. When Rebecca was once again bullied through the new website, she resorted to suicide (Alvarez, 2013, p. 3).

This paper will present cyberbullying as a serious social problem, exploring the relationship between cyberbullying and suicide among teenage girls. First, I will describe the characteristics of cyberbullying in comparison to traditional bullying. Second, I will explore the negative effects of cyberbullying on teenage girls, effects that may culminate in suicide.

There is a growing body of research on cyberbullying. Pirjo, Heini, and Rimpela (2012) showed that for girls from 12 to 16 years old, the rate of being cyberbullied was almost twice as high as for boys in the same age group (p. 4). According to Bauman, Toomey, and Walker (2013), cyberbullying is more likely to lead to "reciprocal behavior" than traditional bullying, where physical power differentials more often determine perpetrator and victim (p. 347). Further, Bhat, Chang, and Linscott (2010) note that 30-40% of teens who are cyberbullied do not seek help and that when cyberbullied teens do seek help they most often turn to friends rather than adults (p. 36). Ultimately, research has shown that cyberbullying has detrimental social-psychological effects, such as inducing suicidal thoughts that lead to attempted and completed suicides. For example, Hinduja and Patchin (2010) reported on a survey of Internet use conducted on 1,963 randomly selected middle-school students. Students who had been victims of cyberbullying were more likely to attempt suicide than those who had not (p. 207). Hinduja and Patchin observed that girls, in particular, are at a greater risk of suicide. Thus, I argue that cyberbullying is a unique social phenomenon whose "virtualness" further isolates victims and often leads to suicide among teenage girls.

## The Unique Characteristics of Cyberbullying

In the early twenty-first century, technology is integrated into almost every aspect of human life in industrially developed countries around the world. Bhat, Chang, and Linscott (2010) note that over 1.8 billion people used the Internet in 2009: 42.4% were Asian users; 23.6% were European users; and 14.4% were North American users. Furthermore, it would appear that approximately 1/3 of these users worldwide are between the ages of 13 and 25 (p. 35). Such widespread use of technology has created a new set of problems and challenges, one of which is a phenomenon known as "cyberbullying" (Bauman, Toomey, & Walker, 2013, p. 342). Given that teenagers spend more time on the Internet than any other age group (Bhat, Chang, & Linscott, 2010, p. 35), it is perhaps not surprising that cyberbullying occurs mostly among adolescents (Schneider, O'Donnell, & Stueve, 2012, p.171). In general, cyberbullying has been defined as a harmful, repetitive, and aggressive action conveyed through the Internet or any electronic device (Dooley, Pyzalski & Cross, 2009, p. 182). As we will see, however, certain aspects of this general definition may be open to question and debate. In any event, the intent to psychologically "hurt," shame, or intimidate another person through electronic communication appears to be an essential characteristic of cyberbullying.

Granted, cyberbullying and traditional bullying both involve offenders (or perpetrators) and victims. In this respect, both types of aggression have similar processes: offenders choose targets and humiliate them, sometimes ruining their social life. However, there are some significant differences. In the context of cyberbullying, for example, offenders do not have to expose their real identity and this gives them freedom to express themselves anonymously, seemingly without *any* accountability. As Bhat, Chang, and Linscott (2010) observe, "Cyberbullies can hide behind anonymity or by using pseudonyms, and as a result are often emboldened to say things they are unlikely to say face to face" (p. 37). Thus, it would appear that such anonymity can remove inhibitions and increase the severity of verbal assaults. According to Hinduja (2011), "it is easier to be hateful using typed words rather than spoken words" (p. 23), so one could argue that cyberbullies are actually able to gain greater license than traditional bullies because the former enjoy the double buffer of both anonymity *and* written versus spoken communication. In sum, cyberbullies appear to have greater freedom than their face-to-face counterparts, and this apparently gives them greater freedom to act as they choose. Indeed, the anonymity of the online world may even make it harder to catch cyberbullies.

Further, from a victim's perspective, there can be a perception of wider humiliation in an online environment because the "onlooking" community is not limited to those who are physically nearby. Thus, just as the perpetrator may be anonymous, the onlooking community may consist of innumerable anonymous "bystanders." Dooley, Pyzalski, and Cross (2009) noted that an offender can upload shameful pictures of a victim, which anyone can see. This action can intensify the humiliation of the victim because of the reach of the Internet (p. 183). This results in what Bauman (2013) describes as an increased sense of "thwarted belongingness" and "perceived burdensomeness" (p. 342). In such instances, an insult or taunt can "go viral" (Hinduja, 2011, p. 22). The burden of online bullying can, in fact, be unusually heavy, leading victims to feel that "everyone" is against them, or that "the whole world" has witnessed their humiliation. Paradoxically, therefore, while online communities can expand our social connections, they can also make us feel lonelier than ever before.

Because cyberbullying occurs online, it may seem as though victims can more easily escape their tormentors simply by going offline; yet such an escape may not be as simple as it appears. For example, Wolak, Mitchell, and Finkelhor have said that online bullying may tilt the balance of power in favour of victims because they can go offline. Yet these same researchers have also noted that "there are instances of online victimization that cannot be easily terminated, such as the difficulty of removing information" from the Internet, regardless of whether or not the victim maintains an online presence (as cited in Dooley, Pyzalski, & Cross, 2009, p. 183). Further, as Rebecca's case indicates, teen dependency on online communication makes it difficult for teens to simply stop using the Internet. Dooley, Pyzalski, and Cross describe a condition in which our addictedness to online communication leaves no "reprise" or "relief" (p. 184). Accordingly, online bullying can be particularly insidious and omnipresent, becoming an inescapable part of everyday life for contemporary teenagers. Ultimately, online victims may be more powerless and vulnerable than their traditionally-bullied counterparts.

Cyberbullying is also unique because its virtual nature may raise questions about whether bullying has actually occurred. Physical bullying on playgrounds often leaves physical marks. Online, however, there may be some uncertainty about precisely when taunts or subtle insults become bullying. Even the apparent necessity of repetition, noted in some sources, is perhaps questionable. Indeed, in a study of traditional bullying, Tattum argues that "frequency may be unimportant since students may experience repeated bouts of anxiety, self-doubt, and stress from a single incident" (as cited in Dooley, Pyzalski, & Cross, 2009, p. 183). Likewise, Guerin and Hennessy have found that "over 50% of their sample of children did not consider the frequency of occurrence to be important, with over 40% of those believing that an act that occurred once or twice could still be bullying" (as cited in Dooley, Pyzalski, & Cross, 2009, p. 183). Therefore, even though a teenager has been cyberbullied only once, he or she may still become embarrassed, humiliated, and depressed.

Additionally, teen victims of cyberbullying may lack the kinds of adult support available to victims of traditional bullying. Hinduja (2011) acknowledges that many adults simply do not understand the online world. In turn, when adults try to assist teen victims of cyberbullying, adults may try to solve problems in their own way without really understanding the victims and their larger situation (p. 23). Rebecca's case, as described by Alvarez (2013), is a good example of this. Rebecca's mother tried to help Rebecca when she was being bullied by making significant changes to Rebecca's life: changing her school, closing her Facebook account, removing her cell phone. However, Tricia Norman did not know Rebecca was being bullied again because Rebecca laughed all the time. Norman later realized that Rebecca pretended she was fine because she was afraid her new cell phone would be taken away (para. 6). In regard to cyberbullying, then, it seems as though there is often a generational technology gap.

It follows that in cases of online bullying, teens may be more inclined to attempt to resolve their situation without adult support. In a study conducted by Bhat, Chang, and Linscott (2010), 30-40% of youth who were bullied did not consider they would need help. If they did consider getting help, they would rather ask their friends than their teachers or parents; while 19% of witnesses told adults about cyberbullying, only 9% of victims actually reported their situation to guardians (pp. 35-36). Hinduja and Patchin (2011) reported that this is because most adults do not have as much technological knowledge as most adolescents; therefore, it is hard to talk with youth about cyberspace and how it works. Additionally, some adults do not deal with cyberbullying promptly; as a result, offenders believe that "there are little to no consequences for their actions" (p. 23). This slow response often allows offenders to discount the seriousness of cyberbullying.

Cyberbullying may be unique in other respects. For example, Bauman, Toomey, and Walker (2013) contend that cyberbullying tends to be more "reciprocal" in nature than traditional bullying. That is, the victim is more likely to bully someone else. Thus, an individual may be both victim and bully. Bauman, Toomey, and Walker describe this as "dual bully-victims" (p. 347). Elaborating on the situation, these scholars have claimed that participation in cyberbullying is less likely to be defined by traditional measures of power, whether physical or social. In the schoolyard, the big kid picks on the little kid. Yet, in the online world, anyone is potentially vulnerable (p. 347). Bauman, Toomey, and Walker also note that cyberbullies are more likely to regard their activities merely as a form of "entertainment" (p. 347), at least at the outset. Further, Bhat, Chang, and Linscott (2010) have observed that cyberbullying "often has a component of sexual harassment .... For example the cyberbully may spread rumours about the sexual orientation of the target or may circulate a nude or partially nude photograph of the target" (p. 37). Overall, while cyberbullying shares some characteristics with traditional bullying, it is also a unique social phenomenon that has arisen through our technological age.

Cyberbullying may, in fact, be a social experience that is common among teens everywhere. Wherever the Internet is, someone will be using it for harm.

## The Negative Effects of Cyberbullying[2]

Cyberbullying, like traditional bullying, can lead to a variety of negative effects. In general, it is clear that bullying or aggression from peers can disrupt adolescents' emotional and social development" (Raskauskas & Stoltz, 2007, p. 564). Hodges et al. note that "victims of bullies are more rejected by peers and less likely to have friends than nonvictimized classmates" (as cited in Raskauskas & Stoltz, p. 564). However, Raskauskas and Stoltz also observe that "electronic bullying may have more impact on youth's emotional development and well-being than traditional bullying because of an even greater power imbalance created by the fact that many victims of electronic bullying may never know the identity of their bully" (p. 565). Ybarra and Mitchell agree that "electronic bullying may pose a greater threat than traditional bullying because electronic bullying is often anonymous and can transcend school grounds such that children are vulnerable even in their own homes" (as cited in Raskauskas & Stoltz, p. 570). In some respects, then, the unique characteristics of cyberbullying increase the likelihood of negative outcomes for victims. Additional factors considered earlier, such as a wider sense of humiliation, a greater sense of isolation, an absence of effective parental support, and the high likelihood of sexual harassment all make cyberbullying a particularly distressful experience for teens.

In cases of cyberbullying, victims commonly experience general problems with psychological and psychosocial development. Hinduja and Patchin (2011) note that victims often experience sadness, anger, frustration, embarrassment (p. 22). Furthermore, Bauman, Toomey, and Walker (2013) added that victims also felt low self-esteem, hopelessness, and uselessness after being bullied. Indeed, "anecdotal evidence suggests that electronic bullying can increase students' level of stress and general anxiety, threaten self-esteem, and contribute to school failure and dropout" (Leishman, Tench, & Wendland; as cited in Raskauskas & Stoltz, 2007, p. 565). Similarly, Hinduja and Patchin (2011) quote one teenager who reportedly said: "[Cyberbullying] makes me hurt both physically and mentally. It scares me and takes away all my confidence. It makes me feel sick and worthless" (p. 22). Victims of ongoing cyberbullying are also prone to more serious forms of psychological distress, such as depression. Hinduja and Patchin (2007) describe the case of a twelve-year-old Massachusetts girl who said: "[Cyberbullying] lowers my self-esteem. It makes me feel really crappy. It makes me walk around the rest of the day feeling worthless, like no one cares. It makes me very, very depressed" (n.p.).

On the whole, then, research shows that cyberbullying is connected to a broad spectrum of negative feelings and thoughts that can have many detrimental effects on the lives of victims, including depression.

Among victims of cyberbullying, depression may also lead to suicidal thoughts and behavior. Hinduja and Patchin (2011) mentioned, "Cyberbullied youth also reported having suicidal thoughts, and there have been a number of examples in the United States where youth who were victimized ended up taking their own lives" (p. 22). Bramwell and Mussen cite the case of a sixteen year old boy who received harassing text messages for months. Eventually, this boy "jumped from a cliff near his home." The boy's mother informed reporters: "text messaging isn't going away. Bullying isn't going away. That combination killed my son!" (as cited in Raskauskas & Stoltz, 2007, p. 566).

Notably, however, cyberbullied girls are twice as likely to attempt suicide as cyberbullied boys. According to Hinduja and Patchin (2010), 4% of boys who were bullied at least once a week attempted suicide, whereas the girls' rate was twice as high. Also, bullied boys had suicidal thoughts 3.8 times more than non-bullied boys, while bullied girls had suicidal thoughts 8 times more than those who were not bullied. This study shows that girls respond more severely than boys to cyberbullying (p. 209). Bauman, Toomey, and Walker (2013) indicated that among teenage girls, the experience of being cyberbullied is strongly associated with depression, and continuously being depressed could lead to attempting suicide. Because girls tend to be more sensitive and self-conscious, girls' rates of attempted suicide are higher than boys'. In support of this, Bauman, Toomey, and Walker (2013) found out that "because many cyberbullying actions are attempts to publicly humiliate the target or damage her friendships and social status ... the entire social world in which the target interacts is aware of her humiliation, contributing to the development of depression." Thus, girls can be at higher risk of attempting suicide and suicidal thoughts (p. 346).

## Conclusion

In conclusion, this paper has focused on the relationship between cyberbullying and suicide among teenage girls. I have demonstrated that cyberbullying is a distinct social occurrence that isolates victims and often leads to suicide among teenage girls. Traditional bullying and cyberbullying share some basic victim/offender relational dynamics, but cyberbullying is unique in some ways.

The offenders may have an anonymity that emboldens them to be particularly hurtful. Further, victims themselves may experience a sense of wider humiliation because the onlooking community can be so vast. Victims of cyberbullying may also lack any escape route because online participation is such a prevalent aspect of their lives. The verbal nature of cyberbullying may raise questions about whether bullying has actually occurred because the physical marks of playground assaults are absent. Cyberbullying is also distinguished by a particularly acute absence of adult support and by violations of privacy that may include sexual humiliation. Ultimately, cyberbullying may lead to a series of increasingly negative effects such as sadness, humiliation, depression, suicide ideation, and even suicide. Unfortunately, teenage girls are particularly prone to suicide as an escape from cyberbullying.

As a result, researchers and social organizations have been trying to solve these problems. Some of the solutions Hinduja and Patchin (2011) suggested that students, parents, and educators could try in order to reduce the occurrence of cyberbullying were: students should let their parents know which websites they use and trust parents and teachers; parents should put more effort into communicating with their children; and educators should keep "a safe and respectful school climate" (p. 24-26). However, because victims of cyberbullying often feel reluctant to report incidents of bullying to their guardians, and because most parents are not aware if their children are being bullied, and because preventing cyberbullying is hard for educators when students are out of school, the amount of cyberbullying is increasing. In the face of this increase, there is a need for more research and new practical solutions to deal with the reluctance of victims, the unawareness of parents, and the lack of empowerment of educators. We need to protect countless young women whose mental health and lives are at risk.[3]

## References

Alvarez, L. (2013, September 13). Girl's suicide points to rise in apps used by cyberbullies. *The New York Times*. Retrieved from http://www.nytimes.com

Bauman, S., Toomey, R. B., & Walker, L. J. (2013). Associations among bullying, cyberbullying, and suicide in high school students. *Journal of Adolescence, 36*, 341-350.

Bhat, C. S., Chang, S., & Linscott, J. A. (2010). Addressing cyberbullying as a media literacy issue. *New Horizons in Education, 58*, 34-43.

Dooley, J. J., Pyzalski, J., & Cross, D. (2009). Cyberbullying versus face-to-face bullying. *Journal of Psychology, 217(4)*, 182-188. doi: 10.1027/0044-3409.271.4.182

Hinduja , S., & Patchin, J. W. (2007). Offline consequences of online victimization: School violence and delinquency. *Journal of School Violence 6*(3), 89-112.

Hinduja, S., & Patchin, J. W. (2010). Bullying, cyberbullying, and suicide. *Archives of Suicide Research, 14*(3), 206-221. doi:10.1080/13811118.2010.4 94133

Hinduja, S., & Patchin, J. W. (2011). Overview of cyberbullying. White Paper. *White House Conference on Bullying Prevention.* Retrieved from Cyberbullying Research Centre.

Lindfors, P. L., Kaltiala-Heino, R., & Rimpelä, A. H. (2012). Cyberbullying among Finnish adolescents—a population-based study. *BMC Public Health, 12*(1), 1-5. doi:10.1186/1471-2458-12-1027

Schneider, S., O'Donnell, L., Stueve, A., & Coulter, R. W. (2012). Cyberbullying, school bullying, and psychological distress: A regional census of high school students. *American Journal of Public Health, 102*(1), 171-177. doi:10.2105/AJPH.2011.300308

Thom, K., Edwards, G., Nakarada-Kordic, I., McKenna, B., O'Brien, A., & Nairn, R. (2011). Suicide online: Portrayal of website-related suicide by the New Zealand media. *New Media & Society, 13*(8), 1355-1372. doi:10.1177/1461444811406521

**Instructor comments:**

1. An emphasis on teenage girls does not really appear until late in the paper. Could you do more to highlight the connection between girls and cyberbullying earlier in the paper?
2. This section is still too slight. In fact, we've lost some guiding sentences that appeared in the guiding sentence outline. Could you return to your sources and more thoroughly unpack the negative effects? Is there a progression of increasingly negative effects, for example, sadness → isolation → depression → suicide ideation → suicide?
3. You've worked very diligently on your essay, Jenna! Clearly, as much of our sociality shifts to online expression, so will our aggressive behavior.

# Idea for Further Study

1. To prepare for peer proofreading, it might be helpful for all members of the class to review a sample draft paper. Instructors will likely have material that could be used for this purpose.

# Reference

Rosen, L. J., & Behrens, L. (Eds.). (1994). *The Allyn and Bacon handbook* (2nd ed.). Boston: Allyn & Bacon.

# Copyright Acknowledgements

Roe, Steve and Students of Northern Lights College. "'If the Story Could Be Heard': Colonial Discourse and the Surrender of Indian Reserve 172." *BC Studies* 138/139 (2003): 115–136. © 2003 BC Studies.

Smyth, Heather. "'Lords of the World': Writing Gender and Imperialism on Northern Space in C.C. Vyvyan's Arctic Adventure." *Studies in Canadian Literature* 23.1 (1998): 211–229. © 1998 Studies in Canadian Literature, University of New Brunswick.

Society for the Promotion of Japanese Animation. "AX Anime and Manga Studies Symposium Call for Submissions." Available at https://call-for-papers.sas.upenn.edu/node/55513. Reproduced with permission.

Tang, Susana. "Angel or Devil?: The Environmental and Social Effects of China's Three Gorges Dam." Unpublished student paper, Northern Lights College. Used by permission of author.

Theberge, Nancy. "A Feminist Analysis of Responses to Sports Violence: Media Coverage of the 1987 World Junior Hockey Championship." *Sociology of Sport Journal* 6.3 (1989): 247–256. © 1989 Human Kinetics. Reproduced with permission.

Wanapia, Barnabas. "Beyond the Game: Fan Violence in European Football." Unpublished student paper, Northern Lights College. Used by permission of author.

Wilson, Joy. "Sesame Kale Salad with Roasted Almonds." Available at http://joythebaker.com/2014/03/sesame-kale-salad-with-roasted-almonds/#more-14049. © 2014 Joy Wilson.

Zecchi, Barbara. "All About Mothers: Pronatalist Discourses in Contemporary Spanish Cinema." *College Literature* 32.1 (2005): 146–164. © 2005 West Chester University. Reprinted with permission of Johns Hopkins University Press.

Zhu, Hong. "Burden of Hope: Educational Challenges Faced by Canadian Immigrant Children." Unpublished student paper, Northern Lights College. Used by permission of author.

# Index

abstract, 18, 22, 24, 64, 104, 117–118, 119, 123, 176, 270, 272, 273
abstraction, 20, 22, 23, 24, 25, 26, 27, 28, 29, 35, 36, 37, 38, 39, 66, 72, 73, 98, 113–117, 125, 129, 134, 152, 157, 190, 198, 271, 291, 296
    *see also* prestige abstraction
Academic Search Premier, 26, 35, 39, 176
academic writing, 56, 71, 90, 99, 103, 112, 190, 201, 211, 268, 269
active voice. *See* voice, active
adverbs
    limiting, 245
allusive phrase, 73, 97, 113, 114, 115, 116, 184, 270, 271
American Psychological Association style. *See* APA style
Andersson, C., 262
APA style, 83, 85, 88, 90, 116, 118, 211, 212, 213, 215, 216, 220
argument, 2, 41, 42, 66, 69, 135, 144, 153, 154, 157, 158, 182, 183, 184, 189, 201, 205, 207, 230, 243, 265, 297
    *see also* knowledge claim; thesis
Arruda, Tony, 124, 183–185, 188, 193, 201
article
    academic, 32, 108
    databases, 34, 35, 176
    indexes, 34, 35
    titles, 19, 24, 29
Ashley, S., 260–261
attribution, 231, 232, 233, 234, 239, 241
attributive
    frame, 224, 226, 233, 237, 239
    noun phrase or expression, 119, 217, 219, 221, 222
    verbs, 222
authorial voice. *See* voice, authorial
Aydogan, Ismail, 30

Bader, Rudolf, 132
Bartsch, Dallas, 109–110
Bazerman, Charles, 11, 53–54
benchland topography, 196, 198, 200
    *see also* paragraph topography; topography
Berger, John, 224–226
Bishop, Wendy, 253
block and label, 75, 227, 256
block quotes, 59, 238

blogs, 3, 9, 13, 14, 33, 34, 224
Boeving, J. N., 130
Bostock-Cox, B., 258
Brown, S. 250–251

call to action, 244, 250, 251, 255, 256, 264
call for papers, 14–19, 24, 71
Carlick, Alice, 108, 213
case study, 26, 88, 231
causal analysis (cause and effect), 183, 186, 209
    *see also* method of development; rhetorical, mode
certainty, 101, 247, 248, 268
Chicago style, 74, 211, 212, 215, 216, 220
chronology, 136, 184, 188–189
    *see also* method of development; rhetorical, mode
citation, 211, 212, 237, 274
citation behaviour, 220, 223
classification and division, 182
    *see also* method of development; rhetorical, mode
close reading, 276
Cloud, Dana L., 158
Clouse, Barbara, 182
coherence, 60, 65, 112, 165, 211, 241, 297
    structure. *See* rhetorical, feature
colloquialism, 101
common knowledge, 238–240
    disciplinary, 238–239
    non-disciplinary, 238–239
community of discourse. *See* discourse, community
comparison and contrast, xiii, 182, 184–185, 188–189
    *see also* method of development; rhetorical, mode
complex terminology, 102, 103–105
composition, xiii, xiv, 1, 112, 120, 182, 198, 215, 245, 246, 253, 288, 294
concluding sentence, 191, 196, 226
    *see also* retrospective sentence; transitional sentence
conclusion, xiv, 64, 65, 73, 79, 111, 144, 153, 160, 184–189, 206, 208, 210, 238, 243–250, 252–253, 255–265, 269, 272, 280, 284–285, 295, 296, 297, 304
content analysis, 128, 145, 146, 156, 174

context, 2, 4, 71, 72–73, 95, 96, 107, 111, 120, 122, 155, 160, 161, 162, 165, 184, 186, 187, 188, 218, 233, 244, 252, 274, 282, 298
core, 244, 249, 269
    paragraph, 41–42, 56–57, 181, 200, 229–230, 255
Council of Science Editors style. *See* CSE style
Cowley, Malcolm, 102
Cox, Donna, 195
Cruikshank, Julie, 151
CSE style, 78, 211–212, 214–216
    *see also* documentation, styles of
cut-and-paste, 56, 59, 234, 238
    *see also* plagiarism

Davis, Ann, 248
Davis, Richard C., 27, 158, 188–189
definition, 9, 103, 112, 123, 152, 155, 182, 183
    *see also* method of development; rhetorical, mode
definition of key terms, 72–73, 155
del Mar, David Peterson, 249
den Ouden, Pamela, 126, 197, 212
description, x, xiii, 72, 73, 74, 78, 102, 103, 107, 108, 148, 174, 182–183, 188, 221, 279
    *see also* method of development; rhetorical, mode
Dews, D., 258
discourse, 36, 54–55
    academic, 95, 101, 269
    channel of, 36
    community, 2, 4, 107, 233
    community of, 98, 234
    level of, xiv, 297
    scholarly, 2, 99, 121, 221
discursive situation, 4
discussion, 270
documentation, 2, 54, 74–75, 117, 189, 211, 212–216, 219, 221, 225, 233, 238–239, 255, 286, 296, 297, 298
    *see also* APA style; Chicago style; CSE style; Harvard System of Referencing; MLA, style; SBL style
    styles of, 74–95, 211, 215–216, 219, 286, 298
Dressler, Laurie, 151–152

Egan, Susanna, 141
Eklund, M., 262
email, 1, 33
English language learners, 240
envelope technique, 225, 297
epigraph, 14, 38, 73, 111, 112, 119, 142, 255
epistemic, 112
epistemological, 243
epistemology, 112

evidence, 14, 66, 69, 74, 85, 102–103, 107, 108, 109, 112, 144, 153, 181, 190, 201–202, 222, 244, 254, 258, 277, 283, 284, 303
exemplification, 182, 186, 188, 209
    *see also* method of development; rhetorical, mode
explanatory phrase, 73, 97–98, 113–116
    *see also* allusive phrase; topic; two-part-title

Facebook, 3, 34, 83, 113
Ferch, Shann R., 254–255
first page of text, 117–119, 272
forecasting, 72, 137
    general, 73, 136, 184, 277
    specific, 73, 74, 95, 98, 162, 163, 165
Fouts, Gregory, 131, 146–147
freight-train nouns, 103, 268, 291
    *see also* nominalization
Friesen, David W., 140
front matter, 111, 113, 120, 270

Gage, Bren, 78–79
Gawthrop, M., 257
generalization, 116, 189, 190, 196, 198, 200, 201, 255
genre, xvi, 1–4, 9, 17, 18, 39, 66, 67, 71, 98, 101, 103, 121, 158, 186, 201, 211, 216, 234, 270
    theory, 1–4, 9, 216
Gerlinsky, Christy, 172–174
Gillespie, Greg, 121–122
Giltrow, Janet, 1, 4, 20, 24, 71, 125, 129, 133, 136, 137, 189, 245, 248
"gist," 56
Google Scholar, 35
grammar, 100, 102, 108, 288
grammatical
    constructions, 221
    correctness, 100
Grant, Shelagh, 57–64, 106–108, 136
guiding sentence, 59, 64, 65, 98, 189, 190, 191, 192, 196, 202–205, 211, 224, 226, 297, 306
    outline, 202, 205, 207, 209, 228, 230, 241, 306

Hamer, David, 128, 214, 246
Harrassowitz, Christiane, 251–252
Harrison, Shari, 116, 117, 118, 213
Harvard System of Referencing, 211
header, 117–119
hedging. *See* limiting expression
Heiskanen, J., 275
Helms, Gabriele, 141
Herndl, Diane Price, 143
Herrero, Stephen, 199, 200, 274–275
Higgins, Andrew, 199, 200, 274–275
Higton, H., 261–262

Hill, Annette, 159, 195–196
Hobbs, H., 136–137
Hookimaw-Witt, Jacqueline, 139
Hunter, Kendra, 81–83
Hyde, Pamela, 124
Hyland, Ken, 200, 216–217, 220, 241
hypothesis, 160, 277–279, 280, 284

I
    see also self-disclosure, 137–144
    autobiographical, 137, 142–143
    as emotionally engaged researcher, 141
    merely discursive, 137, 138
    as witness, 139–140
Iacovetta, Franca, 138
Idlout-Paulson, Leah, 105–106, 107
integrated reference, 98, 126–128, 217, 219–220,
    221, 222, 224–227, 233, 241, 275, 297
    see also attributive noun phrase or
        expression; non-integrated reference;
        reported speech
interlibrary loan, 34, 35
Internet, 14, 25, 33, 54, 233, 235, 270
    formal searches, 33–34, 38
    informal searches, 33–34
in-text acknowledgement, 211
    see also attributive noun phrase or
        expression; integrated reference;
        non-integrated reference; plagiarism;
        reported speech
introduction, xiv, 111–112, 119, 134, 144, 153, 155,
    156, 157, 159, 160, 161, 162, 163–165, 166, 167,
    171–176
    and research and topic, 27, 28, 29, 38
    compiling a research notebook, 41, 56–57,
        64
    and conclusions, 243, 244, 252, 255
    core paragraphs, 183–189, 218
    and proposals, 74, 88
    revising, 296
    and scientific writing, 269, 270, 272–274,
        276–277, 278, 289

Janosik, Steven M., 128–129, 148–149, 156–157
jargon, 102, 289
Jenna files, xv, 4, 25, 37, 42–45, 95–99, 163, 164–
    165, 209–211, 228–230, 264, 265, 287, 298, 306
Jones, M. V., 259

Kanev, N. N., 260
Katsioloudis, P. J., 259
Keller, James, 185–186, 205–207, 241
key words, 68, 113, 272, 273
Kirby, Mark, 194

Kirschner, Cheryl, 127
Knott, Helen, 75–77
knowledge
    see also thesis
    claim, 35, 38, 73, 99, 144, 153, 154, 157, 160,
        244, 252, 269, 284
    deficit, 72–73, 78, 129–132, 162, 163, 165,
        184, 253, 265, 274, 276, 281
    domain, 65, 129, 131–132, 201, 275
    gap, 82, 129, 162, 166, 173, 274, 276
    limits, 245
    making of, 2, 13, 14, 31, 99, 107, 112, 120, 125,
        129, 144, 152, 157, 220, 223, 243, 269, 276
Knowles, Richard Paul, 122–123
Kostiuk, Tammy, 171–172

Lainsbury, Greg, xiv, xv
    see also Jenna files
Langenau, Edward E., Jr., 149–150
Lawson, Andrea, 131, 146–147
Leslie, Mary, 252
Levine, Samuel J., 68, 69, 187–188
librarian, 14, 34–35
library, 19, 33, 34, 102, 103, 109, 215, 276
limiting
    see also marker of obviousness
    expression, 245, 246, 248, 265, 284
    prepositional phrase, 246
LinkedIn, 34
Livshits, A. A., 260
Loveland, T., 259
low-level detail, 41, 45, 181, 190–192, 198, 200,
    203–204, 224, 228, 297
    see also paragraph topography;
        topography; valley

MacAulay, Scott, 123–124
MacDonald, Susan Peck, 275–276
MacTavish, Kari, 174–176
marker of obviousness, 248, 265
    see also limiting, expression
Martin, J. A., 250
Martin, Janice E., 128–129, 148–149, 156–157
Mayes, Andrew D. H., 155–156
McCreery, John, 30
McGowan, A. J., 263
merely discursive I. See I; self-disclosure
metadiscourse, 29, 112, 134, 157–158, 244
    see also I; self-disclosure
metadiscursive verbs, 134, 157, 246, 284
    see also knowledge-making
method of development, 182–183, 185, 186, 189,
    202, 209, 241, 296
    see also rhetorical, mode

methods section, 2, 72, 73, 75, 111, 117, 144–150,
151, 163, 165, 174, 175, 184, 269–270, 275, 279,
280, 288, 289
Miller, Carolyn, 2–3
Miller, Talia, 45, 46
Mitchell, Jennifer, 207–208
MLA
Bibliography for English Studies, 35
style, 75, 81, 119, 211–212, 213, 215–216, 220
Modern Language Association style. *See* MLA, style
Möller, H. H., 260
Montemurro, Beth, 165–166
multiple submission, 238
*see also* plagiarism; self-plagiarism

narration, xiii, 182
*see also* method of development; rhetorical,
mode
narrative coherence, 205, 207, 211, 241, 297
nominalization, 103, 220, 247, 250, 262, 287, 289,
290, 291, 297
*see also* freight-train nouns
non-integrated reference, 98, 126, 128, 217–218,
219, 220, 221, 224, 225, 227, 233, 241, 274–275,
297
*see also* integrated reference; in-text
acknowledgement
Norris, Frank, 67, 186–187
note-taking, xiv, 41, 53, 54, 56, 202
Nowacki, G. J., 129–130

objectivity, 105, 108–109, 112, 137, 244, 268, 279
O'Connor, Patricia, 125
Olien, Diana Davids, 35, 55
Olien, Roger M., 35, 55
opportunities for further research, 253, 255, 285
*see also* conclusion
original research, 14, 78, 145, 174
Orr, Jeff, 140
Orsini, Michael, 253
outline, guiding sentence. *See* guiding sentence,
outline

paragraph topography, 189–192, 196, 198, 202,
223
*see also* topography; valley
paraphrase, 41, 42, 53, 55, 60, 64, 68, 162, 181, 190,
217, 218, 219–222, 226–227, 233, 235, 237, 240,
274, 297
*see also* attribution; integrated reference;
non-integrated reference; quotation;
reported speech
Parsons, Catherine, 160–161
passive voice. *See* voice, passive

personal
*see also* I; self-disclosure
essay, 105, 112
pronoun, 138, 219, 272, 289
writing, 13
Phelps, M. S., 254
Pierson, D. P., 30
plagiarism, 54, 59, 232–234, 237–238, 240
*see also* attribution; cut-and-paste; multiple
submission; references
self-, 238
Pomeroy, Elizabeth C., 249
portfolio of sources, 36–37, 39, 41, 46, 66
prairie topography, 198
*see also* paragraph topography; topography
prestige abstraction, 20, 22–27, 29, 36, 66, 72, 73,
113–115, 117, 125, 134, 152, 157, 271, 296
*see also* abstraction; research, site; topic
process analysis. *See* chronology
proofreading, xiv, 294, 297, 298
peer, 307
proportion, 200, 205, 207
*see also* guiding sentence, outline; narrative
coherence; relevance
proposal, xiv, 41, 56, 71–75, 78, 85, 88, 95, 100,
103, 109, 111, 134, 160, 161, 163–165, 176, 183
*see also* introduction; rhetorical, feature; topic

questions for further research, 244
*see also* conclusion
quotation, 42, 45, 54, 55, 68, 73, 98, 112, 113, 119,
181, 190, 217–219, 221, 222, 226, 233, 234, 235,
237, 297
marks, 33, 42, 54, 63, 68, 234–237, 238
quote, 34, 41, 53, 54, 60, 64, 65, 68, 217, 219, 235
block, 59, 238
dropped, 218

Ramsey, Marleen I., 254–255
recap the argument, 265, 297
*see also* conclusion
reference, integrated. *See* integrated reference
reference, non-integrated. *See* non-integrated
reference
references, 71, 74, 95, 233, 270
relevance, 25, 32, 65, 72, 73, 78, 160, 186, 187, 188,
205, 207, 244, 252, 255, 256, 264, 265, 283, 297
statement of. *See* statement, of relevance
reported speech, 98, 191, 190, 196–198, 200–201,
216, 217, 218, 224, 230, 241, 255, 262
*see also* attribution; integrated reference;
non-integrated reference; paragraph
topography; paraphrase; quotation;
topography; valley

research
    *see also* academic writing; knowledge;
        prestige abstraction; thesis; topic
    article, 12, 21, 38, 99, 105, 106, 153, 269
    domain, 252
    notebook, xiv, 41–42, 45–53, 55, 57, 67, 69,
        74, 75, 165, 181, 183, 202, 203, 205, 228,
        241, 265
    opportunity. *See* opportunities for further
        research
    paper, xiii, 11–14, 19, 25, 26, 29, 31, 64, 105,
        111, 112, 121, 181, 200, 201, 228, 232, 233,
        269, 289, 297
    prose, xiii, xiv
    question, 72–73, 148, 156, 187
    site, 20–22, 24–27, 29, 31, 35–36, 37, 38, 57,
        72, 73, 75, 83, 98, 108, 113–116, 125, 129,
        134, 138, 140, 152, 153, 157, 186, 271, 291
retrospective sentence, 190–192
    *see also* concluding sentence
report format, 269–270, 276, 279
    genre, 270
results, 33, 103, 269, 270, 272, 274, 278, 279,
    280–283, 284
    *see also* scientific writing
rhetorical
    building blocks, 25
    feature, xv, 64, 65, 73–75, 78, 109, 111, 112,
        134–135, 144, 145, 153, 159, 161, 165, 171,
        176, 192, 244, 255, 256, 257, 262, 265, 270
    function, 74, 244
    mode, xiii, 182, 183
        *see also* method of development
    structure, 270
Ridington, Robin, 120, 127
Roe, Julia, 83–85
Roe, Steve, 167–171
Ross, R. J., 273
running head, 271–272, 291
    *see also* APA style; title, page
Ryan, J., 131

SBL style, 211
    *see also* documentation, styles of
scientific
    discourse, 268
    writing, xiii, 103, 128, 200, 268, 278, 290
Scott, Britain, 251–252
Seiler, Robert M., 154
Seiler, Tamara P., 154
self-disclosure, 88, 107, 109, 111, 137, 138–144, 269
    *see also* I; knowledge-making;
        metadiscourse; metadiscursive verbs;
        personal, pronoun

setting the stage, 274
Sin, Jenna. *See* Jenna files
Slakov, June, 252
Smyth, Heather, 38–39
Society of Biblical Literature style. *See* SBL style
solutions to a problem, 73, 244, 249–250, 256,
    264–265
sources, xiii, 13, 14, 34–37, 38, 39, 41, 46, 53, 54,
    56, 66, 68, 71, 75, 85, 95, 98, 112, 181, 189, 190,
    198, 201, 202, 211, 216–219, 220, 221, 223, 224,
    230, 234–239, 240, 241, 285, 291, 306
    list of, 74, 212
    primary, 31–32, 110, 144, 174
    secondary, 31–33, 78
    tertiary, 31–32, 238
Spak, F., 262
statement
    of purpose, 134, 277–279
    of relevance, 65, 72, 73, 78, 160, 186, 187,
        188, 244, 252, 255–256, 264, 265, 283
St. Jean, Eva, 126–127, 234
Strang, K. M., 263
subjective, 75, 105, 152, 183
    *see also* subjectivity
subjectivity, 105, 107–109, 146, 152, 269
summary, 53, 55–57, 59–60, 63–67, 125–126, 190,
    233, 240, 244–245, 249, 252, 259, 272
    critical, 65–67, 69
Sundh, V., 262
Svoboda, N. J., 250
Swales, John, 111–112, 125, 145, 161, 241, 280

Tam, C. M., 27, 123
Tang, Susana, 91–92
Tenisci, Laney, xv
tense, 265
    past, 272
    present, 272
    present perfect, 244
    simple past, 244
Terrill, Robert E., 155
textbook, xiv, xv, 1, 4, 32, 55, 59, 98, 189
text message, 1
Theberge, John, 289
Theberge, Nancy, 28–29, 192, 201
theoretical framework, 2, 64, 72–73, 81, 117,
    152–153, 157, 162, 163, 167, 172, 186, 188
theory, 111, 152, 153, 154, 155, 200
    *see also* genre theory
thesis, 38, 42, 46, 60, 64, 66, 72–74, 78, 83, 95, 99,
    111, 117, 135, 137, 138, 153–154, 156, 157–159,
    162, 163, 165, 167, 176, 181, 183, 185, 188,
    204–205, 207, 209, 211, 252, 255, 256, 277, 278,
    284, 296

*see also* knowledge claim
delayed, 160, 184, 187, 244
-driven narrative coherence. *See* narrative
   coherence
recap, 65, 186, 188, 189, 244, 264, 265, 297
Thundal, K., 262
title, 19, 29, 34, 35, 38, 54, 60, 98, 113, 219, 291
   *see also* allusive phrase; explanatory phrase
   page, 116, 117, 118, 119, 270–272
   two-part, 72–73, 98, 113–116, 270
topic
   *see also* abstraction; prestige abstraction;
      research, site
   and compiling a research notebook, 42, 46,
      59, 64, 65, 66
   and conclusions, 252, 255
   and core paragraphs, 184, 188, 189, 203,
      204–205, 207, 209
   and introductions, 112–113, 115, 116, 117,
      120, 121, 123, 124, 125, 133–135, 136, 137,
      138, 145, 153, 157, 162–163, 172
   proposals, 71–75, 78, 88, 95, 97, 98, 108
   research and, 1, 11, 13–14, 19–21, 22, 24–27,
      29–32, 33, 34, 35–36, 37, 38
   and revising, 296
   and scientific writing, 276, 277, 278, 285, 286
   sentence. *See* guiding sentence
topography
   benchland, 196, 198, 200
   high-low, 191, 192, 200
   high-low-high, 191, 192, 200
   low, 191, 192, 193, 198, 200, 202, 203, 204
   low-high, 199, 200
   paragraph, 190, 202, 234
   prairie, 198, 200
tradition of inquiry, 57, 64, 72–73, 75, 78, 81, 89,
   95, 98, 123, 125–128, 129, 131–132, 153, 162,
   163, 165, 167, 221, 234, 239, 274–276, 282

transitional sentence, 190–191
   *see also* concluding sentence; retrospective
      sentence
Turabian style, 211, 215
   *see also* Chicago style
Twitter, 34
two-step process, 211, 215
   *see also* documentation

Valery, Joan, 125
valley
   floor, 190, 197, 255
   of low-level details, 190, 191, 290
   of reported details, 226, 255
   of reported speech, 255
voice
   active, 287, 288, 289
   authorial, 107
   own, 189, 198, 202, 233, 240, 255
   passive, 144, 145, 272, 280, 287, 288, 289,
      290, 291
voices, 56, 109, 125, 181, 189–190, 198, 200–202,
   233, 241, 255

Wall, A., 275
Wanapia, Barnabas, 93–95
Warhol, Robyn R., 143
Weaver, Andrew, 245, 247–248
West, D. A., 154–155

York, Lorraine, 142
YouTube, 233

Zecchi, Barbara, 256–257
Zhu, Hong, 88